Scribe Publications
WALKING THE CAMINO

Tony Kevin retired from the Australian foreign
service in 1998, after a 30-year government career
during which he served in the Foreign Affairs and
Prime Minister's departments, and was Australia's
ambassador to Poland and Cambodia. He has
written extensively on Australian foreign, national-
security, and refugee policies in Australia's national
print media, and is also the author of the award-
winning book *A Certain Maritime Incident: the
sinking of SIEV X.*

To Amy Banson, a true pilgrim

TONY KEVIN

WALKING THE CAMINO

a modern pilgrimage to Santiago

SCRIBE

Melbourne • London

Scribe Publications Pty Ltd
18–20 Edward Street, Brunswick, Victoria 3056, Australia
2 John St, Clerkenwell, London, WC1N 2ES, United Kingdom

First published by Scribe 2007
This edition published 2013
Reprinted 2019, 2023

Typeset in Sabon by the publishers

Printed and bound in the UK by CPI Group (UK) Ltd, Croydon CR0 4YY

Scribe Publications is committed to the sustainable use of natural
resources and the use of paper products made responsibly from those
resources.

978 1 921372 33 9 (paperback edition)
978 1 921753 83 1 (ebook)

Catalogue records for this book are available from the National
Library of Australia and the British Library.

scribepublications.com.au
scribepublications.co.uk
scribepublications.com

'The Passionate Man's Pilgrimage'

Give me my scallop-shell of quiet,
My staff of faith to walk upon,
My scrip of joy, immortal diet,
My bottle of salvation,
My gown of glory, hope's true gage,
And thus I'll take my pilgrimage.

—Sir Walter Raleigh (1604)

Contents

Preface

During eight weeks between May and July 2006, I walked a long diagonal line across much of the map of Spain, from Granada—the last Moorish city-kingdom to fall to the Christian empire, in 1492—in the far southeast, to the medieval pilgrimage destination of Santiago de Compostela in Galicia, in the far northwest. My route took me through four Spanish regions, each with its own distinctive history and cultural identity—Andalucia, Extremadura, Castile, and Galicia. I covered around 1200 kilometres in all, walking most days between twenty and thirty-five kilometres. Usually I walked alone, carrying a sixteen-kilogram rucksack and wooden staff, and without back-up support. It was a challenge for a rather overweight and sedentary 63-year-old man. To my surprise and relief, I completed almost all the intended journey on foot, losing eight kilograms' weight in the process. I returned home feeling fitter and healthier than for many years.

But this was not just a very long walk. It was a pilgrimage, following the yellow arrow waymarks of the *Vía Mozárabe* and the *Vía de la Plata*, two of the many centuries-old pilgrim 'ways' *(caminos)* that crisscross the map of Spain and Portugal in an intricate spider's web of walking trails, all leading to the one great destination, the cathedral city of Santiago de Compostela. Santiago in the Middle Ages was Europe's most famous pilgrimage goal, and in recent years it has enjoyed a remarkable and sustained revival of that role. Every morning towards eleven o'clock, hundreds of hot, tired, and dusty pilgrims stream into Santiago Cathedral for the daily pilgrims' Mass there, and to collect their *compostela* from the cathedral office, the precious certificate of completion of journey that will be hung proudly on walls back home, along with family photographs and university degrees, as testament to a significant achievement in their lives.

What is this Santiago pilgrimage about, in our frenetically busy and consumption-driven twenty-first century? What drives hundreds of thousands of people of all nationalities and creeds to take time out from their normal lives to walk long, exhausting, and not particularly scenic routes across the cold mountains and hot tablelands of Spain, in order finally to celebrate a medieval Christian liturgy of spiritual renewal and reconciliation with God?

As I farewelled my family and flew out of Australia in May 2006, excited but scared at what might lie ahead of me, I knew I was looking for something in Spain that I had been unable to find at home: some answers to the complexities of life, a circuit-breaker from the growing stress and pain of living in what seemed to be becoming a more selfish and joyless society. I really did not know what Spain would show me. I feared I might not be up to handling it. Most of all, I feared I might not be able to see the point of it.

This book is a personal and impressionistic account of my eight weeks' continuous pilgrimage walk through Spain. It is not a guidebook or travel diary, but might be of interest to people contemplating a walk to Santiago, as well as to armchair travellers who enjoy reading about unusual journeys from the comforts of home. I have tried here to convey some of the flavour of what it was like to walk each day on the camino from Granada to Santiago. This book is also a look at contemporary Spain, a country that surprised and delighted me in many unforeseen ways. And, unavoidably, because pilgrimage is such a deeply personal experience that has the potential to unlock the deepest recesses of hidden memory, conscience, and aspiration, this book reveals a little about my life and my dreams.

chapter one

What Am I Doing Here?

I am sitting on a carved, granite way-marking stone, at a junction of rough, dirt trails in dry scrubland somewhere in the middle of Extremadura, the hottest and driest region of Spain. It is only eleven in the morning, but the sun is high in the sky and it is already over thirty degrees Celsius. The huge horizon is shimmering, liquifying in the heat. In a couple of hours it will be over forty. It is 28 May, still technically in spring, and all of southern Spain is baking in an unseasonally early summer heat-wave. Maybe it is global warming?

The back of my shirt and my wrists are soaked with sweat. I have walked sixteen kilometres already today, and there are six more kilometres to go before I reach the village of Al-cuéscar and its cool refuge of the Residencia de Hermanos Esclavos de María y de los Pobres (the headquarters of the Spanish order of Brothers, Servants of Mary and the Poor), which I have been told contains one of the most comfortable *albergues por los peregrinos* (pilgrim hostels) in Spain. There are lots of tracks around here, but I won't get lost, because the reassuringly frequent yellow arrow waymarks point me onto the right direction of the camino at every junction.

I have been walking in Spain for three weeks already. I have walked close enough to 400 kilometres, and there are still 750 kilometres to go to reach Santiago, a hard-to-believe dream in my mind of green hills and flowing rivers. Here it is a barren landscape of parched, yellow grassland, dotted with grizzled *encina* trees, a hardy, local dryland oak. Spanish dry-cured ham, *jamón serrano,* tastes so special because Spanish pig-farmers let their black pigs out for free-range grazing in this kind of terrain for a few weeks in the autumn, gorging on fallen acorns before they are slaughtered and the hams cured through the cold, dry winters. This gives to the best *jamón serrano* what maturing in oak barrels gives to wine—a special extra-oaky flavour. The *encina* trees, seen at a distance, could be Australian eucalypts—with similar leathery, greyish-green leaves and twisted, gnarled trunks and limbs.

I started walking this morning just before dawn, at around six o'clock, from the village of Aljucén, enjoying five precious hours of cool walking. But by now, it is hot—no question. A late breakfast—one warm, squashy ripe pear with a wedge of *manchego* cheese, a delicious, hard, salty sheep's cheese from La Mancha province, and the remains of last night's dinner bread roll, washed down with the last litre of lukewarm water from my two 1-litre flasks, balanced one on each side of my pack. It is not a bad meal after your appetite has been sharpened by five hours on the road. I hope this meal and, more importantly, this water will fuel the final burst of energy that I will need to reach Alcuéscar, waiting somewhere behind those low hills up ahead.

You have to carry two litres of water on the camino, especially on hot days like this when you know there is a long stretch between villages with drinking water. And you have to keep drinking every couple of hours, otherwise it is easy for dehydration to set in before you know it. The warning signs are dizziness, fatigue, and pains in the legs and joints, but by then it's too late to get your energy back—you will be walking wounded for the rest of the day. I never knew I could make myself swallow so much water when I wasn't really thirsty. But the more you drink, the lighter the pack gets—and so it is good to stay watered-up.

What am I doing here? Why am I sitting in the blazing sun, in the middle of this harsh, god-forsaken landscape? I might as well be in Arizona or central Australia. This is not the kind of place where sensible people would choose to walk for pleasure. Why am I not at home with my family, enjoying the comforts of suburban Australia—watching football on the telly, reading the papers, getting another cold beer out of the refrigerator? Why is this 63-year-old, overweight, retired man sweating his way across Spain in high summer, lugging a heavy, sixteen-kilogram pack on top of his own ninety-four kilograms, which means 110 kilograms of weight bearing down on four tender sole and heel pads that have been taking the punishment of about 30,000 paces a day, every day over the past three weeks? No wonder I have the biggest and rawest foot blisters I have ever seen.

Yet my completed route already shows up as a satisfyingly long marking-pen trace on my Michelin maps of Spain. It makes me feel that the next 750 kilometres to Santiago might just be feasible, after all. The dream I had a few months ago in Australia, of one continuous walk across Spain from Granada to Santiago, might actually come true.

Maybe it is time to start writing some of this experience down on the camino, before I begin to forget it. It will be hard to recapture the feeling of all this afterwards. With my travel diary entries supplemented by occasional audio reflections on my MP3 player, I just might be able to hold onto some of these memories.

* * *

El Camino means 'the Way'. It is the only walking trail that matters in Spain. There are many possible alternative routes for *el Camino*: all lead to Santiago de Compostela, the famous cathedral city in the far northwest of Spain that is also capital of Galicia, one of Spain's autonomous communities (regions). Santiago is about 100 kilometres inland from Cape Finisterre, the most westerly point of continental Europe—the place where Europe ends. Fearful ancient and medieval mariners used to believe they would fall off the edge of the world if they sailed out of sight of Finisterre. Santiago is about the same distance south of La Coruña (in British history books, Corunna), the site of a disastrous British army defeat in 1809 during the Napoleonic wars in Spain. General Sir John Moore is buried in La Coruña, and each year a ceremony is held at his gravesite. He was the hero of a doomed British expeditionary force sent to Spain to help guerrillas resisting Napoleon's invasion. We learned at school a stirring patriotic poem, 'The burial of Sir John Moore after Corunna':

> Not a drum was heard, not a funeral note,
> As his corse to the rampart we hurried;
> Not a soldier discharged his farewell shot,
> O'er the grave where our hero we buried.

We buried him darkly at dead of night,
The sods with our bayonets turning,
By the struggling moonbeam's misty light
And the lanthorn dimly burning ...

There is a short camino—the *Camino Inglés* (the 'English way')—starting in La Coruña. But most pilgrims from Europe choose to walk the *Camino Frances*—the 'French way', three classic alternative routes from Vezelay, Le Puy, or Arles in France that converge at Roncesvalles in the Spanish Pyrenees into one busy pilgrim trail about 800 kilometres long that then runs due westwards across northern Spain, from Navarre and the Basque region, through the cities of Burgos and León, across the rugged mountains of León and thus finally into Santiago in Galicia. This justly famous route attracts many tens of thousands of pilgrims every year.

But I had chosen a camino far less travelled—the longest, hardest way that I could find, the *Vía de la Plata,* which starts in Seville in the south. I also opted for a longer feeder variant from Granada, the *Vía Mozárabe,* which is 400 kilometres long and joins with the *Vía de la Plata* at the old Roman city of Mérida, 200 kilometres north of Seville and 800 kilometres from Santiago.

My walk had started in Granada three weeks before, and I had just enjoyed two days of resting and sightseeing in Mérida. I had seven more weeks to try to reach Santiago, to collect my *compostela* (the official certificate of completion of pilgrimage) from the cathedral authorities there before my booked air-flight home. The authorities will check my *sellos* (overnight accommodation stamps) in my *credencial*—my 'pilgrim passport'—to satisfy themselves that I have truly walked the pledged pilgrimage route. Then it will be home again to the family and normal life.

My passport is already up to its third page of *sellos*, from churches, town halls, *hostals*, pilgrim *refugios*, and bars encountered on my way so far. There is something very satisfying about all the complexities of your life reduced to the simple daily goal of walking twenty to thirty-five kilometres, carrying everything that you own on your back, and having only one target to meet: to get a pilgrim stamp in the travel-record book at the end of each day.

All the *sellos* count, but the most valued are those from churches or monasteries, for they suggest your walk did have some religious purpose. Lowest in the pecking order are the stamps from bar-restaurants where you ate and drank on the way. As the guidebook delicately puts it, the ecclesiastical authorities in Santiago might not be too impressed by a pilgrim's *credencial* that looks like nothing more than evidence of a sustained pub-crawl across Spain. Tonight, I'll get a suitably prestigious stamp from the brothers in Alcuéscar.

Where did it start, this middle-aged folly? Interestingly, I have not yet met a single Spaniard on the camino who thought me mad or eccentric, or at least those I have met were too polite to say so if they did. The closer I get to Santiago, and the better known is this camino, the less likely that I will. Even in rapidly secularising Spain there seems to be a fondness still for the idea of el *camino*, and an affection and respect for those who take on its challenge. It is partly about religion, and partly about nostalgia for the old Spain.

The new Spain is a modern country of big cities, factories, and highways with huge lorries and fast cars whizzing by. A pilgrim with his staff and backpack and cockleshell pendant and floppy sunhat walking along the verges of a Spanish highway is about as anachronistic as a person of similar appearance would be walking along a highway in Britain or the United States or Australia. Sensible Spaniards travel between towns by car or bus or train. Only penniless vagrants or pilgrims would walk along the edges of busy highways.

I rarely met Spanish walking pilgrims. Spaniards on pilgrimage to Santiago seem to prefer the faster and more modern option—doing their camino fast, on sturdy mountain-bikes, laden with heavy saddlebags and dressed in the latest resplendent multi-coloured lycra gear, with snazzy winged helmets and goggles. By superhuman feats of endurance, riding fast over the same rough trails that I am walking, they can complete the 1000 kilometres from Seville to Santiago in incredibly short times (fourteen days, even ten days). It is not my thing—for how could a pilgrim really meditate and let his mind go loose, steering a heavy bike at speed over rough bumpy paths?—but they seem to enjoy it. They come in all shapes and sizes, from super-fit athletic types to potbellied deskbound companions struggling to keep up with the leaders in the group. What they all share is a boundless enthusiasm and loud *macho* jollity: the *bicyclista* pilgrims always make their presence seen and heard on arrival in a village.

Coming up the track behind me now are some other, more unusual, pilgrims. Four horsemen, businessmen from Barcelona, are having the time of their lives riding the camino on four elegant Spanish thoroughbreds. I met *los quatros caballeros* in the pilgrim *albergue* in Aljucén last night, where they stayed, tethering their horses in the backyard. They are doing it in style, with a back-up carry-van driven by a fifth alternate rider, carrying all their gear and going ahead each day to scout out suitable accommodation and stabling. Riding calmly out of the heat haze towards me in their sleek and creamy Texan hats, they look as if they have just stepped out of a spaghetti Western movie. It's an efficient operation, as you would expect from a group of well-off restauranteurs and winemakers armed with mobile phones. This year they are riding the first half from Seville to Salamanca. Next year, they will complete their pilgrimage to Santiago. They are not rushing, walking their horses comfortably in the heat. Some genial '*Holas!*', a photo, and they are on their way again, clip-clopping into the blue haze ahead.

Next come two walkers chatting amiably in German, moving almost as fast as the horsemen: two fifty-ish athletes, built like greyhounds and as thin as whipcord, power-walking at a pace far beyond my dreams. They stop for a quick break and chat. They have already walked thirty-three kilometres today, all the way from Mérida. We are to meet again this evening in the Residencia, where one of them, a friendly Englishman living in Berlin, Bill Attwood, gives me the secret to overcoming my chronic blisters. Throw away your heavy wool outer socks, he said. Always wear two pairs of lightweight walking socks, the expensive kinds like Coolmax or Bridgestone—worth every cent. Keep your feet as dry as possible: stop halfway through the walking-day, take your boots and socks off, dry your feet well and rest them for half an hour, propped high up on a bench or on your backpack, to cool them and ease the swelling. Then talcum-powder them well before you put on two pairs of clean socks and your boots, which by now should be marginally drier. Bill's advice, which I followed exactly, worked wonders. A week later, my blisters were healing fast, and the soles and heels of my feet were at last hardening up. After Salamanca, there would be no more blisters.

Another group of walkers go by me, five fit young Germans (whom I had met last night at Aljucén), moving effortlessly with light day-packs—for they also have a back-up car. They started two hours after me. I had better get moving; it is depressing to be passed by so many fitter people. I pack up my breakfast remains, hoist the pack onto my extended knee, swing it smoothly over my shoulders, cinch up the waist-belt as tight as it will go to get the weight off my shoulders and down onto my hipbones, clip the chest-strap tightly to stop the pack bouncing around on my shoulders, grab my trusty wooden pilgrim's staff, and away we go again. After a while, with a well-packed and well-adjusted rucksack, you can forget you are carrying anything—until the end of the day, when soreness under the shoulder straps starts to remind you again.

Up into the last range of low hills, small farms start to appear in the scrub along the track: there are fences, olives, grapes, a few cows and sheep, modest farmhouses. Over the crest and it is greener now, more cultivated. I have entered an irrigated mixed-farming area of small fields, vegetable and cereals plots, orchards, vineyards. The path slopes gradually downwards into a shallow valley, looking ahead to a village up a slope on the horizon. It must be Alcuéscar. Distances to villages are deceptive: you can see a church-tower from up to ten kilometres away, but I had learned that only when you can distinguish the windows in the church-tower will the village be less than two kilometres away. As we get closer, I see a very large isolated building over to the left on its own, surrounded by wheatfields and vineyards and orchards. This must be the Residencia of the Brothers, and so I turn my steps towards it.

A few minutes later I am showing my pilgrim passport to a welcoming doorkeeper brother who escorts me upstairs to the *albergue por los peregrinos:* a self-contained pilgrim hostel area on the third floor of the Residencia, with a common room, a few small individual bedrooms, a large dormitory tightly packed with steel bunks, and a communal bathroom with lots of hot showers and clean toilets. It is all unisex and it is all free, though there is a discreet donations box on the wall—I dropped in a five-euro note. Because there were not many pilgrims that day, I scored a single room. It was spartan—a bed, a desk, and a chair were all it contained—but it offered all I needed. Looking out the window, writing, I saw a group of Africans, singing as they hoed and weeded vegetable gardens. Later I learned that these were penniless boat people who had come into Spain without papers, by *cayuco* (canoe) from Senegal to the nearby Spanish Canary Islands. They were being cared for by the brothers, learning Spanish and preparing for entry into the general community.

This order of brothers has quite a recent history. It was founded in 1939, just as the fratricidal Spanish Civil War was drawing to its bitter close, by a charismatic and visionary parish priest in Alcuéscar named Leocadio Galán Barrena. Father Leocadio started this charitable order of brothers, seeing the urgent need to address the terrible poverty and neglect of children in this part of Spain, after years of depression and civil war. There were so many orphans and homeless children—many, I suspect from the photographs I saw of the early years of the order, being the traumatised and orphaned children of civil war victims: they gaze out with hurt and anger in their dark-shadowed eyes. They are not smiling.

The order started with no resources, but gradually built up its numbers and properties over six decades. Now it has houses across Spain, and the central Residencia is a handsome, imposing, three-storey brick building, with chapel and gardens and dining room and a museum of the order's history. It has an impressive sense of solidity and permanence about it, reminding me of my old Jesuit boarding school in Sydney, Saint Ignatius' College.

I have a refreshing shower, change my clothes, and then walk slowly up the hill to the village, trying not to raise a sweat again. I find there a welcoming bar-restaurant, Casa Alexandro. It is already 3.00 pm, but the dining room is still full of diners enjoying a leisurely late lunch. Then coffee and a chat with some locals at the bar, before drifting back down the hill to the Residencia for a couple of hours siesta. Already, the rigours of the morning seem long ago and far away—has it really been just a few hours ago on this same day that I walked twenty-two kilometres in thirty-five-degree heat?

This is the most wonderful quality of pilgrimage—how it slows down and separates time into discrete bundles. The walking and resting parts of the day are so sharply distinct that they almost feel like separate existences. Maybe farmers and manual workers experience this same soothing separation between their arduous working hours and their precious free hours of rest afterwards. In modern white-collar society, most of us have lost that happy capacity to put the working day behind us once it has ended. We carry our workplace worries and stresses home with us, and they never really leave us, even in sleep.

But on pilgrimage, once the day's work of walking is done, it is as if it had never happened. Having done your daily work of walking, you enter a different world of human civility and comfort and clean clothes, of good food and drink and leisurely conversation. Yes, the hard work of pilgrimage walking will start again at dawn the next day, but tomorrow seems a long time away. I feel something of Homer's *Odyssey* today, those remembered accounts of a dusty and travel-weary Odysseus arriving in a fine palace, to be welcomed, bathed, given clean clothes, and then wined and dined by generous and gracious hosts. Pilgrimage walking, with its daily renewals of the spirit, is a kind of Odyssey.

The brothers had a final welcome surprise in store. Waking from my nap in the early evening, I found that we had all been invited to dine in a special pilgrims' dining room. There were cold cuts of ham and chorizo sausage with home-baked bread, platters of fried rice, fruit, chocolates even, washed down with carafes of good house-red wine. It was the usual Residencia hospitality to pilgrims, and it was served by a brother with a matter-of-fact grace and generosity. For these brothers, helping travellers is just part of the day's job—be they pilgrims or penniless African immigrants without papers. 'This is normal for us, this is what we are here to do' was the brothers' unspoken message. As we finished our meal, the attendant brother gave us little prayer cards, with this inscription (in my rough translation):

Welcome, brother: because your visit honours us; because we can share knowledge with you; because we consider you as our brothers, sons of the same Father; because this house has room for all who come here; because we promised Him to extend peace and friendship towards all; because Christ sends rebirth to us with His open arms, and as we would welcome Him here; because our faith and our vocation requires us to offer kindness and hospitality; and because your visit allows us to practise the charity between brothers which is the essence of our holy servitude. Thank you!

As I looked at the faces of the happily chatting men and women pilgrims around me—English, Germans, Spanish, Dutch, Canadians, Japanese—I began to feel the spirit of the Santiago pilgrimage starting to enter quietly into my soul. There was fellowship here, human solidarity, and generosity of spirit. It wasn't just about endurance walking and blisters on hot, dry roads: there was something more happening here.

chapter two

The Idea of Pilgrimage

I stumbled across the pilgrimage to Santiago accidentally a couple of years ago, happening to hear a public radio documentary on it. It caught my interest—an Australian radio journalist was out on the *Camino Frances* with a microphone, talking with pilgrim walkers at random, asking what they were doing there. As people replied, I could hear the steady crunch-crunch of their boots on the gravel paths. It was quite hypnotic just to listen to that background noise, and to try to imagine what kinds of landscapes they were walking through.

What people said was interestingly diverse. People of no professed religious belief said they were doing this simply because of the physical challenge of a very long walk, or because it was 'the best walk in the world'. In contrast, people of strong religious belief argued firmly that the walk would have no meaning for them unless it were a religiously inspired endeavour; that it was far more than just a long scenic walk (and often, one walker suggested, not particularly scenic anyway). People also debated the Santiago foundation miracle myth: was it true or just superstition, and did it matter whether it was true? Some people said they looked forward to the welcoming rituals in Santiago Cathedral as part of the rich fabric of European and Spanish history. Others felt less comfortable with what they saw as the underlying sectarian triumphalism of Santiago: did they really want to celebrate Spanish Christians' bloody military victories over Spanish Moors, when we all understood now how cruel the consequences of the Christian reconquest had been for Spain's Muslims and Jews? Would arrival in Santiago mean very much, or was it the walk itself that mattered more than the destination? Was it better to walk alone or in groups? How easy was it to make friends on the way? In all this good-humoured diversity of views, everyone agreed on one thing: they would rather be here doing this walk than almost anything else, and it was a memorable and significant event in their lives.

I filed the program away in the back of my mind and didn't much think about it again, until in 2005 I won an unexpected and financially generous 'ACT Book of the Year' award from the government of my home city, Canberra. The prize was for a book I had written in 2004, *A Certain Maritime Incident: the sinking of SIEV X*, which controversially investigated what was known about the unexplained sinking of a small asylum-seeker boat in October 2001, criminally overloaded by a people smuggler. The victims were mostly Iraqi Shia Muslim refugees from Saddam Hussein's regime, and mostly women and children whose husbands and fathers had preceded them to Australia. The boat sank in the Indian Ocean on its way from Indonesia to Australia's nearby Christmas Island. In this huge maritime tragedy on Australia's doorstep, 353 people drowned and only 45 people survived.

My book (and my prior public questioning to an Australian Senate investigative committee about the circumstances of the tragedy) had raised disturbing issues about what Australian border-protection authorities, and Australian police agencies, who were conducting a covert people-smuggling disruption program in Indonesia at the time, might have known about this doomed voyage and whether they had clean hands.

These were polarising questions, going to the integrity of Australian government ministers and senior national security agencies, and my work therefore aroused a flurry of bitter controversy in Australia. Government supporters scorned my questions (questions the government had refused to answer, claiming national security and other reasons), while some human rights and civil liberties advocacy groups accepted the seriousness of the issue and took it up. By 2005 I was pretty burnt out, disillusioned at how my country's national security institutions, on whose basic honour and professionalism I had hitherto relied, had so cynically shrugged off their public-accountability obligations.

I had also come to understood how the disturbing public history of this nameless, sunken boat that I had named *SIEV X* ('Suspected Illegal Entry Vessel, Unknown') was symptomatic of a much larger trend, a disturbing collapse in previously assumed public standards of truth in government and respect for the human rights of all in the community. In these matters, Australia's experience in recent years has paralleled that of the United States and Britain. More and more, the English-speaking democracies—the cradles of modern, representative, constitutional government—seemed to be losing the plot. More and more, our nations' civic discourse seemed to be swamped in moral panic, heartlessness, xenophobia, and artificially fostered 'new realities' promoted by governments now in the business of promulgating the politics of fear and spin against people they define as 'the other'. More and more, our governments' basic operating rules seemed to have become: 'Whatever we do is alright, as long as we are not found out; and, through our management of the news agenda and public information, we will seek to ensure that we are never found out'.

My sense of distress that defenceless groups of homeless people were being gravely abused by my national government, but that the majority of my fellow citizens just didn't seem to know or care about such injustices, or to see the dangers in these trends to their own personal freedoms and security, was curdling inside me. I was becoming bitter, harshly judgmental, retreating from old friendships, sleeping badly, eating and drinking too much. I knew that I needed to break out of what was becoming a self-destructive cycle. I tried to stand back from politics, to walk and garden more, to spend more time with my young children, to change the rhythm and priorities of my life, but nothing seemed to work well enough. I remained at risk of sliding back into the same negative-feedback cycle of corrosive anger. I needed something dramatic, a circuit-breaker.

It came to me one day in December 2005, shortly before Christmas, that maybe I should spend some of my book prize windfall to make the pilgrimage to Santiago. Yes, it would be selfish to leave my family for so long, but maybe I had earned it? I started to research the topic on the Internet. It did not take me long to decide that this was for me. My wife, Sina, wisely understanding the need, generously gave me a three-month leave pass from parental duties (we have three young children). I bought my air tickets and started organising the journey. Almost immediately, I was more focussed, happier. Even in anticipation, the pilgrimage was working a beneficent magic.

* * *

Jonathan Sumption, a brilliant English barrister and, in his spare time, a first-class historian of the medieval period in Europe, cut his teeth as a history writer in 1975 with a fine book, *Pilgrimage: an image of medieval religion*. I read his book a few weeks before I went to Spain to try to fill out my understanding of the curt dictionary definition of *pilgrimage*: 'a journey, often long and arduous, undertaken for primarily religious reasons'.

Sumption details how pilgrimage in the medieval period, a time when rulers and ruled alike took religious belief and obligations intensely and literally, was primarily motivated by three aims: seeking forgiveness of sins and guarantees of eternal salvation through proximity to especially holy relics; seeking cures and better health in this earthly life by the same means; and, simply, getting away from the boredom and restraints of life at home. Going on pilgrimage was a way to see the world in a legally sanctioned way, no matter how poor or obligation-bound your station in life. As long as you were able to walk, you could get permission to set out on pilgrimage, and if necessary beg for food and shelter on the way. For rich and poor alike, pilgrimage was the medieval version of a holiday abroad.

Around these three ideas, in an age when most people were firmly tied to their place of residence by service obligations to their local lord or bishop, and when running away from these obligations was a serious crime, a rich tradition of Christian pilgrimage grew up and flourished for hundreds of years, from about 800 A.D. until the Reformation era. In the Dark Ages, the practice of pilgrimage cast a ray of warm light that persisted until the Renaissance. Then the growing rationalism and scepticism of the European Enlightenment discredited the notion of pilgrimage as nothing more than a superstitious medieval relic. It faded away.

Yet the idea of pilgrimage had never been exclusively Christian or European. The sense of a quest or epic journey with spiritual elements is embedded in pre-Christian pagan sagas, and has been a constant thread running through the world's great literature. The story of humanity's urge to travel and engage with a larger world is as old as time, from the first stories of tribesmen who went to explore what was over the next hill. Think of Gilgamesh, the Icelandic and Norse sagas, Polynesian and Vedic sagas, Hiawatha's journeys, Australian aboriginal legends of spiritual journeys through the Dreaming, Jason's search for the Golden Fleece, the voyages of Odysseus and of Sinbad the sailor, the Christian-era epics of a search for the Holy Grail, the Buddhist monk Tripitaka's journeys across the Himalayas to bring back the sacred books, and the travels of Marco Polo. In imagining Bilbo Baggins' journeys and Frodo's quest to return the Ring to its maker, Tolkien taps into such rich universal themes: Bilbo and Frodo are both pilgrims as well as explorers.

The idea of an arduous but sacred journey far from home strikes chords in many religions and cultures, even in the more contemplative and cerebral ones. Hinduism and Buddhism are full of the imagery of holy mountains which one had to climb, and holy rivers where one had to go and bathe, in order to earn spiritual merit. Think of all those devout swimmers in the River Ganges at Benares; all those well-trodden ancient pilgrim trails up into the heart of the Himalayas through the mountain passes of Nepal, Kashmir, and Yunnan; those steep paths and steps up to myriad hilltops with their crowning shrines and monasteries throughout Buddhist Asia; and the great temple of Angkor Wat in Cambodia, symbolising in the very architecture of its towers and steep-sided staircases the mighty Himalayas themselves.

The idea of religious journey is even more strongly embedded in the Abrahamic religions, with their emphasis on humanity's active quest for revelation and salvation. Moses wandered fruitlessly for forty years in the Sinai desert in search of the Promised Land of Israel, and Jews in exile yearned to return to their holy places, praying for 'next year in Jerusalem'. It is still the religious duty of all devout Muslims who can afford the trip to make the pilgrimage to the holy sites of Mecca before they die.

For Christians in the Middle Ages, visiting pilgrimage sites was a central part of their religious experience, as natural as attending church on Sundays. These sites sprang up like mushrooms wherever there were credible stories of miracles or apparitions or saintly events, or simply the claimed discovery of sacred Christian relics such as fragments of the true cross, Jesus's shroud, or the bones of saints or martyrs. It took little to start a story of miracle cures or holy relics, and once such stories began they quickly gained a credibility and surrounding theology of their own. In the end, it mattered little whether the original story was true or imagined. The site became holy and religiously significant simply because so many believed that it was, rather in the manner of a self-fulfilling prophecy. Sometimes the institutional church tried vainly to put the genie back in the bottle, to get some sort of order and discipline and 'consumer protection' into verifying these stories of relics and miracles. They were usually too late, for the people had already decided what they wanted to believe.

From a huge array of local or national pilgrimage sites that came and went out of fashion (local sites close to home, like Canterbury in Britain, or Vezelay and Le Puy in France, could be most easily accessed by people from the same nation and language group) there emerged three favourite destinations for long-distance European pilgrimage: Jerusalem, Rome, and Santiago de Compostela. Some of the local sites then acquired new functions as starting points or way-stations for these longer pilgrimage routes (for example, Cologne, Paris, Vezelay, Le Puy), thereby ensuring their own longer-term popularity and prosperity.

But why Santiago of all places, tucked away in the remote northwest of Spain? How did the fame of this pilgrimage destination come to rival for hundreds of years the appeal of Rome or Jerusalem itself? There were practical reasons of accessibility and security, but there was also a uniquely powerful Christian foundation legend that raised Santiago to the level of Rome or Jerusalem. Santiago became known as 'the Jerusalem of the West', and certainly at its height its resident clergy thought of it in that way.

As a practical matter, Jerusalem in the Middle Ages was expensive to reach, and was for long periods dangerous to access, and insecure and culturally frightening even when one got there. The land route across the Balkans and Anatolia became increasingly perilous for pilgrims after the Arab occupation of Syria and Palestine in the seventh century, and impossible after the Seljuk Turks occupied much of Asia Minor following their crucial victory over the Byzantine Christians at the battle of Manzikert in 1071. The sea route to the Holy Land, on Venetian or Genoese trading ships, was safer but prohibitively expensive for all but the very rich. In the Holy Land itself, pilgrims were barely tolerated under the unsure and grudging protection of Muslim caliphs who had bitter memories of Christian perfidy and cruelty during the eleventh-century Crusades. Rome was difficult and dangerous to access through an unruly Italy of endemically warring and anarchical city-states, and the papal city and territories were often corrupt and insecure.

The road to Santiago, by contrast, offered an appealing combination: remoteness and hard walking, but with a reassuring degree of organisation and security. It was a satisfyingly long distance away from home, but still within the west European cultural space, and it passed through fairly well-governed Christian regions that became safer as the Christian–Muslim frontier zone in Spain moved further south. It is interesting that Chaucer's Wife of Bath—not a lady, I would think, to seek out too much danger or hardship on pilgrimage—had made a pilgrimage to Santiago.

From the eighth to the fifteenth centuries, and in particular under the wise guidance and sponsorship of the Benedictine monks of Cluny in France, led by their great abbot Peter of Cluny (1092–1156), who understood the unique importance and value of the Santiago pilgrimage as an educational tool to broaden Europe's cultural horizons, an impressive infrastructure of cathedrals, colleges, and hostels developed in the now-thriving city of Santiago and along the routes to it. Huge numbers of pilgrims travelled each year along the *Vía Frances* through Roncesvalles, then as now the most popular route. So many walked the Way that their footsteps wore down stone steps along its route.

The powerful founding myth centred around the life and death of St James the Apostle played a crucial role. St James (*Santiago* in Spanish, a compression of *Santo Diego*), was one of the three brothers commanded by Christ to leave their fishing nets on Lake Galilee and follow Him. He was said to be buried in Santiago. After a lifetime spent preaching the gospel in Spain, so the legend goes, James returned to the Eastern Mediterranean, where he was martyred. His headless body was then brought back to Spain in a stone ship, and buried secretly near the site of Santiago. There, several centuries later, in a legendary battle at Clavijo in 844 A.D. between Christian and Muslim armies, St James appeared in a vision to the despairing Christian fighters, inspiring them to victory. His bones were then discovered nearby, and a pilgrimage shrine established, which became the city of Santiago.

St James has two religious *personae*: *Santiago Matamoros*, 'The Moorslayer', portrayed in armour on horseback, energetically killing Moors; and *Santiago Peregrino*, the gentle, Christ-like pilgrim with scallop-shell, staff, water bottle, waist-purse, and robe. The image of *Santiago Matamoros* is the cruel face of the Crusades, Christianity's holy wars. To kill Muslims in the name of Christ was not a sin, but a sacred duty. I cannot warm to *Santiago Matamoros*—his imagery in Spanish churches as a mounted knight with sword in hand, slashing at helpless Muslims crushed beneath his horse's feet, chills my blood—but the reality of the historic duality in Christianity between peaceful pilgrimage and warlike crusade cannot be ignored. Santiago expresses that duality.

To better comprehend the Crusades and the complex Christian–Muslim–Jewish cultural dynamics they involved, I turned to a great work of medieval history: Sir Steven Runciman's *History of the Crusades* (1951–54). The Crusades were first inspired by the same pilgrimage ideal—the desire to be able to travel freely and safely all the way from Christian western Europe to the holy places of the Bible, through Christian-ruled lands without let or hindrance. The same motivations were there for crusading as for pilgrimage—redemption, healing, expiation of sins, adventure, escape from a dull or dreary life at home—but there was a crucial difference.

Crusaders went a-pilgriming with sword in hand, armed with the dispensation to kill Muslims or Jews (or even Eastern Rite Christians) in the name of Christ. So, together with the excitement of leaving behind a poor, cold, and primitive western Europe still trapped in the ignorance and discomfort of the Dark Ages, and entering the warm, sunlit world of the higher post-Roman civilisations of the eastern Mediterranean, these military pilgrimages offered the adrenalin rush of righteous war, conquest, and booty.

All this is brilliantly captured in Ridley Scott's moodily atmospheric 2005 film about the Crusades, *Kingdom of Heaven*. The lead character, Balian the Blacksmith, in deep despair at the death of his beloved wife, desperately (and unlawfully) flees from his bleak and lonely home village, departing by sea from southern Italy to Palestine with monks intoning the ritual blessing, 'To kill a Muslim is no sin'. To

Balian's wonder and delight, he sails to the glowing sunshine and luxury of the short-lived Christian kingdom of Palestine, where he comes to love and respect Muslim chivalry and culture.

Meanwhile, at the other end of the Mediterranean, in what is now Spain, the small and embattled remnant Christian kingdoms in León-Castile and the Asturias had no role in the Holy Land Crusades, because their hands were full with their own national crusade at home: to fight to win the peninsula back from Moorish rule. These little kingdoms on the northern periphery of rich, Muslim-ruled Spain were situated in territory too mountainous and forested for the Moorish cavalry to subdue easily—and they were never worth the trouble to conquer. These states were, in every way (economically, culturally, militarily), weaker than the powerful Muslim-ruled state of al–Andalus that dominated Spain for over 300 years from its magnificent southern capital at Córdoba.

Yet these little Christian kingdoms gradually consolidated as the spearhead of the Christian reconquest of the Spanish peninsula. Over three centuries, with frequent reverses and temporary accommodations, the frontier of Christian state power moved southwards. Even before the idea of Spain had any real meaning, a martial Christian crusader culture had developed in the north of the Iberian peninsula, with *Santiago Matamoros* as its central symbolic inspiration.

Protecting the pilgrim route of the *Vía Frances* from the Pyrenees to Santiago was an integral part of the Christian reconquest project. Periodically, Moorish mounted raiding parties, swiftly crossing the no-mans-land of the high unpopulated *meseta* (tableland) from their great fortress cities such as Zamora and Salamanca, would fall on bands of pilgrims, seeking booty and ransom money. In self-defence, military orders of armed monks (Spain's own Knights of Santiago, as well as the Templars who were also very active in Spain in this era) built strong castles from which they defended the camino routes and made their own raiding sorties into the Muslim-ruled south.

But the southern frontier was rarely an impermeable military or cultural barrier in these years. The Santiago pilgrimage not only nourished the dream of a united Christian Spain, it also stimulated a rich trading and cultural interchange between Christian Europe and the higher civilisation of Muslim al-Andalus. Spanish Christian pilgrims from the southern region—because there was freedom of religion there—and seaborne pilgrims from Italy, disembarking in the seaports of Cádiz or Seville, came up along the ancient *Vía de la Plata*, the old Roman 'Silver Road' linking the south and north of the peninsula. They brought with them ideas and knowledge from the East, sharing them with Christian pilgrims from northern Europe.

What an exciting melting-pot of knowledge and ideas Santiago must have been in those years; what mind-expanding conversations must have taken place in its inns and libraries and plazas. From the *Vía Frances* grew up safe and well-marked routes south through Muslim lands to cities like Toledo, then a brilliant centre of Muslim–Jewish–Christian scholarship. Peter of Cluny went to this region and met scholars from Toledo in 1142, an event that was momentous in the cultural history of Europe.

Finally, I think, Santiago always had another unique asset: the unspoken attraction of the older pre-Christian civilisation of this region, the haunting aura of the times when this was a place of Celtic magic and runes and druids. Santiago and Finisterre, indeed all of Galicia, still give off a mystical, pagan Celtic spirituality, and it must have been even more pronounced then.

Both the Crusades and the pilgrimage to Santiago—at opposite ends of the Mediterranean world—became powerful vehicles for the transmission of higher learning and culture from the post-Roman east into western Europe, finally ending the long night of the Dark Ages, laying the foundations for the European renaissance that began in the twelfth century. The classical Graeco–Roman achievements in art, science, and philosophy—this precious repository of knowledge and culture that was mostly lost in western Europe during the disruptive barbarian invasions of the western Roman empire—had been cherished and preserved (and expanded) in the libraries of the old eastern Roman empire maintained by the Arab invaders, in Egypt and Syria in particular.

Through the pilgrimage to Santiago, Christian western Europe was able to connect with the classical learning and high culture of al-Andalus and its successor states. European Christians readily acknowledged in those centuries that Moorish Spain was the most advanced and enlightened culture in the western Mediterranean. Much of the great body of classical Graeco–Roman learning reached western Europe and England by this circuitous indirect route through Moorish Spain. Texts that were first translated from the original Greek or Latin into Arabic by Greek and Muslim scholars in the eastern Mediterranean areas were retranslated on the Spanish peninsula into the declining language of medieval Latin or increasingly into the young, developing

Romance languages of Europe and thence finally into English. This circuitous process took many centuries. Much of this learning was still fresh and exciting, even as late as Shakespeare's time in England. We can sense this excitement in Shakespeare's and Marlowe's plays.

***

I was fascinated to learn more about how, for some 500 years between 850 and 1350 A.D., as the pilgrimage to Santiago grew in fame and cultural importance, the rich societies of Moorish Spain—being al-Andalus, based on its capital city of Córdoba, and its smaller successor city-states—had nurtured an advanced culture of knowledge, urban civility, and religious freedom.

Al-Andalus was a powerful and dynamic Moorish state with its capital at Córdoba, founded in 755 A.D. by Abd al-Rahman, a brave and brilliant young refugee prince from Damascus, the last survivor of his massacred Umayyad line—why has Hollywood never made a film about his epic life? His new state of al–Andalus, nominally owing allegiance to the far-away Baghdad caliphate, but effectively independent, soon conquered most of the Iberian peninsula from weak Visigothic states, beginning a golden age of stability and prosperity that lasted for three hundred years. Then, in 1031 A.D., dynastic failure led to the dissolution of al-Andalus into a confused jumble of smaller warring city-states, some ruled by Christian and some by Muslim princes. But this very political instability, as in Renaissance Italy, stimulated a rich and fruitful interchange of Christian, Jewish, and Islamic trade and scholarship. Wandering merchants and scholars carried knowledge and culture throughout the peninsula and beyond into Europe proper.

This inspiring story, and much more, is told in the book that became my third major reference-point in preparing for my pilgrimage walk from Granada to Santiago—María Rosa Menocal's brilliant work of cultural history, whose title speaks for itself: *The Ornament of the World: how Muslims, Jews and Christians created a culture of tolerance in medieval Spain* (Little, Brown, 2002).

I chose to begin my walk in Granada, passing through Córdoba, the magnificent capital built by Abd al-Rahman, because I wanted to try to get some insights into this great multicultural civilisation. I hoped to get some hints of what it had been like here at its height, before the dark night of religious intolerance and persecution descended on Spain after 1492; to explore what traces it had left in Andalucia, and how much it had influenced the rest of Spain and, through Spain, western Europe. I was as much seeking to explore Spain's glorious Muslim past as its more recent Christian past.

***

Sumption emphasises how seriously and literally medieval European Christians took their religion: they were a superstitious and credulous lot. Once an idea took hold that certain places were especially holy, and that to go there would bring real spiritual and physical benefits, there was no stopping the mass movement of pilgrims swarming in from all directions. Pilgrimage (like crusading) released huge and powerful latent energies in ordinary people. It took them away from the drudgery of growing food and staying alive in cold, wet climates; away from harsh and boring village lives that, for most people, still hovered just above a bare subsistence level. It also released their yearnings for travel and adventure. It was an impulse that the church welcomed for spiritual reasons, at the same time knowing how hard it was to safely channel and control.

Church leaders like Peter of Cluny gave priority to promoting and building safe travel infrastructure, establishing well-marked and well-resourced routes to stop people straying all over the countryside and becoming prey to local brigands, or themselves stealing food and disrupting local populations. So the church encouraged the formation of military monastic orders like the Knights of Santiago, tasked to protect and succour and organise the huge numbers of pilgrims, to build chains of protective pilgrim refuges on the way, to bridge dangerous rivers, and to erect strong forts and castles to guard insecure sections of the route. In these ways, a separate pilgrimage culture and economic infrastructure developed around the camino to Santiago, a phenomenon standing alongside but in some ways separate from the general European political and cultural experience in those years.

For pilgrims, to go to Santiago was an extraordinary adventure of a lifetime. Pilgrimage soon developed its own liturgies and traditions. Its romantic imagery entered into the languages of Europe. England's first great extended literary work, *The Canterbury Tales*, is the story of a group of English pilgrims to Canterbury—the great cathedral where the martyred relics of Thomas á Becket were enshrined—who entertained each other with nightly tales after each day's walking. Shakespeare's plays, and Elizabethan-age literature generally, are full of the exciting imagery of pilgrimage: of travel to faraway places, of shipwreck, losing one's way, meeting strange foreigners, coping with foreign laws and customs, exile, loneliness, and homecoming. All these themes represent the medieval pilgrim experience.

Even centuries later, when the great medieval pilgrimage routes of Europe had lost relevance and were crumbling into disuse and decay, pilgrimage as a metaphor, an ideal, could still inspire John Bunyan's wildly popular allegory, *The Pilgrim's Progress*. The seventeenth-century Puritan religious refugees who colonised New England in the 'Mayflower' were happy be known as the 'Pilgrim Fathers'. Protestant England's most inspiring hymns are filled with the language, metaphors, and imagery of pilgrimage. I still remember as a schoolboy lustily bellowing out the stirring anthem inspired by Bunyan's words:

> He who would valiant be, 'gainst all disaster,
> Let him in constancy, follow the Master.
> There's no discouragement, shall make him once relent
> His first avowed intent, to be a pilgrim.

The idea of pilgrimage, the dream of 'an arduous journey far from home undertaken for sacred reasons', is embedded deep in our culture and history. It is part of us, part of what inspires our urge to travel, to experience foreign places. We may not know it, but each time we leave our homeland to travel the world, we are looking for something more than just 'holidays', fun, and sex in the sun. I think we are seeking, whether we recognise it or not, spiritual enlightenment, wisdom, and the revelation of God in the richness of the great world that lies out there beyond our home town.

Every traveller, especially every young traveller, is a pilgrim: whether they go consciously to seek spiritual rebirth, to escape from oppression or grief or boredom at home, to seek interesting or spiritually rewarding work experience abroad, or simply to enjoy the thrill of unfamiliar places and customs. The desire to go a-pilgriming, it seems, is part of our human condition.

chapter three

Setting Off

In my garden in Canberra, one crisp and sunny autumn afternoon in May, my family and friends—my sister Naomi had even flown up from Melbourne—came to see me off to Spain. But it wasn't just an ordinary pre-holiday farewell gathering. Father John Eddy, a Jesuit priest and a good friend for many years, was there to bless the pilgrimage I was about to set out on.

We were honouring the medieval customary practice. When pilgrims or crusaders left home, everybody knew there was a fair chance they might never come back, or at least not for a very long time. So departing pilgrims would make their personal arrangements with care—paying any debts, collecting any debts due to them, asking reconciliation with their enemies and forgiveness from those they had wronged, and making prudent arrangements for the care of their dependent families while they were away or if they did not return. Finally, they would ask the local priest or bishop to bless their pilgrimage and pray for their safe return home. I thought all those were good rules, and wanted to emulate them.

So there I was, proudly dressed in crisp new khaki pilgrim gear, walking boots, and floppy hat, a scallop shell around my neck, a packed rucksack and wooden staff at my side—no doubt looking rather ridiculous, but I wanted to do this thing properly—as Father John sprinkled me and these meagre belongings with blessed holy water, and offered his priestly pilgrim's blessing. I realised then with a shock that all this was truly happening, that I really was about to embark the next morning on the strangest adventure of my life. I would need all the help and prayers I could get, and was suddenly very glad that my family and friends were there to wish me well and pray for a safe journey and return home to the family. It was a memorable and heart-swelling send-off from my priest and friend John. Looking around at the shining faces of family and friends, I felt more at peace with myself than I had been for a long time.

But the next morning's departure was considerably less happy. Suddenly I was lonely, and scared of what might be in store. I was going to the other end of the world, alone. I looked down at my pack and staff—they seemed both very heavy to carry, and very small. Everything I owned, my whole life-support system for the next two months, was in this little backpack. I was leaving behind—I realised now, for a long time—the warm comforts of home, the joy and love of family, but for what real purpose? Waves of doubt and fear and a sense of my own foolish selfishness swept over me as I made my final packing checks.

The taxi tooted in the driveway, and I gave my wife and children hasty farewell hugs, fighting back brimming tears and incipient panic. It was crazy to be leaving for so long those whom I loved. Why on earth was I attempting this pilgrimage venture on the other side of the world. Had it all been a huge error of judgement?

I caught the bus for Sydney, and tried to drive away such bleak thoughts by closing my eyes and burying myself in Spanish-language tapes for the next few hours. The tapes were a good excuse for not thinking, a mental exercise in keeping fears and emotions at bay. I didn't know it, but the iron discipline of the pilgrimage was beginning.

***

While I patiently waited out the long bus and air and train journey stages from Canberra to Granada—it took over forty-four hours in all, and I did not sleep in a bed once in that time—I thought more about how the Santiago pilgrimage, which by the early twentieth century had become defunct medieval history, had revived spectacularly after World War II and the return of democracy to Spain following Franco's death in 1975. It's an interesting story in itself that says much about the changing mood and values of our times.

There was a combination of powerful cultural trends. In continental Europe there was widespread disillusionment after the century of terrible wars and atrocities that had followed the two centuries of the optimistic Enlightenment. Now, many serious thinkers felt that secular rationalism had taken Europe down a civilisational blind alley that had, in the end, contributed to the perverted nationalist ideologies of the twentieth century, and to the huge crimes against humanity of the Nazi and Stalinist eras. Many thought that something more than secular rationalism was needed to rebuild the foundations for a decent European civic morality. There was a new open-mindedness and interest in religion, and a new readiness to try to re-connect with the noble old ideal of a united Christian Europe. Europeans had had enough of competing nationalisms, except on the football field and in the Eurovision song contest. As the Cold War wound down to its close, and as postwar generations of Europeans grew up, there was a growing conviction that it was essential now to look for new models—new ways to come together in love and friendship, both symbolic and practical, affirming the cultural unity of European peoples.

Spain itself was searching for new approaches to civil society and to church-state relations. Franco's coercive and now discredited clerical-fascist ascendancy had run its course, and with his death in 1975 a new democratic politics was in rapid gestation. Progressive Spanish Catholics were looking for new ways to re-legitimise their church, to restore its standing and connections with younger, democratically minded Spaniards. In this context, the pilgrimage to Santiago was something fresh, holy, and untarnished by past church mistakes and misdeeds. Local voluntary 'Friends of the Camino' societies sprang up across Spain and Portugal to survey, waymark, and restore the old pilgrimage rights-of-way—routes that had in many areas become no more than vague local memories. Soon there were several alternative waymarked routes to Santiago being re-established: not only through the Pyrenees, but also from Valencia, Alicante, Toledo, Granada, Seville, Cádiz, Lisbon. All the ancient caminos of Spain were being re-located and re-signed with the famous yellow arrows.

In Rome in the 1960s, the Catholic Church under the benign influence of Pope John XXIII was itself searching for symbols of a new global ecumenicism and inclusiveness. The Second Vatican Council, 1965–68, launched this new spirit, and pilgrimage fitted into the new ethos perfectly. In 1978, Karol Wojtyla, who had been Archbishop of Cracow in Poland since 1963, became Pope John Paul II. A strong and vigorous athlete, he was throughout his life a priest who instinctively understood the great value of pilgrimage in the re-building of Christian life. As Archbishop of Cracow he had helped restore the historic Polish pilgrimage to the shrine of the Black Madonna in Czestochowa in southern Poland. Defying mockery and harassment from the communist state authorities, young Catholic Poles from the 1960s onwards walked this pilgrimage in great numbers as an act of religious affirmation and symbolic rejection of the Communist Party's pretensions to dominate Polish society. The freedom and joy of the Czestochowa pilgrimage relieved the fear and suspicion that people lived with under the harsh control of the communist national security state. Even the worker-intellectual alliance that became Solidarity, the social renewal movement that eventually toppled communism, was forged on the pilgrim paths to Czestochowa.

Thus, in eastern as well as western Europe, religious pilgrimages became a symbolic rejection by young people of the sterility of both communism and capitalist greed. As pope in 1989, John Paul II presided over a seminal World Youth Day in Santiago that was attended by huge numbers of young people.

Even outside the Church, in Western society at large, there was a new readiness in people who were not necessarily religious in a conventional sense to explore their own spirituality in new ways. Secular rationalism had truly had its day in Europe. For the same sorts of reasons that a lot of people were ready to try yoga, transcendental meditation, Zen, travelling to India to explore oriental mysticism, varieties of tantric sex or mind-enhancing drugs, and experimenting with new communal ways of living together, more and more people were ready to have another look at the Santiago pilgrimage. Going to Santiago became a fashionable 'New Age' thing to do.

Obviously, modern pilgrims no longer expected miracle cures in Santiago, nor were they seeking guaranteed passages into heaven, but they were looking for answers to important questions about the good life and a good civil society that European secular rationalism had failed to deliver. And it turned out that the pilgrimage delivered something of value that many were looking for. Its popularity grew rapidly. This is easy to measure, because Santiago Cathedral keeps statistics of the number of *compostelas* that it issues each year to pilgrims completing their journey.

Here are some published data: in 1986, 2491 *compostelas* were issued; in 1992, 9764; in the holy year of 1993, 99,439; in 1998, 30,126; in the holy year of 1999, 154,613; in the jubilee year of 2000, 55,004; and in the holy year of 2004, 179,944—the highest figure yet. In 2005, a 'normal' year, 93,924 were issued.

The greatest numbers of pilgrims still choose the most popular set of routes from France, the *Vía Frances* from Roncesvalles. But conscious of the dangers of this classic route becoming overloaded and overstressed with too many pilgrims for their own safety and comfort, the Spanish and European Union authorities (Spain joined the Union in 1986) have been working to improve the infrastructure on alternative routes—in particular, the *Vía de la Plata* from Seville in the far south. A lot of money is going into better waymarking and information signage, establishing new pilgrim *albergues* and *refugio*s big enough to handle large groups of walkers—school groups, for example—and protecting and maintaining public pedestrian rights of way on the camino*s* as new motorway-construction projects carve great swathes out of the Spanish countryside. The European heritage values of the pilgrimage trails have been formally recognised and gazetted, and the economic value of the pilgrimage in encouraging remote-area tourism and bringing more economic activity into isolated villages accepted. Of course, the pilgrimage has wider long-term benefits for Spanish tourism: walkers on the camino may not be big spenders, but they may return in later years with their families for more conventional holidays in Spain.

The European Christian churches, both Catholic and Protestant, see the value of the pilgrimage as a stimulus for religious revival and consciousness-raising in the youth. And doctors and mental-health professionals see its therapeutic value for mind and body. So the modern pilgrimage to Santiago speaks to many constituencies, all sharing the central classic motivation of pilgrims, ancient or modern—a hunger for spiritual rebirth, for better answers to deeply felt spiritual needs. That the pilgrimage seems to appeal alike to practising Christians and to non-Christians, even to determined humanists, only confirms that something interesting is happening here in terms of spirituality and personal growth.

***

On the face of it, the people you meet on the camino today might seem far removed from medieval concepts of pilgrimage. But they are not so different, I think, as might first appear.

In the Middle Ages, pilgrims certainly carried a lot less. They might have looked a lot like the statues of *Santiago Peregrino* you see in Spanish churches—in a homespun robe and sandals, a scallop-shell hanging around their neck, and carrying a staff, water bottle, and waist-purse at their belt. No hi-tech backpacks or hiking boots for them!

The Elizabethan courtier and adventurer Sir Walter Raleigh wrote a lovely little poem—which forms the frontispiece to this book—that perfectly captures the uncomplicated and artless spirit of medieval pilgrimage:

> Give me my scallop-shell of quiet,
> My staff of faith to walk upon,
> My scrip of joy, immortal diet,
> My bottle of salvation,
> My gown of glory, hope's true gage,
> And thus I'll take my pilgrimage.
> — 'The Passionate Man's Pilgrimage' (1604)

Raleigh is a link between medieval and modern pilgrims. A versatile Renaissance man—courtly and elegant, a buccaneering sea-captain and knight much favoured by Queen Elizabeth of England, imbued with the cynicism of his worldly age—he was still in spiritual contact with the medieval idea of pilgrimage. And his short poem here is far more than just a pilgrim's packing list. Raleigh lived while England was being torn asunder politically between the old

Catholic religion and the newly established national Church of England. His poem shows a rich empathy with the fast-fading medieval ideals, with the old urge to 'go a-pilgriming'. I want to reflect a little on Raleigh's lines.

My scallop-shell of quiet: this is a lovely image, reminding us of how pilgrimage is fundamentally a search for peace and quiet from the hurly-burly, tensions, and complications of daily life and work. Put the shell to your ear, Raleigh suggests to us, and the noise of the world falls away—all you will hear is the soft sigh of the sea. And wearing the scallop-shell of St James around his neck identifies a pilgrim to Santiago, being his safe-conduct pass through dangerous lands where an unidentified foreigner might otherwise be suspect.

My staff of faith to walk upon: the sturdy wooden pilgrim's staff, shoulder-high or longer with its forked or hooked top, was symbolic both of a shepherd's crook and of Christ's wooden Cross. Raleigh's key phrase here is 'to walk upon'—not just to walk with, but relying upon the staff as companion and helper on the way, assisting the pilgrim over mountains and rough ground, crossing rivers and marshes, and as a weapon of self-defence. Raleigh understood that the staff symbolises the pilgrim's strong faith that, with God's help and protection, he would complete his arduous and dangerous journey to Santiago.

My scrip of joy, immortal diet: literally, the 'scrip' is the pilgrim's *credencial* or passport, his document from his local priest or feudal lord testifying that he has been permitted to go on this pilgrimage. But 'scrip of joy, immortal diet' has a richer meaning that I experienced one wonderful day in high Castile. I was walking alone, my blisters had healed, my excess body weight was gone, and my pack seemed light. It was early morning. Dark-grey storm-clouds were massing in the sky to the west, rolling across the ripe, golden wheatlands towards me. Morning dew still hung heavy on the wire fence alongside my track, and pendant spiderwebs glistened like silver against the gold and grey horizon. Everyday wayside flowers—dog roses, thistles, lupins, bluebells, wild shallots, everlasting daisies, lavender, and much more—were in bloom. This commonplace countryside view suddenly was so overwhelmingly beautiful to me that I wept as the glory of God's creation washed over me. That, I think is the 'immortal diet' Raleigh has in mind: those wonderful moments on a pilgrimage when all pain and earthly care is transcended, when you see with piercing clarity and joy the wonder of the world that God has given us to love and care for.

My bottle of salvation: there are several sly Elizabethan puns here, I think. Without water, we die: it is the essential element in our physical organism, and our bodies are mostly composed of water. When we dehydrate, we die, and our bodies finally become no more than dry dust and bones. So the water bottle a pilgrim carries is his water of life, his essential guarantee of physical survival. Raleigh would have seen other meanings wrapped up here as well. A pilgrim's leather water bottle would have frequently held not only water but alcohol—wine or beer or cider or spirits, all part of the pilgrim's normal diet. Christ turned water into wine; and in the Christian sacrament of Holy Communion, consecrated bread and water and wine—the pilgrim's basic foods—become the body and blood of Christ. To eat and drink from the consecrated bread, water, and wine, in memory of Christ's supreme sacrifice on the Cross, saves us from sin and thereby offers the possibility of eternal life. Finally, the 'bottle of salvation' also good-humouredly reminds us of the benign secular pleasures of human society on pilgrimage. To be a pilgrim is not to be a cheerless lonely traveller, but to journey in groups, to meet people and enjoy convivial relaxation with them after the day's hard walking, to celebrate life and friendship in evenings of eating and drinking with fellow pilgrims and people met on the way.

My gown of glory: Raleigh, who wore the rich and colourful garb of an Elizabethan courtier, speaks here with affectionate irony about the typical pilgrim's rough and dirty brown homespun gown. Medieval pilgrims did not carry backpacks or changes of clothing. The one rough robe was worn through all weathers. They walked, slept, and bathed in it (whenever they found rivers or lakes in which to bathe). The austerity of such spartan clothing was part of their pilgrimage experience. Part of their sense that their act of pilgrimage had value, their 'glory', came from their sacrifice of physical comfort and vanity.

Hope's true gage: what made pilgrimage so powerful an expression of Christian belief was the hope it bore within it, the firm belief that to make such arduous and dangerous journeys to faraway holy places would carry great spiritual and temporal rewards: God's forgiveness of one's sins, the promise of eternal salvation; the healing of disease or disability in oneself or in one's loved ones; the hope of reconciliation and forgiveness from those one has wronged in life. Without those firm beliefs, the privations and risks of pilgrimage would have been pointless suffering.

Thus, in these six tightly drafted lines, Raleigh captures the essence of the medieval philosophy of pilgrimage. How, I wondered, do we modern-day pilgrims measure up to his simple message? A few pilgrims are happy to follow his example, delighting in the spontaneity of just throwing a few clothes in a rucksack and heading off when the idea takes their fancy, trusting in God or Providence to help them on their way. Laurie Lee writes that, as a young man, he just walked out of the door of his mother's house in England one midsummer morning and started walking towards Spain. This reminds me also of a charming story Sumption tells, of how Irish monks in the Dark Ages used to float off from Ireland to preach the gospel to pagan Europe, in little coracle boats without sails or oars, trusting that God would steer their fragile craft to places where their work was most needed. Fortunately, the Gulf Stream would have helped most of them eventually to make a landfall somewhere in Europe. You can do the pilgrimage in that carefree spirit—I met a young Portuguese near Zamora who was moving fast, walking from Valencia to Santiago without maps, without a pilgrim *credencial*, with little money and the smallest of daypacks—and I know he got to Santiago, because other friends met him there later. But most of us would want to go with at least a little more preparation and resources.

***

I will say something here, remembering as I sat through that long flight from Australia to Europe, how I had tried to prepare my body for long-distance endurance walking, about the care of feet, and about what a modern pilgrim might choose to carry. But if you're impatient to start the walk with me, go straight to the next chapter and come back to read the rest of this chapter later.

Long-distance walking on roads or paths for upwards of twenty kilometres a day, week after week, is not a normal sort of exercise. It is a high-intensity physical activity that makes particular demands on human bodies, just as long-distance running or mountain-climbing or high-energy ball games do. So our bodies need to be trained up for it beforehand, if the pleasure of the first weeks on the camino is not to be ruined by muscle stress and fatigue pains, or in the worst case physical breakdown and forced withdrawal. I found that the best way to prepare (about three months before setting out) was to start walking around home, preferably with a laden pack, increasing the distances each day. It is hard for most people to find the time or suitable paths near home to do this. Best are unpaved country lanes or footpaths, preferably not too even, to improve balance and flexibility, and to get your ankles accustomed to coping with movement over rough ground. Also, the hillier the better, to improve aerobic fitness and to get used to balancing the backpack going up and down slopes. Those who live in a big city may use its major avenues and large parks, walking off the paved paths onto grass as much as possible, and looking for slopes to go up and down. Big cities such as New York, Washington, London, or Ottawa have long jogging-trails through accessible, rough parkland (for example, in Central Park, Rock Creek Park, Hampstead Heath). A few longer weekend walks in real countryside, planning routes of two or three days, and walking at least six hours a day, are good training. I was lucky: my hometown, Canberra, is ringed with nature parks on surrounding hills that offer a diverse range of rough walking trails.

Most mornings during the ten weeks before I left, I would get up early and do five to fifteen kilometres fast walking before breakfast. By the time I left home, I had over 500 kilometres under my belt, and presumed I was already quite fit. That was not quite the case, but at least I had gone some of the way.

It is a good idea to lose as much weight as possible before setting off, using the mental spur of the upcoming challenge to help motivate a smaller food intake. Walkers inevitably lose weight on the camino, but it's more enjoyable if you can get down to a fit walking weight before starting. I didn't, and I paid for it later.

Walking in the socks and boots that will be used on the camino prepares feet for what is in store. Although walking two to three hours a day doesn't fully condition feet for walking six to eight hours a day, it helps. As to footwear, some walkers swear by traditional German-style leather hiking boots that need to be broken in, but some prefer modern lightweight athletic cross-trainers. I opted for a compromise—lightweight hiking boots, a cross-trainer-style synthetic trail boot with stiff, lugged rubber soles and high side-ankle support. They were comfortable from first wearing, dried quickly (Goretex-lined), and wore quite well. I used two pairs in sequence, and each pair was good for 600 kilometres. Both wore the heels right down to the slate inserts, but I had new rubber heels glued on when I got back home.

On a hot trail like the *Vía de la Plata* in summer, your feet will sweat and swell; so it is best to size the boots a little loose, while wearing two pairs of lightweight synthetic walking socks. Leave the traditional heavy woollen outer socks at home. By always walking in two pairs of socks, the outer sock sticks to the boot and the inner to the skin; this means that most of the rubbing that would cause blisters takes place between the two sock layers, rather than between socks and skin. Take at least four pairs of such socks for two changes a day, a good talcum powder to dry moist feet, and a good foot cream to soften hard, scaly feet and prevent cracking around the heels. Pampering feet, keeping them clean and dry, and massaging foot cream in generously after a day's walking, means happy feet—the most critical element in the enjoyment of walking.

After the day's trail walking was over, I would change into open, lightweight leather sandals—not unlike what medieval pilgrims and monks wore—for strolling in villages or towns. Sandals aerate and relax the feet, refreshing them for the next day. You can buy such sandals either before leaving or easily and cheaply anywhere in Spain.

***

On my camino route, I never camped out. Pilgrims were few, and there was always cheap accommodation in village bars or pensións, or in pilgrim *albergues,* so there was no need to carry a tent or sleeping bag or groundmat. I had a cotton liner sleeping bag and a baby pillow; but walkers in cooler seasons might want to take a lightweight sleeping bag for use in unheated *albergues*. I took a hammock, thinking it might be good for midday siestas on the trail, walking on in the cool of the evening. But I only used it twice, because I found that you want to complete your walking day as early as possible, and enjoy a real rest on a bed at the day's destination. Though the siesta is a Spanish idea, siestas on the road don't seem to fit the rhythm of a pilgrim's day.

Similarly, I didn't carry food or a cooking stove. A bit of cold food in a carrybag—fruit, leftover bread, some *jamón serrano* or cheese—was useful for early breakfasts and snacks on the way. Sometimes, you could find a workmens' café or bar open early in the morning for a fortifying coffee and *tostada* (toasted breadroll with jam).

Thus the pack only held clothing, toiletries, essential pharmaceuticals and first-aid items, electronic gear of choice (for example, digital camera, radio-cassette, or MP3 player, mobile phone), and essential documents. The weight of these sorts of items soon adds up, however.

Most people take three sets of clothing: one to wear, and two to pack. Many invest in lightweight, synthetic hiking clothing, but I prefer the protection of heavier cotton-drill clothing, which made my pack a few kilograms heavier. Northern European pilgrims like to soak up the sun, stripping down to shorts and T-shirts at the first sign of warmth in the sun's rays. As an Australian with a healthy respect for the medical risks to skin, I always wore long trousers and long-sleeved shirts. A woollen pullover was useful for cool evenings, and a hip-length showerproof Goretex-type jacket for any really rainy days. I also took a lightweight towel, and a light dressing gown or nightshirt for unisex dormitories; a broad-brimmed cotton hat with a chinstrap for windy days; and a swimming costume and bathing cap, to enjoy the hot baths or river swimming spots on the way.

Pharmaceuticals and toiletries are a personal choice, but here are a few tips. I packed these items in three labelled leather bags ('pharma', 'feet', and 'toiletries'), so I could easily find whatever I was looking for. Even the smallest Spanish village has a pharmacy, open in the early evenings and stocking a wide range of inexpensive generic medicines and drugs, so you don't need to carry a lot of just-in case pharmaceuticals and toiletries. I found the pharmaceuticals I used most were ibuprofen (which goes under the brandnames of Nurofen, Panafen, etc.), which I found more effective than aspirin or paracetamol for relaxing tight muscles and easing joint pain, thus helping me get a better night's sleep. Tiger Balm or similar liniment was effective, rubbed into sore ankles, calves, knees, shoulders. An asthma-reliever, hydrocortisone cream (Dermaid, Hydraderm, etc.), old-fashioned Vaseline for chafed skin in the tender parts, and lip balm were all put to good use. I carried—but hardly used—anti-allergenic hayfever tablets, antibiotic tablets, cold-sore cream, a cough and cold syrup, Vicks Vaporub, and sunburn cream. Those apprehensive about food upsets can carry anti-diarrhoea tablets and electrolyte-replacement salts, but every pharmacy sells these without prescription.

My foot kit was simple: bandaids for the odd blister and, for bad blisters, locally made *tiritas*—large oval patches of synthetic skin that one puts on and forgets about. Nail-clippers, a good foot powder, a tube of foot cream, and a roll of lambswool (which Boots The Chemists sell at London Airport) completed the foot kit.

Toiletries: the basics—toothbrush, safety razor, toilet soap, clothes-washing soap or detergent, deodorant, sunglasses, and a spare pair of prescription glasses. You can buy most of these things on the way in village *supermercados* (general stores), so there is no need to load up with spare toothpaste, soap, etc. A shaving cream that works with cold water is useful for men—there won't always be hot water in the mornings. It is good insurance to carry a couple of bath or basin plugs:

it is remarkable how often these are missing in even the best pensións. Similarly an elastic travel clothesline and a few pegs are useful, as is a basic sewing-kit and earplugs.

Other bits and pieces: the indispensable Swiss Army knife (but remember not to pack it in your carry-on bag, or it will be found and confiscated by airport security); a plastic spoon (handy for eating tubs of yogurt or custard or jelly); and bits of cord, spare laces, and a roll of packing tape for sending parcels home or on ahead in the post. Spanish post offices offer a wide range of sturdy padded envelopes and cardboard boxes, so you don't need wrapping paper. If you standardise electronic equipment to run on AA-size batteries, replacement batteries can always be found even in the smallest village. I had a four-pixel digital camera with a large memory chip (enough room for 450 images), ideal for on-the-road photography and making it easy to delete rejected shots. In large towns like Salamanca, there are shops that will transfer all your images onto a CD that can be sent home.

For documents, I bought a big, heavy-duty, plastic waterproof envelope with a neckstrap, designed to keep a trailmap or guidebook dry in the rain. It never rained for me, but the case protected my key documents from trail wear and tear: passport, air tickets and travel insurance, next-of-kin contact data, favourite family photos (laminated for durability), pilgrim *credencial*, roadmaps, guidebook, photocopied city maps, pens, envelopes and writing paper, spare postcards and stamps, pocket diary, Spanish dictionary, Berlitz phrasebook, and instruction booklets for my camera, MP3 player, and mobile phone. This document case was the heaviest item in my rucksack.

With all this stuff on my back, I was a long way from a

medieval pilgrim's few belongings. If I had been confident of my spoken Spanish and had not wanted to carry the technology to communicate with my family and record my journey, the weight could have been a lot less.

To carry this sort of weight, you need a real rucksack—that is, a backpack engineered for trail walking. A lot of backpacks for sale nowadays are really little more than soft carry-bags with shoulder-straps and a waist-belt; they are fine for short walks around towns from airport or bus station to hotel, but not designed for long-distance walking. A 55-litre or 65-litre rucksack is big enough, because you do not want to carry more than 15 per cent of your body weight. The pack needs to fit well because, when loaded and adjusted, it should redistribute most of the packed weight down from the shoulder-straps onto the hipbones. So a strong molded waistbelt and a well-designed adjustable backframe are the most important parts of the rucksack.

I bought a Berghaus Antaeus—sold as their 'entry-level' rucksack—and found it did the job really well. This pack has additional side and top pockets, double-zips above and below in the main compartment, and an inbuilt raincape. I also bought a waterproof rucksack liner bag—a heavy-duty plastic bag that rolls up and clipseals at the top. I'm sure it would have protected the contents from the heaviest downpour, but I never found out.

When I started out from Granada, my pack weighed a foolishly heavy twenty-two kilograms. When I got to the first town with a post office, I got rid of about six kilograms by posting three parcels on ahead with my sleeping bag, sleeping mat, pullover, unneeded clothing, and books. It is really important to keep pack-weight as low as possible, resisting the temptation to pack that extra item 'just in case'. With my body weight of ninety-four kilograms (at the start of the walk) and eighty-five kilograms (at the finish), a 16-kilogram pack was the maximum comfortable load I could carry. That included two kilograms for the two 1-litre water bottles when filled for a long day's walk.

In preparing the pack, it was important to pack tightly, to balance the weight between the left and right sides, and to concentrate the heaviest items in the centre of gravity of the pack—that is, around its middle and behind the small of the back. Putting heavy stuff at the bottom creates an uncomfortably heavy lump down behind your rear, and putting heavy stuff at the top increases problems of maintaining equilibrium and balance over rough ground.

Lifting the laden pack onto the shoulders and taking it off are the times of greatest strain on straps and seams. To prevent rips and tears, I did this as seldom as possible and as gently as possible. Specialist shops that sell rucksacks will adjust the main pack straps at point of sale to suit your size and shape. On the road, you put on a laden pack by first resting it on the extended right or left knee (depending on whether you are right- or left-handed) with the backstraps facing you, and slipping the preferred first arm through its shoulder strap. Taking the weight on your shoulder, you gently swing the pack around behind, and loops the other arm into its shoulder strap. Then, lifting up the pack with both hands behind the back taking its weight, you can sit the straps evenly on the shoulders, making sure the back belt is sitting comfortably just above the hipbones, and then finally tighten the waistbelt strap as far as it will go. The chest strap is tightened as close as comfort allows, in order to stop the top of the pack from swaying. The small shoulder-top adjustment straps are kept as short as possible, for the same reason. Getting these fine adjustments right makes for comfortable walking. After a while, you forget that you are carrying a 16-kilogram pack.

Water bottles are as essential for the modern as for the medieval pilgrim. I like the indestructible aluminium kind, but some prefer lightweight plastic bottles. It's a good idea to have two water bottles of the same size (one litre or three-quarters of a litre), putting one in each side-compartment of the rucksack. That way you can drink from them in turn, keeping the water weight balanced. Some people like to sip water all the time; others take a healthy large swig every couple of hours. If the former, you can carry the water bottle in a small handbag, along with guidebook and snack food, so that you don't have to stop and take off the pack too often.

I didn't know all these things at the beginning of my walk, but I learned by experience and from others on the way, so I am sharing it here. Later in this book I offer some more 'tradecraft' advice about the pilgrim's best friend on the trail—the walking staff—and about the benefits of breaking yourself in, walking gently and keeping within endurance limits, eating and drinking sensibly, having rest breaks, map-reading, and navigation.

chapter four

From Granada to Córdoba

The walk began in Andalucia. I had arrived in Madrid on a Monday afternoon, after a long international flight from Australia with transfers in Frankfurt and London. Catching a fast metro train in from the super-modern Madrid International Airport, I arrived at a main city station just in time to catch the last afternoon intercity *Rapido* train to Granada. As I tried out my first tentative Spanish phrases with the patient barman in the buffet car, the train glided across the darkening, barren high plains of La Mancha. I looked for Don Quixote's famous canvas-sailed windmills, but could not find any. Then the train snaked its way up into the olive-clad mountains of Andalucia. By 10.00 pm I was sinking into an exhausted sleep in my first Spanish pensión, chosen at random not far from the Granada railway station.

The next morning, awakening before dawn, I walked up through the old city to see dawn breaking over the Alhambra with the still snow-covered peaks of the Sierra Nevada beyond—a glorious sight. I went to a busy little café-bar for an early breakfast of coffee, croissants, and an experimental cognac shared with local workmen. Then I found my way to my official pilgrimage starting point, the Real Monasterio de las Madres Commendatores de Santiago. The Mother Superior of this beautiful old convent was wearing the red cross of the Knights of Santiago on her habit, linking her order back to those knights who protected the camino. She received me in the convent reception hall after Mass, ceremonially stamping the first *sello* in my *credencial*. Because I was impatient to be on my way, I did no more sightseeing in Granada, but went straight back to the hotel to pick up my pack. I started walking out of the city, following Alison Raju's guidebook instructions—which worked perfectly.

Six hours and seventeen kilometres later, I was walking into my first Spanish village, Pinos Puente. It had been a pleasant but uninspiring day passing through irrigated flat croplands that I suspect were fed by Granada's treated grey water. In Pinos Puente, a puzzled parish priest, on whose door I had naively knocked, directed me to a large hotel on the nearby main highway. I had a romantic half-hope that he might have offered me dinner and conversation and a bed in his presbytery, but there was no such luck, either now or later. I had no appetite for dinner and fell straight into bed, falling into a deep dreamless sleep for fourteen hours.

Early the next morning, on a cool, calm, and sunny day, I was climbing steadily out of Pinos Puente into rolling uplands covered in geometrically planted olive plantations. Gaining height, glorious views opened up all around. The countryside was like a Harris Tweed herringbone jacket, with tidy stripes of blue-green olive trees radiating off in all directions, as far as the eye could see to faraway mountains. There were millions of olive trees, in land that was clear-ploughed and well weeded. Young trees were irrigated by trickle pipes fed from water distribution tanks. Older, deeper-rooted trees lived on whatever rain fell and on subsoil moisture. Every drop of rain that fell went down to the olive roots, because nothing else was growing except along natural watercourses. Some of the trees looked centuries old, with huge, gnarled trunks. Many were younger, and some were just newly planted saplings. There was a huge, continuing, long-term infrastructural investment here. There were hardly any workers to be seen, just the occasional tractor-drivers ploughing up the ground between trees, or men with trucks pruning unwanted limbs. We waved hellos across the fields. It was very quiet.

The olive trees had already set fruit, and a bumper crop was on the way, ready to be mechanically harvested and trucked to nearby pressing and bottling plants. I saw fields being planted by specialist crews with new baby trees: a precise business of surveying lines and marking planting points, laying water-pipes, and staking saplings. Olive-oil production here has clearly become a highly efficient, mechanised agribusiness in the twenty-first century. Essentially it converts six ingredients—sun, soil, water, olive trees, petrol, and fertiliser—into olive oil. With Andalucia's ideal soil and climate, and the advantages of cheap petrol and huge economies of scale to minimise labour costs, Andalusian olive oil has conquered world markets: nowhere else in the world is this quality of olive oil being produced in such quantities and so cheaply. Spin-off industries are based on bottled olives and fertiliser, made by drying the solid residues left after pressing the olives. Nothing is wasted.

Twelve kilometres later, it was down off the hills into Los Olivares, a little village at the head of the valley, below the mountain pass of Moclín. Here I was first recognised as a pilgrim to Santiago, and enjoyed my first real village hospitality. Lunch consisted of the local draught beer—excellent—and tapas at an attractive little bar-café next to a bridge over a rushing mountain torrent. My Spanish was still tentative, but I enjoyed what conversation I could manage. The friendly barkeeper wanted to know where I had come from and why—the first of many such conversations. He offered tapas over the counter, courtesy of the house, and I had more to drink than I should have, basking in the hospitality and curiosity around the bar about this pilgrim from Australia.

What I thought would then be a leisurely two-kilometre afternoon stroll up a short hill to my destination for the day, the hilltop fortress village of Moclín, turned out to be a demanding climb—around 500 metres' height gain—up a steep, loose gravel track. I stumbled, sweating and exhausted, into Moclín in mid-afternoon, to find there was no accommodation of any kind. I was preparing myself mentally for slinging my hammock overnight between two posts in a quiet chapel porch when a friendly builder took pity on me and asked his wife to open up a holiday apartment they owned.

Bathed and refreshed, I walked up later to see the old Moorish castle on the hilltop, with glorious sunset views all around, and then back down to the only café in the village plaza. At first it was very quiet; but as the sun came down after 7.00 pm, the plaza came to life with people strolling and chatting and little boys playing football. It became a good evening, my first real evening in a Spanish village.

Moclín is a place rich in atmosphere. Its Moorish castle had guarded this strategic mountain-pass on the road between

Córdoba and Granada, the natural frontier of the last Muslim kingdom in Spain. The small emirate of Granada had made a prudent separate peace with the invading Christian armies from Toledo in around 1250, and was thereafter allowed to remain as a remnant Muslim-ruled state for another 250-odd years. Finally their Catholic majesties Ferdinand and Isabella decided enough was enough, tore up the supposedly perpetual treaty, and annexed Granada without resistance from its last Muslim ruler, Boabdil, in 1492.

My pilgrimage had began in Granada rather than in Seville because I had wanted to spend as much time as possible in Andalucia. I was curious to see how much of the rich cultural mix of Muslims, Jews, and Christians who had lived here together during the heyday of al-Andalus from the eighth to the eleventh century, and in the turbulent but creative four centuries thereafter, might still be visible after five centuries of brutal expulsions, forced conversions, inquisitions, and other persecutions of Spain's non-Christian communities by triumphant, imperial Catholic Spain after 1492.

In that fateful year, the year also of Columbus' first voyage and the fall of Granada, the empire offered Spain's large and thriving Jewish communities a terrible choice: forced conversion or expulsion. A century-and-a-half of brutal ethnic cleansing of Spanish Jews and Muslims ensued, with savage cruelties inflicted on these defenceless groups in the imperial-religious quest for a Spain that would finally be, as Spanish historian Francisco Márquez Villanueva bluntly put it in 1991, 'homogeneous, resolutely Catholic, and secure from unwanted outside influences'. In 1614, the last Moriscos (Spanish Muslims who had publicly converted to Christianity, but continued to be suspected by the authorities of practising their old religion in secret) were similarly expelled from Spain.

The role of the Spanish Inquisition was primarily to interrogate and uncover such suspected disloyal elements, as part of a church-state nation-building project whose cruelty to human beings in the pursuit of Spain's religious unity knew no limits. This history makes terrible reading; perhaps more so for me as the son of a Viennese Jewish mother who, in fear for her life, was forced to flee her birth country and cultural homeland, Austria, after the Nazi *Anschluss* in 1939. Following the German 'reconquest' of its Austrian borderlands, the brilliant and thriving mixed Christian–Jewish culture of Vienna was destroyed, in pursuit of the vain Nazi dream of a greater Germany of pure Aryan blood.

There are important similarities. The Spanish Christian conquerors saw themselves, it is true, as cultural-religious unifiers rather than ethnic cleansers. At least in theory, they offered to Spain's populous ethno-religious minorities a conversion option—the acceptance of Spanish Catholic religion and values. But converts were never trusted, and the final result was much the same—an imposed national homogeneity at unimaginable cost in human fear and suffering. So I identified with the ghosts of Spain's persecuted and expelled Muslims and Jews. For me, this was a huge dark shadow over Spain. How could I ever love, or even feel comfortable in, a country that had inflicted such a cruel history on parts of its own people? As a pilgrim to Santiago, I would have to grapple with this harsh Spanish paradox, and Andalucia was the place to begin this—the region that had suffered the most from the cruelly misguided policies of Spain's imperial rulers after 1492.

I read in Menocal how under sustained state persecution, the formerly prosperous societies and economies of al-Andalus broke down. Huge land grants had been given to the invading nobility from the north, who used the land ignorantly and unproductively. Irrigated fertile cropland areas, the patient work of centuries of husbandry, were neglected and destroyed by irresponsible free sheep-grazing. Urban market economies collapsed, as those Jews and Muslims who could afford to—the rich bourgeois families, the business leaders of formerly thriving trading economies—fled Spain for ever. Jews found new homes in exile in more tolerant cities around the Turkish-ruled Balkans, cities like Istanbul, Salonika, and Sarajevo, in the Levant and in North Africa, and also in parts of Christian Europe. Smaller numbers of exiled Spanish Jews settled in Britain.

Many of the poorer Jews and Muslims who could not afford emigration quietly became internal refugees, fleeing the increasingly dangerous Christian-dominated cities, finding safer refuge in remote mountain villages, merging with local peasants and gypsies to form mixed communities of *fellah mengu,* an Andalusian-Arabic phrase meaning 'peasants without land'—from which some scholars say derives the Spanish word *flamenco.*

A hybrid rural outcast culture developed in these poor and remote Andalusian villages over the next few centuries, blending all these elements—the original local peasants, the Muslim and Jewish refugees from the towns, and incoming itinerant gypsies. Meanwhile, Andalucia's cities became increasingly monocultural centres of triumphalist Christianity. Their old synagogues and mosques crumbled away, the carved stone re-used in new churches.

Seville became Spain's new imperial capital. The new ruling class, Castilians from the north, absorbed some good things from the old Muslim culture: its architecture, decorative arts, and gardening. Cádiz became Spain's major seaport, dedicated after 1492 to the new national imperial project—the colonisation of Spain's growing American empire.

Only very few of the most significant buildings from the al-Andalus period survived more or less intact, as cultural showplaces: icons preserved to celebrate the Christian reconquest. In Córdoba, the previously abandoned great mosque, the Mezquita, was restored to its former architectural perfection—but bizarrely, with a Christian mini-cathedral triumphantly constructed exactly in the middle of it. In Granada, the grand fortress-palace of the last Muslim rulers, the Alhambra with its beautiful walled gardens and courtyards, became a showplace complex of museums, churches, and convents. All else was left to fall into ruins, like Moclín Castle.

So had the reconquest and Inquisition purged Andalucia of its separateness, made it just like the rest of Spain? The answer I found was, emphatically, no. There is a subtly different flavour to Andalucia, evident in its landscapes and townscapes, in its flamenco music and dance, in its food, in the faces and physiques of the people. Andalucia is different. Today, Spaniards celebrate and honour its uniqueness.

Andalucia is big in every way. During my first sixteen days in Spain, I walked through three Andalusian provinces—Granada, Jaén, and Córdoba—travelling in a northwesterly direction for nearly 300 kilometres. It is the largest autonomous region in Spain in population terms—nearly 8 million people in 2005, 18 per cent of Spain's total; and the second largest in area, 17 per cent. This autonomous region—a new political unit allowed for the first time under the post-Franco democratic constitution—comprises no less than eight provinces, whose capitals include the most internationally famous cities of Spain: Cádiz, Córdoba, Granada, Málaga, and Seville. The other three city-provinces of Andalucia are the less well-known Almeria, Huelva, and Jaén.

***

Leaving Moclín, my third day of walking was twenty-five kilometres, mostly flat, to Alcalá la Real, a substantial little town of 25,000 people about halfway between Granada and Córdoba. It was lovely walking, much of it gently downhill through green and well-watered highland country, with olives interspersed with orchards of apple and almond and apricot trees, green pastureland and cereal cropland. It was still spring here: wild dog-roses and brambles flowered abundantly in the grassy lanes where I walked under the shade of overhanging trees. I was not to see lush green countryside like this again until faraway Galicia, still seven weeks ahead. The main Granada–Córdoba road was well away, out of sight and earshot. I was starting to feel more confident in my navigation skills: the yellow arrow waymarks and Alison Raju's route descriptions between them were keeping me on course.

I was in high spirits despite exhaustion and worsening blisters as I walked down off the plateau into Alcalá. But I couldn't deny the fact of jetlag any longer. It was time for a good full day's rest. So I spent the next two nights in Alcalá, and it made a world of difference. Alcalá was a pretty town, almost a small city, with a graceful main avenue lined with four-storey office and apartment buildings, a large central city park with cafés and promenades, a good range of shops and bar-restaurants, and my first Internet café. On my rest day I explored the town, and climbed up to the restored medieval castle and Romanesque cathedral on the hilltop above the saddle where the town sits. I bought a Spanish mobile phone and sampled local *fino* sherries—excellent, and truly cheap for the quality—in a few congenial bars. I was beginning to use my Spanish a little less haltingly, starting conversations, shedding my inhibitions. Spanish bars are forgiving places: no one laughed at my mistakes, people were gracious and courteous. I felt I was acclimatising, though it had only been five days in Spain.

The next day was a hilly twenty-four kilometres to Alcaudete, another old Moorish hill town of which I remember little, because I again arrived tired and with red-raw feet, by now badly blistered. I did the arithmetic—it was not encouraging. I had walked only eighty kilometres in four days of hard walking, and I seemed to be already nearing my limits of physical strength and motivation. At this rate, I was never going to get to Santiago, an impossibly remote 1120 kilometres ahead. Indeed, I would be lucky if I even managed to complete the *Vía Mozárabe* to Mérida. It had been crazily proud to think I could do this, but how would I face my family and friends if I gave up so soon? I would just have to keep plodding on, whatever the pain, because the embarrassment of admitting failure would be far worse.

The next day, twenty-two kilometres to Baena, was a little

better: more olive plantations, a harder and drier terrain than on the two previous days of walking. I was coming down now off the hills, into the broad valley plains of the rivers Guadajoz and Guadalquivir. It was good to be going downhill even if it was getting hotter. I passed a huge olive-oil waste-fed fertiliser factory, crossed a new motorway under construction, and walked into the hilltop village of Baena, famous for its high-quality olive oil and a centre of traditional Andalusian culture.

Baena, a beautiful place, lifted my spirits again. It was more of a small town than a village, and the most attractive town I had stayed in so far. Just below the usual hilltop church and Moorish castle, where the main road curved around the base of the old town, I found a welcoming and sophisticated pensión–restaurante, the Hostal Rincón, with a large shaded outdoor café area in front, where lots of people were finishing a late lunch. The food looked good. The lady in charge offered me a cheap and quiet little room at the back of the hotel at pilgrim rates, 15 euros. I showered and changed, had a rest, and then went out in the early evening to explore Baena.

A delightful surprise awaited me. Up on top of the hill, on a large terrace between the church and the Moorish castle ruins, a local dance festival event was getting underway, in preparation for the next day's local saint's day procession. It was a flamenco dance competition between village and neighbourhood youth groups. Young girls and women, all in gorgeous traditional dance costumes, were gathering excitedly and limbering up. Families were expectantly setting out chairs and picnics to watch. A small orchestra of professional musicians and singers were tuning up their instruments and voices. As night fell, the concert began ... and what a magnificent evening it was. One dramatic dance followed another, as the girls twirled and spun in well-trained routines to the beautiful and dramatic sounds of flamenco vocal and guitar music. This was no tired and over-practised tourist nightclub routine: it was the real thing, Andalusian flamenco at its most authentic, with teams of beautiful young women dancing with all their passion and skill and strength, for the sheer joy and excitement of it. I loved their crisply defiant body movements, their tossed heads and flashing eyes, their tense steps, forward like a coiled spring, then the releases and scornful turnings away as from an unwanted suitor ... The music spoke to me of a fierce national pride and a controlled passion. It did not matter that I barely understood a word of the songs. The young dancers were mostly thin, with olive skins, slim legs and ankles, finely chiseled noses. I thought I saw Arab and Berber features, as well as Ibero-Hispanic features, and blonde Castilian–Norman–Visigothic faces as well. I mentally kicked myself—tonight of all nights, I had left my camera and music recorder in the hotel room. I went to the festival bar and got another glass of sherry and some local cheese, went back to my chair and surrendered to the music and dancing and my thoughts.

I was thinking about the unique cultural place Andalucia occupies in modern Spain. The central paradox is that for foreigners, Andalucia represents all the essential iconography of Spain: fierce sun, flamenco song and dance, gypsies, handsome bullfighters in their flamboyant costumes, sparkling whitewashed villages with red roses and geraniums tumbling over wrought-iron balconies, sherry, olives, *tapas*, golden beaches, romantic trysts with dark-eyed beauties, and so on. Yet within Spain, Andalucia seems exotically different, historically mistrusted as not authentically Spanish. Andalucia is foreign, mixed-race, sexy, sinful. Andalucia is 'the other' Spain, the out-of-bounds Spain of uncensored dreams. It is where Spaniards can go to escape from the mundane realities of modern industrial Spain, where they can cut loose from their inhibitions ...

A tourism commercial was being heavily promoted on Spanish television while I walked through Spain. The soundtrack was a female voice singing an achingly bittersweet flamenco melody, music that to my ear sounded more Arabic or Jewish than Spanish. As she sang, one saw a succession of familiarly beautiful images: ruined Moorish castles, the Mezquita in Córdoba, riders galloping on white horses, bronzed lovers on a beach ... the concluding voiceover was '*Andalucia—que tu quieres*' ('Andalucia—it's whatever you want').

I believe that underlying this Spanish image of Andalucia as a very different place is also the acute, if unstated, awareness of Andalucia's glorious but tragic history—and perhaps a residual guilt at how cruelly Catholic imperial Spain treated the land and people of Andalucia. Federico García Lorca (1898–1936), the great and passionate Andalusian poet murdered early in the Civil War by Francoist police, understood and did much to articulate the complex debt that Spain owes to Andalucia. He is not a crudely political poet, but consider these subtle lines:

Soledad: por quién preguntas
sin compaña y a estas horas?
—Pregunte por quién pregunte,
dime: a ti qué se te importa?

Vengo a buscar lo qué busco,
mi alegría y mi persona.
—Soledad de mis pesare,
caballo qué se desboca,
al fin encuentra la mar
y se lo tragan las olas.
—No me recuerdes el mar,
qué la pena negra brota
en las tierras de aceituna
bajo el rumor de las hojas.

Soledad, who do you ask for
so late and so alone?
—No matter who it is,
what is it to you?
I want whatever I want,
my person and my joy.
—Soledad of my sorrows,
the horse that runs away
finds the sea at last
and is swallowed by the waves.
—Don't remind me of the sea,
for the black pain springs
from the lands of the olive
under rustling leaves.
(From *The Gypsy Ballads, 1924–1927*)

Lorca knew that the Spanish civilisation of al-Andalus and its successor city-states had flourished in multicultural brilliance for many centuries, while the north of Spain and western Europe languished in the Dark Ages. Andalucia had been Spain's window to the civilised Mediterranean world. It had been the region of Spain most open to Phoenician, Carthaginian, Greek, Roman, Arab, Berber, and Jewish trading and colonisation. During the Roman Empire, and again from the eighth to the fourteenth century under Muslim rule, Andalucia was the cultural, economic, and strategic heartland of Spain. Here, under tolerant Umayyad rule, Muslims, Jews, and Christians had lived together in harmony and prosperity, attaining the highest economic and cultural level in Western Europe. Córdoba, 'the ornament of the world', had been the fabulously wealthy and elegant capital of the stable Umayyad-founded regency (later Caliphate) of al-Andalus for some 300 years, from 756 to 1031 A.D. And even after this great state broke up, powerful Muslim successor city-states (known as the *taifa* states) competitively flourished in southern and central Spain for another 300 years: great city-states like Seville, Toledo, Granada, and Valencia.

Ethnically, as well as religiously, the Andalusians were a richly complex mix of peoples. Before the Moors came, the base population had been Hispano-Roman and the aristocracy Visigothic. Abd al-Rahman, who invaded in 756, brought small numbers of Arab princes loyal to his Umayyad clan from his native Syria. They became the new ruling class. Most of his Muslim warriors were Berbers from North Africa. Menocal comments on the subsequent mingling of peoples that followed, during long processes of inter-marriage and religious conversion. She notes that the ancestors of a Muslim living in Córdoba around 1200 A.D. were as likely to be Hispano–Roman as Berber, with smaller infusions of either Syrian–Arab or Visigothic blood. As in

Bosnia before Milosevic's ethnic-cleansing wars, Spanish Muslims, Christians, and Jews looked very much the same.

Andalucia was bordered to the north by Toledo. This was the first of the Muslim *taifa* city-states to be conquered by the expanding Castilian empire. In 1085, King Alfonso VI of Castile made Toledo his new capital, but it remained for centuries thereafter a multicultural city of tolerance and learning and a magnet for European scholars. Even as the Christian–Muslim political boundary moved southwards, there remained free cultural and political exchange between Christian and Muslim Spain, and continued acceptance in Christian-ruled as well as Muslim-ruled states of a pluralistic society where mutual tolerance and co-existence generally prevailed among the three religious communities.

After the dynastic collapse of al-Andalus in 1031 came two disruptive invasions from North Africa of fanatical Muslim Berber sects: first, the Almoravids, who conquered what was left of the lands of al-Andalus in 1090, and then the even more fundamentalist Almohads, who crossed the straits about fifty years later. Menocal comments that the Andalusians were restless colonial subjects, whose culture their new Berber rulers could not understand or tolerate:

> They had irretrievably lost their political freedom, but the story of Andalusian culture was far from over: although bloodied, the Andalusians were unbowed, and their culture remained their glory—viewed with suspicion, yet often coveted by all their neighbours, both north and south.

A crucial battle between Almohad and Christian armies, which decided the fate of Spain, was fought in 1212 at

Las Navas de Tolosa, about 100 kilometres north-east of Córdoba and just south of the Sierra Morena mountains, which form the natural northern boundary of Andalucia. Alfonso VIII of Castile led a coalition of Christian princes and foreign crusaders. His victorious army finally broke the power of the Almohads in southern Spain. Under Alfonso's son, Ferdinand III, the remaining Muslim city-states quickly fell like dominoes: Córdoba in 1236, Valencia in 1238, and Seville in 1248.

So it was that by 1248 most of Andalucia had come under Castilian Christian rule. Initially, it did not seem to make much difference. Life went on. But state and church intolerance and harassment of non-Christians gradually increased. The turning point came in 1492, when institutionalised state persecution of Jews and Muslims finally ended 800 years of intercommunal harmony.

In the succeeding centuries, Andalucia went backwards, becoming a stagnant and socially and economically dysfunctional society, sharply divided between the Castilian-dominated upper-class cities whose affluent lifestyle depended on New World gold and the profits of their great, landed estates, and the landless, poverty-stricken outcast villages hidden away in the remote hills. There was severe economic exploitation of poor agricultural wage-labourers by rich landowners, who were quite indifferent to the people's acute poverty. The church sided with the landowners, defending the status quo. Frequent peasant uprisings, driven by desperate hunger, were brutally suppressed. Unemployed and starving surplus populations were forced to emigrate to the new lands of the Americas or to the industrialising north of Spain. A tradition of armed resistance and banditry became endemic.

The Andalusian poor were a despised underclass, stereotyped by the bourgeois city-dwellers as gypsies—*gitanos*.

All this is reflected in flamenco music, a music of sadness and angry resistance, which can be harshly dissonant but can also speak movingly of tender love and the anguished desolation of separation, dispossession, and exile. Flamenco, heavily Arab-influenced in its tonalities and rhythms, became the secret musical language of a physically broken but still proud Andalusian people, who refused to surrender their unquenchable spirit of liberty. The lyrics may at times be banal, even commonplace, but the intense passion of the music itself, the rawness and pain in the voices, reveals much more than the words. And flamenco, in its modern 'new flamenco' form, fusing easily with other genres (rock, jazz, folk, etc.), has broken through its folkloric boundaries and become the leading influence on the distinctive modern popular music of Spain.

The abuse of the Andalusian people continued up to and through the Franco regime. In the Civil War, the military garrisons in the conservative-leaning cities of Cádiz, Seville, Granada, and Córdoba welcomed the Francoist insurgents, but the Andalusian coastal strip centred on 'Red Málaga' held out for the Republic until the end of the war. There followed a vindictive retribution by the victors, with mass executions of tens of thousands of republican supporters.

Andalucia under Francoist rule remained a desperately poor, mistrusted, and politically alienated region. In the late 1960s, parts of coastal Andalucia started to become internationally fashionable holiday resorts. A foreign-inspired tourism property boom began along the Costa del Sol, centred on chic Torremolinos and Marbella. It brought new economic opportunities, and the regional economy at last began to revive and to become self-sustaining. Meanwhile, under the influence of new, Christian social-justice thinking in Spain, the great family-owned landed estates were gradually surrendering some land to be distributed into co-operatives owned by the people.

Today, Andalucia has found a new confidence and social cohesion. It is one of the most prosperous, economically dynamic, and politically assertive regions of Spain, with a burgeoning, distinctive cultural identity. Andalucia's new economy is driven by tourism and by retirement-based coastal resort development—the coastline is now almost one continuous resort zone—and inland by the world's most efficient olive-oil export industry. In Spain's flexibly federalist constitution, Andalusians have voted overwhelmingly since 1978 to reclaim as much regional autonomy as they can from a liberal national government. While I was in Spain, a historic National Assembly vote in Madrid gave new powers to a proudly autonomous Andalusian political community.

I found Andalucia a wonderful place, of charming and gracious people who carry in their genes, architecture, landscapes, music, and food the imprint of nearly 800 years of a successful, pluralist Christian–Muslim–Jewish high civilisation. That heritage is still there, just beneath the surface, when you look for it.

***

Leaving Baena the next day, stopping for early morning coffee and *churros*—fried finger doughnuts dipped in chocolate sauce—it was another twenty kilometres to Castro del

Río, a town I don't remember a lot about, except sparkling clean white houses with cascades of beautiful red geraniums spilling off first-floor balconies. Exhaustion and blisters had set in again, and I was apprehensive about the next day's prospect—a very long thirty-seven kilometres, with little shade and no accommodation, into Córdoba. I did not think that I could do it. Fortunately there was a shorter alternative: a midway detour to a little town on the main highway, Santa Cruz. This avoided the last thirteen kilometres of walking. When I came to the pathway fork, my feet made the decision for me—we turned off the main path and detoured into Santa Cruz. An hour later, I was climbing gratefully onto a bus bound for Córdoba.

Córdoba was everything I had hoped for: big, urban, a city with buzz and style. I found a comfortable pensión in the old city area, the Hostal la Fuente, near the Fuente de San Francisco in the street of that name. It was a lovely old area, close to the river Guadalquivir and the Mezquita. On my first night in Córdoba, I drank icy cold water from the fountain, and then strolled down to the banks of the river. From the south bank, I looked across at the darkening skyline of the city, listening to wonderful trumpet and drum anthems echoing to and fro across the river, calling and responding. Where was this gorgeous medieval-sounding music coming from? They were groups of young players, improvising traditional melodies as they strolled the banks.

The golden copper domes and spires of Córdoba's many cathedrals and churches glowed and slowly darkened in the twilight. It was a restful skyline, older buildings of even height with no jagged modern glass towers, and the ramparts of the Sierra Morena ranging to the north behind them.

I found a local family restaurant, near my hotel, where wonderful food was brought out to the bar and tables with Verdian panache and drama. The patron was one of those intense artists of Spanish food, who demanded absolute perfection from his long-suffering wife and children, all working hard in the kitchen, cooking and serving up tapas at the bar and at table for an appreciative and knowledgeable clientele. If a dish was not perfect and perfectly presented, he would let us all know loudly what the problem was. His watchful eyes roved everywhere, and his memory of what each guest had had to eat and drink was prodigious. I loved the professionalism and pride in good cooking of this little place, and ate there throughout my two days in Córdoba.

It was an imposed longer rest in Córdoba, because I had to bus down to Seville Airport—a day's journey there and back—to pick up two important pieces of lost luggage, my walking staff and second pair of boots, that had been lost in transit from Australia to Madrid. They were found and sent to the Seville International Airport baggage area to await my personal identification and collection. The detour gave me a brief glimpse of Seville, and more time to heal my feet.

I went to Mass in the famous Córdoba Mezquita, in the proud little central cathedral. It has a solid gold altar, gold from the New World that must now be worth millions of dollars. Then I wandered through the nearby 'Jewish quarter' as it was called. I could not see anything particularly Jewish there except the name—the streets just looked like any other old Spanish urban district—except for a synagogue in the early stages of restoration, and a nearby bronze statue of the famous twelfth-century Córdoba-born Jewish philosopher, Moses Maimonides (1135–1204). His family was expelled from Córdoba by the invading Almohads in 1148, who offered Jews the same cruel choice of conversion, emigration, or death. He studied at the university of Fez (in Morocco), and was greatly influenced by the work of Aristotle. His own work was admired by the Christian scholastics, in particular by Saint Thomas Aquinas. He ended his life and work in Egypt and is buried in Israel. Spain has since claimed him as one of its cultural treasures. The great philosopher's big toe is glistening yellow, polished by the hands of many hopeful visitors. I duly rubbed Maimonides' toe too, hoping a little of his wisdom might rub off on me.

The next day involved more strolling, shopping, writing postcards, sipping coffee, admiring the elegance and fashion sense of the women of Córdoba, trying to read local newspapers, and practising my spoken Spanish. It is hard to describe such days, because not much happens, but to spend a rest day like this in a Spanish city is relaxing and therapeutic. You enjoy the quiet pleasures of a gracious and unstressed urbanity, in a traditional streetscape where commercialism does not scream out. Córdoba was a city dedicated to life, not just to shopping. Somehow, the shops—and there were good ones—and banks and business offices blended into a harmonious, people-centred streetscape. Shops and banks did not dominate the city. I remember that parts of the Australian city where I grew up, Sydney, had a similarly graceful quality in the 1950s. I thought about how and why we had lost it while the Spanish cities I had so far seen were still able to retain it. Was it good city-planning management, with tight restrictions on advertising and shopfront design? Or was it simply a popular sense of urban grace and proportionality, an instinctive understanding of how a city should function, a sense of good design keeping mass marketing in its subsidiary place?

I found a lovely Jesuit church, St Ignatius, its white interior and altar-screen *retablo* austerely beautiful—a welcome change after the gilt Spanish baroque and rococo angels I had come to expect in churches. After Mass, I introduced myself to one of the priests as an Australian pilgrim to Santiago and a former Jesuit school pupil, and received a warm blessing from him in return.

It was carnival time, and Córdoba was in festive mood. It was exhilarating just to be there, sharing the mood of this cheerful and vibrant city. I was beginning already to feel a little bit Spanish myself. I had not yet made any friends, my exchanges so far had been quite fleeting, but I was breaking the ice, making contact with the people and culture. I did not feel yet like a pilgrim—Santiago seemed still a world of time and space away, a purely theoretical goal—but I did not feel like a foreign tourist either. I was a lone traveller with a rucksack, drinking in the subtle pleasures of a lovely region of Europe. I sat in a little bar–café, asking the young woman behind the bar (she was Portuguese) what was in the delicious tapas she passed over to me in little dishes, where she came from, who was her husband, how many children did they have ... the pleasures of making simple human conversation in a new language.

The beautifully groomed hills and villages that I had spent my first week walking through, and now this charming city, were working a good magic on me. Spain, at least Andalucia, already felt right for me.

chapter five

From Andalucia to Extremadura

I left Córdoba in good spirits, having completed 160 kilometres, nearly 150 on foot, during my first nine days in Spain. The distance arithmetic now seemed a little more hopeful: I had already done one-eighth of the journey. The ancient Roman city of Mérida, at the end of the *Vía Mozárabe*, lay an attainable 240 kilometres ahead. I was heading into what looked from the map like more remote terrain, with fewer roads or villages—I anticipated a refreshing contrast to the well-tended olive-growing country I had walked through so far.

I avoided a long uphill walk out through the city's uninspiring northern dormitory suburbs by catching the first morning commuter bus up to Cerro Muriano, a village above Córdoba in the Sierra Morena mountains. The bus was full of workers. Cerro Muriano turned out to be the site of a large and busy Spanish Army base. As I walked out of the village past the base, a huge convoy of military trucks and armoured vehicles was just returning from somewhere—manoeuvres? NATO service in Afghanistan?

I learned later a little of the history of this military base, oddly located in the middle of Spain. Córdoba, guarded by the Sierra Morena and this key army base at Cerro Muriano, had fallen into the hands of the Franco rising at the beginning of the Civil War in July 1936. In ensuing months, Republican forces made a determined but unsuccessful effort to re-occupy this politically significant city. A pitched battle was fought right here at Cerro Muriano, during which a Hungarian Jewish photographer Robert Capa took what became one of the most famous documentary photographs of the Civil War, 'The Falling Soldier', of a Republican soldier being shot dead while charging forward gun in hand. This photo had a huge contemporary impact in Europe. The battlefront stabilised just north of Cerro Muriano, and remained that way for the rest of the war. The front line extended north-westward from the mountains just north of Córdoba to just east of Mérida, and thus was very close to my line of walk. The villages of Villaharta and Alcaracejos, which I was soon to walk through, were both just inside a large bulge of territory that Republican forces held onto for most of the war, defending the southwestern approaches to Madrid.

I walked through challenging mountain country that day, playing hide-and-seek with a huge motorway construction project that seemed bent on obliterating every trace of the old walking trail. This is one problem with guidebooks: their truth can be overtaken by events. But adjusting Raju with careful use of the Michelin road map, and keeping an eye on the sun to check my general direction, I did not lose my way. Halfway up to the pass, I lunched in a tiny village called El Vacar, in a village bar–delicatessen called Casa Laura, which had the most wonderful local cheeses, *jamón serrano*, and homebaked bread. After listening to a spirited conversation between Laura and two customers, of which I understood barely a word, I resumed walking with reluctance. My path lay high above a new motorway tunnel. Coming down steeply into a valley, I found a highway-side motel below the pretty hillside village of Villaharta. Villaharta had two bars but no *hostal*.

I set off the next day from Villaharta on my longest leg so far—thirty-eight kilometres through high remote countryside, with no villages or roadside bars on the way—in fact with no roads of any size at all—from Villaharta to Alcaracejos. It was a deeply satisfying walk though beautiful semi-wild rangelands. I was very alone: I met two sheep herders in a four-wheel-drive, a Rumanian immigrant repairing boundary fences, lots of sheep and cows and goats and dogs, but no one else all day. Even after I came down out of the range onto a dry *meseta* (tableland), there were almost no farmhouses. There were a few large cattle properties, ringed with expensive wrought iron and brick-pier boundary fences and huge electronic driveway gates. Whoever lived in these places—if anyone did—clearly would not welcome pilgrim callers. Outside their well-fertilised and watered pastures, it was rough gorse scrubland—awful country. There was no flowing water—whatever water had flowed must have been dammed upstream for the benefit of these rich pastoral estates.

I could not walk any faster than three-and-a-half kilometres per hour, and by 3.00 pm—nine hours after I had started—I had reached the end of my strength, with Alcaracejos still six kilometres ahead. My two litres of water had disappeared down my throat alarmingly quickly during the day, and I had found nowhere to refill my bottles safely. Luckily, I now saw two young builders working on a new house not far from my path, and approached them. '*Agua, por favor*', I croaked in my best tourist Spanish. They looked at me as if I was from Mars, but kindly passed their large chilled water container to me. I took a litre, thanked them profusely, and limped off towards the village. 'How far? Six kilometres? It's nothing', I said proudly—having already walked thirty-two that day and still standing ...

Fortunately, my blisters were by now well anaesthetised while I was moving. They only began to hurt again whenever I stopped. Raw blisters do this—some natural painkiller kicks in when you are walking rhythmically, and it is only when you stop—especially at the end of the day, when you gingerly peel off your stuck-to-the-skin socks and wash your stinging feet—that the injury comes back with a vengeance, in great throbbing waves of pain. That is the time to lie motionless on a bed until two Nurofens have taken effect, allowing you to hobble again—very carefully, after talcuming your dry feet and easing on a pair of open sandals—down the stairs to the bar.

I limped into the village, coming down from an *ermita* chapel on a nearby hill where I had rested for a while on a cool shaded stone bench. There was a choice of accommodation at the main highway crossroads in the village. I chose the grungiest-looking, the Hostal Fonda Nueva, a seemingly rundown hotel with a faded sign, *Bar, Comidas, Camas* (bar, food, beds). I was badly in need of all three, though the place looked like a set from a Sergio Leóne Western. I got a cheap room with bath, with one unmade slept-in bed and one clean bed. The hot-water tap was not working, and the bath was dirty. It was shaping up to be the Spanish hotel stay from hell—my worst pre-trip fantasy come true. But initial impressions were, as I often found in Spain, deceptive. The hotelkeeper, Juan, apologised handsomely for the state of the room: there had been a big *fiesta* in town the night before (Friday), the hotel had been full of guests, and the maid had not yet had time to do the rooms (or maybe she was still sleeping it off after the party). He set to, quickly cleaning the bath and reconnecting the hot-water tap himself. His wife, Isabel, thoughtfully offered to put a load of my clothes through the hotel washing machine—what bliss it was to have really clean and fresh clothes again, after a week and a half of my ineffective hand-washing. I had a luxurious bath, dressed my blisters with about five *tiritas*, and went downstairs to the bar where I spent a happy evening with Juan.

The bullfighting season had started, and it was all over television. I watched it desultorily, with little joy. Most others in the bar did not seem terribly interested either. They were more interested in talking to each other, eating and drinking, looking at newspapers. Let me dispose quickly of bull-fighting, then mention it no more. It does not attract me in any way. I find it cruel, ritualistic killing, involving the taunting and torture of defenceless domestic animals in our human care. I am a moderate meat-eater, so I cannot object to animals being killed for meat. But to take pleasure in killing in unequal contest, to erect a whole 'sporting' culture around it, down to television commentators scoring the finer points of the play as if in a football game, and discussing play statistics—that is an unpleasant thing to me. Most of all I was disturbed by the cruelty in the faces of the bullfighters, their evident joy in killing as they worked themselves up for the final sword thrust through the heads of the by now exhausted and tormented bulls, looking at them dully with hurt and pain-filled eyes. What kind of men could enjoy doing this for a living? What kind of men and women could enjoy watching it?

I also sensed that most Spanish people nowadays would really far rather be watching football, but feel it is patriotic to show at least a polite interest in bull-fighting because the sport is part of their national tradition. It certainly has the active patronage of the monarchy and upper classes—at every televised bullfight I saw, there were members of the royal family prominently in attendance, along with well-suited Spanish people and a certain kind of well-heeled tourist. People dress up for a bullfight—I did not see many T-shirts and baseball caps, but lots of men in well-cut suits and women in summer dresses and hats. It was unsettling to watch the evident pleasurable excitement on some of the women's faces as bloodied matadors came up to receive the acclamations of the VIP stand after killing their bull.

Watching these bullfights at close range on television—for the TV crews make liberal use of close-up filming of the matadors and bulls—I could see a direct line of descent from the cruel recreations of ancient Rome. Even the architecture of the bullfighting arenas is much the same: they look exactly like Roman arenas. I could not help but be reminded of the movie *Gladiator*, another kind of thoroughly uneven contest put on for the perverse entertainment of rich and jaded Romans. I also thought of what had happened in Badajoz, not so far from here, after the city fell to Franco's forces early in the Civil War, on 14 August 1936. One thousand five hundred Republican captives were systematically herded in batches into the Badajoz bullring, there to be slaughtered by machine-gun fire. The bullring was drenched with human blood that day.

In sum, bull-fighting to me is a cruel and anachronistic cultural practice—I can see nothing noble, romantic or beautiful about it—but it is part of Spanish tradition and national pride, and so I suppose some form of it will be around for many years yet.

* * *

Meanwhile I was enjoying getting to know my landlord Juan, a delightful character with Marty Feldman-like eyes and more than a hint of Monty Python zaniness about him. He had done a pilgrimage to Santiago along the *Vía Frances*, and we talked about what it had meant to him, and later he brought out his pilgrim staff to show me. We compared lengths, and had a ceremonial photo taken, in which we both look intensely serious. Juan, a fine fellow, brought out his best Montillo extra dry sherry for me, with Isa's very good homemade tapas—lamb kidneys, marinated vegetables, smoked fish, potato omelette, smoked *chorizo* sausage. Then he served up a three-course dinner at a special table in the bar restaurant area. It was a great evening, finishing up with good coffee and Spanish cognac. Juan recommended that I try the 'Carlos' range, named after Spanish kings. Carlos I *(primero)* is hugely expensive; Carlos V *(quinto)* is the everyday brand and a bit rough; but Carlos III *(tercero)* is just right, a lovely smooth aromatic cognac at the right price. I was getting to really like these Spanish village bars: Alcaracejos didn't feel like the Wild West anymore, and

Juan was the most hospitable and delightful innkeeper any lonely pilgrim could hope for. Through our clumsy Spanish exchanges, there was real warmth: I felt Juan understood why I had wanted to do this pilgrimage, because he had done it himself and said it had enriched his life. Like me, he was Catholic, but not with excessive fervour. We were kindred spirits. Interestingly, he did not seem to know that his village lay on the *Vía Mozárabe* pilgrimage route from Granada to Mérida—I was discovering that this route was still a fairly well-kept secret in Spain.

* * *

I stayed two nights in Alcaracejos, having a rest there on Sunday. The Civil War was still on my mind: the local church where I went to Mass was a modern building, in which all that remained of the original thirteenth-century stone church was an arched stone doorway. I read on a plaque that the church had been destroyed in battle in the Civil War. I do not know which side was defending and which side was shelling the church; the inscription was diplomatically silent on this.

It got me thinking more about the Spanish Civil War (1936–39). One cannot understand modern Spain without knowing this war's history. I sensed real reluctance to talk about it, certainly in public places like bars. So I read books. The best and most objectively balanced general histories of the Civil War period are by English writers: Hugh Thomas *(The Spanish Civil War,* 1977*),* Antony Beevor *(The Spanish Civil War*, 1982, replaced in 2006 by a substantially rewritten new book with the title, *The Battle for Spain*), and Gerard Brenan *(The Spanish Labyrinth,* 1943, an illuminating early account of the social and political background to the Civil War, written soon after it ended). Spaniards on all sides value the work of these English historians because the Civil War is still too close for Spanish historians to confront without painful emotional involvement. While few Civil War veterans are still alive, many of their children are. Memories of terrible atrocities, and of loss of parents on both sides in battle or by political reprisal-killings afterwards, are still disturbingly fresh for people my age. And people whose Civil War family histories are mutually well known still have to live and work alongside one another.

There is consensus now in Spain on two points: the war began with an illegal coup, an act of armed rebellion against the legally elected Republican government by troops based in North Africa and the Canary Islands, who are now commonly called the 'Nationalists'; and thereafter there were great crimes against humanity committed by both sides. Most but not all Spaniards would now agree that more such crimes were committed by the Nationalists than by the Republicans. It was a brutal, unrelenting war, typified by the exemplary reprisal killings that took place after Nationalist military conquests of Republican-held cities.

The Nationalists thought of the war as a second *Reconquista,* and saw themselves as crusaders against the forces of evil and atheism. Their duty was to restore Spain to a well-ordered Christian state; their battle cry was *'Viva España'*. As the war proceeded, and even in the early years after it ended, their leaders showed their defeated enemies no more mercy than the Spanish Inquisition had shown Spanish Moors and Jews four centuries earlier.

The Republicans initially believed they were defending

Spanish democracy and constitutionality. Their battle cries were '*Viva la Constitucion*' and '*Viva la Republica*'. The Republicans enjoyed popular support in Western democracies, except in Franco-leaning conservative Catholic circles, but never had the active military support of Western governments. Hitler and Mussolini, on the other hand, sent powerful military aid to the Franco forces from the beginning.

It is nearly impossible for British or American people to conceive of the depth of political and social breakdown in Spain in the early 1930s that precipitated such a dreadful war. Their national civil wars are now respectively 350 or 160 years ago—long enough to look back on them with emotional distance.

The British historians I read agree that the pre-war Spanish Republic's parliamentary democracy had extremely weak support. Spain had only recently, in 1931, set up a Republic. Popular enthusiasm for the Republic was strong in the lower-middle and working classes, and in major cities like Madrid and Barcelona. But powerful interests at both ends of the political spectrum had no loyalty to the Republic's new and untested institutions. It was under bitter attack from the Right: the large landowners and very rich, the highly conservative Spanish church, most of the military officer class, the Spanish fascist party the Falange, and die-hard monarchist supporters of the former King Alfonso XIII, who had abdicated under popular pressure in 1931. It was also mistrusted by the radical Left: the then very popular anarchists, the still small Communist Party, radical anti-clericalists, and various groups of regional separatists. The highly factionalised democratic government was under many pressures from parties of the Left: to distribute land to the poor, to more effectively tax the rich, to nationalise factories, to constrain the power of the church, to set up a secular school system, to grant more autonomy to independence-minded regions like Catalonia and the Basque region.

The government's agenda was overloaded. It was trying to do far too much far too soon, and civil society was rapidly breaking down, polarising towards the extremes. There was absolutely no social consensus on where Spain was going, or how quickly it should try to get there. The impatient Left, as well as the desperately frightened Right, were both readying to take matters into their own hands by armed force.

The great poet W. B. Yeats was no doubt reflecting on the looming civil war in his own country, Ireland, but these immortal lines in his 1921 poem 'The Second Coming' seem to me to eerily foreshadow the onset and course of the war in Spain fifteen years later:

> Things fall apart; the centre cannot hold;
> Mere anarchy is loosed upon the world,
> The blood-dimmed tide is loosed, and everywhere
> The ceremony of innocence is drowned;
> The best lack all conviction, while the worst
> Are full of passionate intensity.

Initially, there were idealists on both sides of the war, people fighting for a better Spain. The military rebels were hoping for a quick and relatively bloodless victory. Their leader General Franco, a coldly calculating Galician from the coastal city of Ferrol, sensed that most military commanders would fall his way, once the coup's credibility had been proven. And so it almost happened. Over the first few days, Nationalists quickly gained control over the western third of the country: the western parts of Andalucia including Cádiz and Seville and extending up the River Guadalquivir valley as far as Córdoba, and a huge swathe of territory in the north, across Galicia, Castile, and Navarre—Spain's most conservative regions. But Madrid and eastern Spain, the northern Atlantic coastal zone, and Catalonia, together containing most of Spain's population and industry, stayed loyally Republican for most of the war. The government kept its nerve, retaining the all-important national gold reserves in Madrid, and held the loyalty of national army units in areas still under Republican control. It appealed for international aid.

A military front line quickly consolidated, with many untrained Spanish and international volunteers coming forward to supplement what was left of the Army's manpower on the Republican side. The war dragged on for three terrible years, with the Nationalists steadily gaining territory, population, and resources—their iron rule was never to lose ground that they had won. The Republican forces continued to muster enough resources and courage to go on fighting, even as the tide turned inexorably against them. There was enormous courage and enormous brutality on both sides.

There are many reasons why the initially economically stronger (on the face of it) Republican side did not win, and why the war dragged on for so long. From the start the rebels were better led. Franco was a superb political and military tactician. He knew better than anyone else how to balance off the disparate factions on the Nationalist side, and also how to neutralise potential military or political leadership rivals within the Nationalist camp (more than a few of whom mysteriously died in air crashes). He was a master manipulator of words and symbols, an artful consensus builder. He was utterly ruthless in the war, giving no quarter and using deliberate terror as a military weapon. He was interested in nothing less than total victory. By the end of the war, he had achieved total personal control over Spain. The Falange fascist movement, the Church, the officer corps, the rich, the monarchists, were all now under his thumb. Spain had become a totally centralised authoritarian state, becalmed under the iron rule of this one deceptively ordinary little man. And so it continued until Franco's death from natural causes in 1975.

The Republic, by contrast, never had a strongly charismatic or skilful leader. It lacked a Churchill or Cromwell or Lincoln or Napoleon to mobilise the people and throw back the nationalist insurgents. The Republic had weak, often vain, populist leaders, who fell increasingly under the clandestine control of ruthless and disciplined communists, who worked quietly throughout the war to expand their power base in Popular Front governments. The Spanish centre did not hold. The Republic, to a large extent, destroyed itself from within by disastrous factionalism—in particular, the disruptive purge-and-control strategies of the communists.

The initially popular but politically naïve anarchists questioned the legitimacy and authority of the government from the beginning. The communists, always mistrusted and initially very weak, grew stronger as the democrats and anarchists weakened. As the war's end neared, the communists were effectively running the government, while secretly taking orders from Stalin. They were always more interested in purging opponents than winning the war. Only at the last moment, far too late, were they expelled from the despairing and failing Republican government. Their treacherous conduct had played into Franco's hands, lending some credibility to his claim to be fighting for Spain and for Spanish values against an international communist conspiracy. The loss of a strong democratic centre in the end destroyed the Republic, even as its soldiers were heroically dying to defend it against better-armed and increasingly numerous Nationalist forces.

International intervention, or the lack of it, played a key role in influencing the course of the war. The Western democracies were always shamefully deaf to the Republic's urgent appeals for help, proclaiming the war was an internal matter and maintaining official neutrality; though they knew full well that Hitler, Mussolini, and Stalin had no such inhibitions about giving massive military aid to their preferred allies in Spain. For Nazi Germany and Italy, the war was an ideal training area for their growing armed forces and testing ground for their latest weapons and war-fighting strategies. Superior German and Italian airpower and artillery played a crucial role in breaking more heavily manned but poorly armed Republican frontlines. The West imposed an arms embargo on both sides, which they knew the fascist and communist powers were ignoring. Major British and American corporations secretly dealt profitably with the Nationalists, having correctly forecast that they would win this civil war. Looking back, one reflects sadly on the cowardice, hypocrisy, and short-sightedness of the Western democracies.

Stalin played a shrewdly cynical double game. He kept the

Republic weak, so that they would have to rely on the Soviet Union more and more, thereby increasing the leverage of the Spanish communists. Arms were supplied parsimoniously and with conditions. The Spanish gold reserves were sent to Moscow 'for safety' soon after the war began: Spain never saw them again. It is doubtful if Stalin ever wanted the Republicans to win. His interest was to keep the war going, building the Spanish communists' power in the Republican government, and using the Civil War to try to stimulate an anti-fascist European military coalition with the Western democracies against the Axis powers. In this, he failed—the democracies remained cravenly set on isolationism and appeasement of fascism. In 1938, Stalin gave up this strategy: he made his own separate peace with Hitler, the Nazi-Soviet Treaty which partitioned Poland. With that treaty, the Republican cause in Spain was doomed.

The Nationalists were never interested in a negotiated peace: their agenda was always unconditional surrender. A large reason why the Republican armies fought on so resolutely to the end, despairing of Western help that they knew would never come, was because they knew that nothing awaited them but death in reprisal killings—it was better to die with a gun in your hand than to be slaughtered like an animal.

The war attracted huge international emotion, and changed the thinking and lives of a whole generation of young Europeans in the 1930s. It broke the spell of post-World War I pacifism, and its tragic course steeled the European democracies' nerve to finally confront Hitler's aggression in 1939—almost, but fortunately not quite, too late to save Europe. It radicalised some of the best and brightest in the British upper class, who went off to Spain as international volunteer fighters for the Republic. Think of Orwell and Auden and, from the USA, Hemingway; think also of the Burgess, Philby, and Maclean 'nest of traitors', a ring of undercover British communist agents that originated in Kim Philby's bitter disillusionment as a war correspondent in Spain, seeing the West's betrayal of the Spanish Republic. I don't know if Graham Greene went to Spain in this period, but his Civil War-based novel, *The Confidential Agent* (1939), wonderfully evokes the moral desperation and cynicism of the time.

I was thinking about what main conclusions modern-day Spaniards might draw from their experience of the Civil War and the Franco dictatorship. Domestically, I think, they would have drawn three lessons.

First, Spain has developed a firm commitment to democratic pluralism, to respecting the rights of minorities: people of other religions or no religion, homosexual people, immigrants and temporary immigrants, refugees. Spain no longer aspires to political, religious, or racial homogeneity. It celebrates and protects diversity.

Second, Spain now places a high value on procedural correctness in political life: on respect for democratic institutions and constitutional forms, and a scrupulously civil language of politics. Spaniards have learned that the use of dishonest political manoeuvres, and the resort to extremist and abusive public language as an intimidatory tactic, break down the moral inhibitions to physical violence. Also, they know that once constitutionality and respect for the law and its institutions are abandoned, for whatever reason, it is very hard to restore them.

Third, there is firm support for efforts to devolve and decentralise government power, to institutionalise a separation of powers, making it harder for any politicians whose instincts may be to seek to abuse the agencies of a highly centralised state to expand personal power. Spain has the recent memory of thirty-five years of such a state, and does not want to return there again. I do not see this changing quickly, because Spaniards know now that in a highly decentralised and layered system of governance, coups are harder to engineer. Thus, the economic efficiency or political cohesion arguments for centralisation of power that we are so accustomed to hearing in Anglophone countries cut little ice in Spain—now a resilient, regionally based, and pluralist democracy. To Spaniards, centralism is the enemy of democracy.

Internationally, I think the unspoken lesson (I did not hear it said, because the Spanish are a polite people and would not wish to offend an Anglophone guest) would be to trust no foreign government with Spain's national security. In particular, they are determined not to become captive to Anglosphere-led international agendas, because Spain knows from experience that 'perfidious Albion' in the end will put its own interests first. Thus, there is a prudent determination to stay out of foreign wars and entanglements that do not serve Spanish national interests. The best example of this was the Spanish electorate's dramatic decision, after the Islamist terrorist train bombings in March 2004 in Madrid, to throw out the conservative-populist pro-US government of the PP (*Partido Popular*, the People's Party). In a large swing, they voted in the PSOE (*Partido Socialista Obrero Español,* the Spanish Socialist Worker Party), led by José Luis Rodríguez

Zapatero, which was committed to withdrawing Spanish forces from Iraq.

The surprising thing, in terms of Spain's recent history, was not so much the new PSOE government's withdrawing the troops, as its predecessor government's initial eagerness to supply them. For, ever since the loss of their American continental empire, and more recently their rich island colonies, Cuba and the Philippines, to the USA, Spaniards have mistrusted *Imperialismo Yanqui*. There is perhaps more residual respect in Spain for Britain, and Tony Blair's enthusiastic participation in the Iraq invasion might have helped convince the former prime minister, José María Aznar, to offer Spanish troops for the occupying coalition forces in Iraq in 2003.

Zapatero is at pains to emphasise his government's continuing support for the European Union, including its new defence community, and for NATO. That is why Spanish troops were still, at the time of writing, in Afghanistan as part of the NATO presence there.

The young soldiers I saw on convoy into Cerro Muriano were spic-and-span, with excellent modern equipment, and obviously proud to wear their uniform. Spanish people are proud of their army now. If there are any Civil War resentments still there, I could not see them. The last attempted military coup in Spain was in 1981, six years after Franco's death, when an obscure lieutenant-colonel at the head of 220 Civil Guards occupied the National Assembly for a few hours. The army did not support him, and Colonel Tejero's coup attempt fortunately ended in farcical failure. It is hard to see a military coup ever being attempted here again. Parliamentary institutions are stronger and more resilient now. Power has been decentralised, and Spain is firmly locked into the democratic culture of the European Union, which it joined in 1986. The country has moved on, and Spanish fascism is no more than bad memories.

As I walked around Alcaracejos that Sunday, I wrestled with another paradox: how can a country that was so unstable and brutal to itself just three generations ago, be so stable and civil now? But maybe it was not such a paradox: countries seem to recover from serious trauma more quickly than individuals and families can. Think of the United States as it was three generations after the Civil War—by 1914, already a strong and confident democratic nation. Or think of Germany three generations after the 12-year Nazi nightmare, today a firm liberal democracy. Individuals and families can suffer bitter memories of civil war through many generations. States, it seems, are much better at pragmatically leaving painful histories behind. That is probably a good thing.

***

I had now crossed the Sierra Morena, leaving the Guadalquivir River valley behind me, and entered the large catchment of the Río Guadiana, which flows westwards through Mérida and Badajoz into Portugal. After Alcaracejos, the country had levelled out into gently rolling plains, though there were still ranges of low, blue hills on every horizon. It was not as rich as the country between Granada and Córdoba, and it was getting drier and browning off already, though it was still May. There was wheat and other cereal croplands, and pastureland dotted with holm oak. This useful tree is a hardy evergreen, native to the dry Mediterranean lands. Its Spanish name, *encina,* derives from the Late Latin word for oak, *ilicina.* Spanish colonists took it to America, and it is known in the US as Live Oak. Spanish farmers value these trees highly. Once established, they are pretty well indestructible. They provide shade and shelter in all weathers for grazing animals, and the fallen acorns are fed to grazing black pigs in the autumn, giving Spanish free-range pork products, such as *jamón serrano* or chorizo, their special flavour. The grasslands between the trees are regularly ploughed, fertilised, and re-seeded, and cropped for winter hay. I was to see much of this mixed wheat and *encina* grassland country throughout the Spanish dry plains and tablelands all the way to Galicia.

It made for nice walking country, as long as it was not too hot. There were often cool breezes, and it was good to watch the ripening grainstalks rippling in the wind. The hills were never too steep for walking comfort, but there were enough for variety, and for curiosity as to what lay over the next hill to spur me on. People I met in small farms on the way—pig farmers, sheepherders, agriculturalists—were friendly and conversations were easy. But I still seemed to be the only pilgrim doing the *Vía Mozárabe,* as confirmed by the absence, in places where the track was soft and sandy, of any sign whatsoever of footprints or bicycle tracks. I did see a cross that someone had rubbed into lichen growing on an old waystone. But still, the yellow arrows were there whenever I needed them, and the guidebook worked. I ploughed on.

From Alcaracejos it was thirty-five kilometres to the Río Zújar, a river marking the boundary between the Andalucia and Extremadura autonomous regions, and between the provinces of Córdoba and Mérida. I had one more overnight stay in Andalucia, in Hinojosa del Duque, population 7000, a handsome rangelands town with many ham factories, an impressive church known locally as the Catedral de la Sierra, an equally lovely convent church nearby, and a bizarre structure, which I first saw from about fifteen kilometres away, which looked like a very high, double-nave church towering over the rest of the town. I was curious to see this building close-up. When I got into the town, I found it was a huge pair of grain silos with two decorative, faux church-like architectural follies built on the top, so that views of the town from the distance would not be spoiled—a charmingly contradictory example of Spanish urban aesthetics. Hinojosa, for me, had something of the feel of a large Australian country town, a friendly no-frills place, perhaps a bit rough on a weekend night. I went to Mass in the convent church, with the nuns behind a grille—another closed order—and I dined on good rangeland steak back at my hotel on the highway.

My trail took me through or close to many small farms and feedlots. I saw and smelled the Spanish black pig at close quarters, in pens and enclosures along the way: not an attractive animal, with the personal hygiene habits that one expects of penned pigs. But these sturdy black pigs were very different from the flabby, obese pink pigs that we are used to in our factory farms. If you met one of these large black pigs in the bush, you could be forgiven for thinking it a wild boar, and I suspect that if these pigs went feral, their offspring very soon would become just that. I could see where the huge difference in taste between Spanish pork products and our bland offerings comes from: these Spanish pigs are real free-range animals.

Pork products are very important in the Spanish cuisine

and everyday diet. Beef is seen more as a luxury, because historically—before the petro-economy revolutionised traditional agriculture—beef cattle were more expensive to raise than pigs in the dry Spanish climate. Now the cultural preference for pork is well-ingrained. Pork fillet (*lomo*) and chips is the Spanish equivalent of steak and chips; it is on every café–bar menu.

I saw a lot of sheep too, the same breed as we are used to seeing in Australia—the merino—which is not surprising, because Australian merino sheep were originally brought out from Spain to thrive in the similarly dry environments of inland Australia.

There were many herds of cows: mostly our familiar dual-purpose beef–dairy breeds, but a few creamy Brahmin types as well, bred for drylands and hot weather. Goats came in all shapes and sizes, from the usual grey-white goats to big, handsome, multicoloured mountain goats with long curved horns. There were also horses—lots of them—Spanish thoroughbreds, Barbs, knockabout utility horses, draught horses, which were always good company on the road. They usually came over to the fence to say hello to me, and to have a sniff of my hand and sometimes a quiet nuzzle.

And there were many farm dogs—everything from British border collie or Scots kelpie types to huge St Bernard-type mountain shepherd dogs, dangerous-looking guard dogs of the German Shepherd or mastiff type, and small, yappy dogs of every kind. Fortunately, the guard dogs were mostly penned or on chains—I suspect because they did not take kindly to pilgrim passers-by.

* * *

I had had a few days now to get used to my walking staff, which had been my silent but loyal companion on the journey since Córdoba. How quickly had I come to depend on this sturdy wooden staff! I loved its historical associations with the medieval pilgrimage, its firm warm grip in my hand, its reassuring weight and solidity, its hand-hewn sinewy knobbliness that gave it character. Now it hangs on my study wall. It is remarkable how an inanimate piece of wood became so important to me on the long journey to Santiago.

My wife Sina and I had put some effort into making it. We had chosen the straightest upward-growing branch we could find, about 4 centimetres in diameter, from an old plum tree in our garden that I had pruned heavily a few years before and that had re-sprouted vigorous new wood since that time. This is a good way to get hard fruitwood poles that make great staffs, if you can plan your pilgrimage enough years ahead. I cut a length about 150 centimtres long (that is, level with my shoulder), with a little forked stub near the top, handy for resting a hand or hanging bags from when stopped, propped against a tree or wall. Sina had de-barked it and rubbed it to a white satiny smoothness with a kitchen knife, and then I wiped in a generous dressing of olive oil that gradually darkened it under the Spanish sun. I took it to a metal workshop to hammer on a protective steel ring at the base, to stop the staff wearing and splitting. I screwed on a brass name plaque, and finally whipped a leather boating-moccasin lace, boy-scout style, around the top to serve as a good handgrip. It finished up a handsome, powerful staff that Santiago himself would have been proud to use.

I know some people prefer the modern lightweight aluminium, adjustable-length ski-pole staff—easily packed, no problems getting it through suspicious airport security checks—but such a staff leaves me cold. My traditional pilgrim's staff was actually highly functional. It was a kind of third leg, an additional source of spring and energy and balance. Having walked the first 150 kilometres of my pilgrimage on my own two legs without the help and companionship of a staff, I could now see the difference a staff made. With this staff in my hand, I felt we could together make it to Santiago.

I whiled away some pleasurable time on the road thinking up real and imagined uses for a wooden staff. Here's my list:

1. Most importantly, a good companion on the journey.
2. A symbol of the wood of Christ's Cross.
3. A link with home and family.
4. A protective weapon to deter an oncoming hostile dog. This happened to me only once—most guard-dogs were on chains or behind fences—but I think if I had not had the staff to jab at this one threateningly, he might well have taken a piece out of my leg. His negligent owner was nowhere to be seen.
5. A tool for poling along flat roads. Putting the staff down firmly in the ground at every fourth step, English-umbrella style, actually helps the miles go faster, because it takes some of the weight and forward thrust off your feet. It definitely makes for more energy-efficient propulsion, especially on softer trails where you can get a good, springy push off the pole.
6. An aid for getting up hills. The staff transfers some of the work of lifting your body up hills from your legs

and feet to your arms, shoulders, and back — exactly
as cross-country skiers uses poles to help them up
hills.

7. An aid for coming down hills without overbalancing.
Going downhill is the most risky time when walking
with a rucksack. Many times, using my pole as a
balancing third leg saved me from potentially nasty
falls after a misstep on loose or uneven ground.

8. A means of testing the depth in any watercourse or
soft, marshy ground I had to cross.

9. A balancing tool when crossing same, on wobbly
stepping stones or in slippery mud.

10. A weapon for knocking people off logs over rivers, in
the style of Little John in Sherwood Forest.

11. A means of practising one's baton-twirling technique,
in marching-band style, when one is in a cheery mood
and nobody is looking.

12. A life-saver if you were to fall down a bottomless
crevass (it never happened to me, but my staff was
certainly big and strong enough to have carried my
weight if I ever needed it to do so).

13. A tool for digging a hole in the ground and refilling it
afterwards, if caught short in the bush.

14. A centre-pole for a sun or rain shelter.

15. A conversation starter in Spanish bars (e.g., 'Señor,
that is not a staff, it is a war club!')

16. A memento to hang proudly on the study wall when
you return home, along with the framed *compostela*
and route map.

When I flew home from the pilgrimage, I nearly lost my

staff for good. Conscientious Australian quarantine officers at Sydney Airport were determined to confiscate it. With difficulty, I managed to persuade them that it had left Australia with me (apparently I should have got official certification of this on my way out of Australia) and that it did not need to be impounded and fumigated for three months.

Like Pinocchio the wooden puppet, my staff—an occasionally inconvenient but always true friend—had come to have a life of its own for me.

chapter six

Spanish Villages

Regretfully farewelling the Andalucia I had come to love, I crossed the Río Zújar by a high road-bridge into Extremadura, Spain's driest and harshest region. Extremadura is rather like inland New South Wales in Australia: reasonably large rivers run through it, fed by mountains to the east, which are heavily utilised for irrigation; but once away from the fertile river valleys, it is 'extremely hard' low-rainfall country.

Eight kilometres of uphill roadside walking from the river took me into Monterrubio de la Serena: an attractive hillside town in iron-rich, red-earth country (hence the name — there were ancient iron-mines here), and back in olive-growing country. I got a room in the Hostal Vatican, a neat-as-a-pin hotel in the central Plaza de España, close by the sixteenth-century church and the *ayuntamiento*. Around the plaza were streets of particularly lovely, old, three-storey townhouses with climbing roses and solid, double-hung, carved-wooden front doors, and wrought-iron upstairs balconies filled with red, potted geraniums: it was chocolate-box pretty, like a stage set for an old-fashioned production of *The Barber of Seville* or *Carmen*.

I was struck by the conservatism of the folk in the Vatican Bar. For a start, they were all men (there were no women), and noticeably more taciturn than the outgoing people I had been meeting in Andalusian village bars. Here there were quiet card and dice games going on, and less animated conversation. There wasn't the same easy grace; people here seemed a little stiff and more wary of strangers. Maybe I was in the wrong bar, maybe the action was somewhere else in town? I did not force myself on people, but sat quietly and had a leisurely browse through the bar's usual supply of in-house newspapers. Every Spanish bar provides daily newspapers to read as a service, but woe betide any customer who accidentally walks off with one under his arm. I had a quiet dinner, watching television in the dining room.

The next day was an easy walk to Castuera, a gentle eighteen kilometres ahead through undulating red-earth olive plantations, with views across plains to a mountain range, where terraced villages were strung out along a high mountain road. Hawks and kites were wheeling gracefully overhead, searching for prey—rabbits, hares, smaller birds. They rarely caught anything as they ceaselessly scouted the terrain. Then, as if on cue, I heard the deep drone of propeller aircraft. Looking up, I saw what looked like three 1940s-era planes—they could have been old German- or Italian-supplied bombers, they had that look about them—flying overhead in a loose wedge formation, heading north-east in the general direction of Madrid. Maybe these were veteran Spanish air force pilots from Seville or Cádiz, on their way to a vintage-plane rally? I involuntarily shivered—these aircraft looked and sounded just like Nazi bombers in those old World War II movies. Inevitably, Guernica came to mind: that terrible

Nationalist-ordered air raid in 1937 against a loyalist Basque town, carried out by pilots of the German Condor Legion, the air raid that first broke the taboo against deliberately bombing civilian cities in wartime. One third of Guernica's population were casualties of this war crime—1654 killed and 889 wounded. The town, which had been a Republican stronghold, was left as an exemplary burnt skeleton. It was a sight that was soon to become all too familiar in Europe.

Arriving in Castuera, I had to walk through the village: the hostal I had chosen from my guidebook was on the other side of town, on the highway. It was a mistake: this hostal was new, pricey, soulless. I slept badly in a stuffy room with windows sealed to keep out highway noise and dust, full of newish plastic furniture and fabrics whose fumes triggered an allergenic asthmatic reaction in me.

But, before that, I had chanced on a delightful hole-in-the-wall bar, where I enjoyed my first real conversation with ordinary Spanish farmers and workmen. As I stumbled in through the fly-curtain, out of the heat and glare of the street, and with relief dropped my pack in the corner—it was 2.00 pm, the hottest time of the day—it took my eyes a few moments to adjust to the cool semi-darkness inside. The tiny bar was crammed full: farmers and workmen were having an after-work drink with their friends before going home for lunch and their afternoon siesta. Everyone was in good spirits and curious to know who this strangely dressed foreign person was. After the initial ice was broken, we enjoyed some friendly relaxed talk—a bit of football, a bit of politics, a bit of Spanish and Australian comparative geography and agriculture. One man wanted to know how much houses cost in Australia, and how much ordinary people earned. Another asked, what did it cost to fly to Australia, how long did it take, was it a good place for a working holiday? What sort of people were Australians? Were we like British or Americans? Where did most of our immigrants come from now? What languages were spoken? What sort of a government did we have? What were our troops doing in Iraq? People bought me drinks, introduced me to the local wine and tapas. They told me Castuera was a good village, there was prosperity now, plenty of work on new construction and on surrounding farms. The local government was honest and efficient, they had no complaints. One man identified himself as on the Left politically, though most of them seemed to be Right-leaning. It did not seem to interfere with their mutual friendships, though. Gradually the Bar la Cabra emptied out, as people drifted off home for lunch. Soon, regretfully, it was time to go myself.

After a restless siesta in my plastic room, I went out in the still sunny early evening to explore the town, go to evening Mass, and decide where to eat. The lowering sun was still hot, and the houses and pavements were still giving off the heat of the day. There was barely a soul yet to be seen on the silent shuttered streets. When the sun goes down behind the houses and the cool of the evening creeps in at around 7.00 pm, doors open, people come out of houses and start to walk and talk, do a bit of local shopping, have a drink on the bar terrace, go to Mass ... that is the time of day that Spanish villages come to life again.

But for now, as I wandered through the empty winding streets of Castuera trying to find my way back to the central plaza that I had passed on the way in, the fierce afternoon sunlight was still casting sharp blocks of light and shade onto roofs, walls, and pavements. Every street was a de Chirico townscape composition, bright colours and sharp angles, *sol y sombra*, the stark contrasts of sun and shade, no fuzzy-edged impressionism here. A cat, and a child sitting playing in a house doorway, were the only signs of life.

After a few false turnings, I found the plaza, overlooked by an impressively large church. Mass was at seven. Waiting for it to start, I watched some boys kicking a football expertly around the plaza. The massive main church doors—only opened for feast day processions of the Madonna and saints' images—served as the goal. Bang! thundered the doors as well-aimed shots hit home past the goalkeeper. No one seemed to mind—but the boys did stop playing during Mass. Afterwards, I sat again in a shady corner of the plaza, watching the resumed game. The evening seemed endless, a time for quiet contemplation.

I thought about the near-perfect grace and beauty of these Spanish villages. Castuera, in terms of its street layout and architecture, was a model village. And it triggered some old childhood memories, that might be a clue as to why I found myself on this walk through Spain now, almost a lifetime later.

As a rather solitary nine-year-old boy, the only child of separated parents, I lived with my mother and grandmother in a small flat in Sydney's Elizabeth Bay, a cosmopolitan, immigrant-dominated enclave of tight-packed apartment buildings and crowded small parks. During school holidays I used to visit my father, a senior Australian public servant and diplomat who lived and worked in Australia's bush capital Canberra, when not on official duty overseas (which was for much of the time). I stayed with him in the government hostel where he lived alone in a spartan single room. It was a strange sort of father-son contact we had, though I always loved seeing him. His room was piled high with books by his favorite authors Graham Greene, Evelyn Waugh, George Orwell, and with back issues of literary magazines like the *New Yorker* and the London *Spectator*. His room always smelt musty, like a library archive. I used to read a lot when I was with my father, because he encouraged me to and often there wasn't a great deal else to do.

In the hostel reception office hung a large old *papiermaché* relief map of the mountainous Australian Capital Territory region that surrounds Canberra. I used to gaze for hours at the steep contours moulded into this map, imagining myself plunging into those deep-green, forested river valleys, and skiing over those mysterious high, white Brindabella Mountains—which, in those days, always had deep snow cover in winter. I used to gaze across from Canberra at the white Brindabella peaks just 30-odd miles away, at mountaintops with melodic aboriginal names like Bimberi, Ginini, Gingera, Tidbinbilla ...

I was also fascinated by the little villages shown on this map, strung out along the highway and railway lines running south from Canberra towards the country town of Cooma with the Snowy Mountains beyond. These villages had names like Colinton, Royalla, Williamsdale, Kellyvale, Michelago, Bredbo. They were shown by little crosshatched street plans, with symbols or initials designating a church, a school, a post office, a hotel. I used to imagine life in these villages: a lonely child's storybook fantasy of happy Australian families living in real houses and gardens in real small towns. It was a disappointment a few years later to see these places as they really were: forlorn semi-abandoned postal localities along the highway, places that if you blinked twice you would miss as you drove past, government surveyors' hopefully pegged-out townsites a century before that had never grown into real human settlements. Most were just postal names, with maybe two or three farmhouses clustered near a road junction for company, a forlorn rural church or one-room school set in a few pine trees surrounded by open fields, a ramshackle post office/petrol station on the highway, a few empty sheds marking an agricultural railway stop. I had dreamed of those villages as a sort of fantasy escape from the lonely realities of my transitional, immigrant-child Sydney life: but they had never existed.

But in Spain, fifty years later, I found the villages of my dreams: lovely little communities of neat, whitewashed houses draped in climbing roses and cascading geraniums, clustered together in streets that wound randomly around hillsides; town squares tucked away in the middle, with a big church and, facing it, a town council building draped in bright flags—always three, the flags of Spain, the region, and the province; boys cheerily playing football in the square; young mothers sitting together in the sun or the shade near the fountain, with their small children in prams or crawling at their feet; older men playing cards and gossiping in the café overlooking the scene; young men showing off their shiny new motorbikes with lots of testosterone-fuelled standing revs; girls walking demurely in twos and threes, arms linked together; families out for a stroll together in the cool of the early evening; and old ladies putting out their chairs in the street in front of their houses for a communal knit or sew and conversation at the end of the day. Such villages as I had dreamed of, such communities, did exist after all. In a kind of way, even though I did not know anyone and Spain was not my country, I had come home.

Let me describe a place that is like Castuera, but also blends in memories of similar villages I stayed in during my walk through Spain. So much of the joy of pilgrimage for me came from afternoons and evenings wandering around these villages in which I stopped to eat and sleep along the way. I never got tired of walking slowly through the maze of village streets, always finding my way out in the end, checking out the endless variations of Spanish domestic architecture.

The joy begins on arrival: it is such a striking contrast and relief to pass in a few steps from a hot, dusty rural road or pathway through open fields into a cool village street shaded by close-set, two-storeyed houses down each side, with spotlessly clean, tiled footpaths flanking narrow, cobbled roadways just wide enough for two small Spanish cars to pass, with cast-iron streetlights, climbing roses in bloom ... you immediately enter a different world. Like C. S. Lewis's children walking through the wardrobe into Narnia, the pilgrim's transition from countryside to village is sharp and thrilling. If the day's walk has been especially hot and tiring, the pleasure of stepping into a shady, cool village street is all the greater. Your weary pace quickens and your bent back proudly straightens as you walk the last few hundred metres to a cool, welcoming café–bar or *hostal*.

Spanish villages are usually very old. They overlay Iron Age and pre-Roman Iberian settlements. These locations were well chosen. More often than not, villages developed on small hilltops overlooking nearby fertile river flats, or (in hillier country) on a slope or ridge with commanding views of lower country. Such sites were chosen to enable the defence of a central fortified area against attack, and to have a good view of the village's grazing and croplands, providing a warning if needed of approaching enemy armies or robber bands trying to steal livestock or to ravage ripening crops. They were also protected on hilltops from floods, and stormwater drained away safely and healthily after heavy rains. They were easier to see from a distance when finding one's way home from a journey.

Those villages continued to grow through the settled and prosperous Roman Empire era, and then survived through the more unsettled years of barbarian invasions that followed (Spanish historians refer to this as the Visigothic period, after the Germanic tribe that established a weak post-Roman hegemony in Spain), until around 750, when better-armed and better-led Muslim armies quickly took control of most of Spain. Menocal tells us what followed thereafter:

> Over the course of the subsequent three hundred years until roughly the turn of the first millenium as it was calculated in the Christian calendar, the sort of political order and cultural flourishing that had once graced Roman Spain returned to the peninsula ... There was a vast economic revival: the population increased, not just in the invigorated and ever more cosmopolitan cities, but even in the once decimated countryside, where the introduction of new crops and new techniques, including irrigation, made agriculture a prosperous concern; and the pan-Mediterranean trade and travel routes that had helped maintain Roman prosperity, and which were vital for cultural contacts and continuities, were reconfigured and extended.

So these villages, and the old rural roads and paths that I was walking on between them, had a long and rich history of human life and commerce. The *Vía Mozárabe* and the *Vía de la Plata*, initially Roman roads, became the main roads of Muslim-ruled Spain, safe trade and pilgrimage routes through the empire of al-Andalus and beyond, and northwards to the kingdoms of Christian Europe.

And here is a delightful thing to contemplate—these gleaming white villages would not have looked too different in the al-Andalus period from the way they look now. There are, of course, differences: the mosques and synagogues are long since gone, torn down as in the cities, their dressed stones recycled into the large, beautiful post-reconquest Romanesque and Spanish Gothic churches that replaced them. Water and sewerage pipes, electricity, and Internet cables are now cleverly retro-engineered invisibly into the architecture of the old cobbled streets.

But these village houses were built to last. Houses might still have the same old stone or brick walls from al-Andalus times, buried and protected under many centimetres of new whitewash painted on through all the centuries since. The heavy wooden doors and window shutters cut from long-gone, old-growth forests might be hundreds of years old. The street layouts would not have changed. There is so much proud history all around you, even in the smallest and poorest Spanish village.

These villages—not so different from other villages around the old Mediterranean, in southern France, Italy, Greece, the coastal Balkans, Turkey, Syria, and Lebanon, North Africa—were designed for '*convivencia*' ('living together'). Christians, Jews, and Muslims would have coexisted peacefully in extended families, living in large houses extending back a long way behind deceptively narrow street frontages. Their occupants would have rubbed shoulders together in the same thriving, easy-going culture of medieval Spain, working, trading, having families, making friends and intermarrying across religions. Some villages, like Hervás up on the Extremaduran–Castilian border, still remember and street-sign their Jewish quarter, nestling under the Catholic church on top of the hill (had it once been a synagogue site, I wonder)—streets that look just like the rest of the old town. It must have been a good time to live in Spain, the time of al-Andalus, and you can still get a sense of it in these peaceful and dignified villages.

I also remembered that these were the kinds of villages that the internal Muslim and Jewish refugees fled to after the *Reconquista*, the remoter the better, away from the frightening religious intolerance and vengeful inquisitions of the conqueror-dominated cities. These were the villages where you might have relatives or trusted friends to shelter you, places where you could hide inside these secluded and shuttered houses in their narrow, twisting lanes, burying your past, praying that you might be able to protect your wife and children from the waves of hate and madness sweeping through the cities of imperial Spain—the cities that used to be your homes.

***

I had not expected the clean, tidy prosperity I found in most of these villages, especially in the south. I had been expecting scenes of abandonment, poverty, of old people struggling to survive and live meaningful lives in already depopulated and crumbling villages, with their adult children having long ago fled away to jobs in the cities. I was to see something of this later, in northern Castile and Galicia, but not here in Andalucia or Extremadura. Here, villages seemed to be doing well. True, there were more children and elderly people, and fewer young working-age adults about, than one might expect—but not disturbingly so. There were few obviously abandoned houses, though I could not know how many of the well-painted locked front doors still housed full-time resident families, or how many had become weekend second houses for people living in flats in the big cities. Most houses were well-tended and some were undergoing building renovations: more signs of prosperity. And though I saw plenty of good newish cars, I did not see foreign number-plated cars; these villages had not become enclaves of foreign part-time residents and transients.

A lot of the new prosperity in these villages, I was told, has to do with the social welfare benefits of European Union membership. There used to be a lot of poverty and joblessness in these villages as recently as twenty years ago. Spanish social security payments were miserly under Franco. In these villages, poorer people used to live hard, on subsistence incomes and without running water or sewerage or electricity. But now, their incomes and social amenities seem well up to European Union community standards. Spain, as an initially poorer Mediterranean entrant in the first round of EU expansion in 1986, benefited disproportionately (as did Greece and Portugal) from the generous social welfare systems of the original six member countries. I suspect that generous EU retirement pensions have fuelled a lot of the manifest prosperity in these villages: a stable retiree population with new pension money to spend creates service jobs, more demand for food products and homewares. Children left in the week-day care of grandparents need schools and sporting facilities, clothes shops and toy shops. And when the young adults working in towns see the home village is livening up again, they come back more often at weekends to see the grandparents and their former school friends, maybe they look for economic opportunities to open up small businesses or workshops in the old village ... in this way, a virtuous circle of reviving village prosperity develops, all stemming from generous provision for retired people. I wondered why we could not do something similar in our declining country towns in Australia.

I was impressed by how skilfully the modern necessities of urban living have been grafted into these villages, without damaging their architectural and social character. Spaniards seem to cherish their local history and hate to knock down old buildings. They will use unlived-in village houses as cow stables, fodder-storage sheds, garages, or small workshops—anything. But the stone walls and roofs will be kept in good repair until there is new money in the family to make the old houses habitable again, and there are new requirements for family members to re-occupy them. The Spanish seem to be instinctive conservationists and recyclers of human habitats of value.

Next to the old village is usually (depending on the village's size) a modern services zone, concentrated on or near major roads, roads which would usually be re-routed carefully around the village proper to protect it. Here would be the all-important bus station, the village's lifeline to the outside world. Spanish bus routes go everywhere: they are cheap, frequent, and reliable, with fast express-bus services between provincial cities; smaller, local bus-routes in spider-web networks radiating out all around; and even on-call minibuses serving the remotest small villages. In my whole time in Spain, I was never more than a day away by bus from Madrid.

In the service zone would be schools, parks, and playing fields, larger supermarkets, motor-repair garages, local factories, produce depots and bulk-goods warehouses, and highway motels and roadhouse bars. And these modern facilities would be concentrated efficiently, in one or two particular areas of the village perimeter, not sprawled aimlessly all around, gobbling up farm land and cutting off the original village from its agricultural hinterland.

I discovered that this had not been done for the aesthetic pleasure of walkers or pilgrims like me, but for the best of practical reasons—because the villagers want to have close and convenient access to their nearby fruit and vegetable plots and small animal and poultry lots, where much of the village's food comes from. Some villagers own or work nearby small farms, livestock pens, fruit orchards, vegetable gardens, and vineyards. They would rather live in the village than in isolated farmhouses—only the rich or urban weekenders choose to live that way—but villagers want to retain close access on foot or bicycle to tend their nearby plots and animals.

These dense and compact stone and brick villages are highly energy-efficient in maintaining human-friendly temperatures throughout the year. Their thick walls moderate the hottest and coldest extremes of the harsh Spanish continental climate without need for air conditioning or much winter heating. Human proximity has advantages: there is so much concentrated thermal mass in these densely packed and thick-walled houses (rear gardens are very small, not much more than shaded grapevine-clad patios), that they store the sun's heat during the day and then let it out again on chilly nights, insulating house interiors from the heat of summer and cold winds of winter. And the narrow winding streets cut back the worst of the winds all year round, keeping the streets themselves cooler and shadier in summer, and milder and warmer in winter. In the blazing mid-afternoon heat of the day, I could always find cool shady spots to sit in a Spanish village. I would walk in from the countryside, out of glaring 37-degree Celsius heat (100 degrees Fahrenheit), confident that in the village streets it would be at least five degrees cooler, and five degrees cooler again once I had stepped inside a stone building.

Shopping is quite a minor aspect of Spanish village life. There are only a few shops tucked away in houses: often a butcher–delicatessen–grocery combined (sometimes grandly called a *supermercado*), a pharmacy, a books and newspapers shop (*librería-papelería*), a gift shop, a toy shop. Shops are often unmarked by signs. You have to ask locals to be told that this particular fly-curtained open door is a shop (fairly hard, when so many houses have similar plastic-ribbon fly-curtains across their open doors). People would do their bigger bulk-goods shopping in nearby larger towns, or in the commercial zones on the edges of larger villages. Clearly, a lot of food is still grown locally and exchanged informally by gift or barter: this is still the kind of economy where people can make their own wine from their own grapes, pickle their own green olives, keep hens and bees and honey, slaughter their own livestock and poultry for meat, cure their own hams, grow their own fruit and green and root vegetables ... It is not that every family would try to produce everything that it consumes, but that people would give reciprocally or barter informally with their neighbours, or buy local fresh produce in weekly street markets—food that in more urbanised economies is grown, packaged, and traded through the mass retail sector, and is always several days if not weeks old by the time we get to eat it.

What kind of quality of life do people have, living in a village like this? Do they become dull and ignorant country bumpkins, lacking in civility and sophistication and knowledge of the world? Quite the contrary: my observation was that it makes them more civilised, happier, more neighbourly, more interested in one another's welfare. I could not conceive of an elderly person dying alone in his or her house or flat in a Spanish village, with no one discovering that fact for weeks—something that happens too often now in big cities everywhere. People look out for one another in villages.

Similarly, village streets are safer for children to play and grow up in—the risk of hit-and-run accidents or 'stranger danger' child-abuse incidents would be very low in a close-knit Spanish village. So children can enjoy the freedom of safe street play, protected by large extended families and attentive neighbours, which makes the weekday absence of many working parents less of a problem. Mentally and physically handicapped people are nourished and treated with dignity, secure in the social fabric of communities that have known and cared for them since their childhood. I saw quite a lot of handicapped people in bars, always treated with familiarity, respect, and love.

I saw that these villages offer an alternative, no less good, lifestyle to that in big cities—not a poorer, more deprived, or even less sophisticated lifestyle. Behind the carved double doors and shuttered windows of these houses that keep their secrets so well might live highly educated people with rich personal libraries, art collections, musical instruments, CD and DVD collections, Internet access ... and celebrating proud, richly layered family histories, with a strong sense of their own family's acquired place in the village community. And at the public level there are public libraries, health services, pediatric and aged care facilities—these villages do not lack the fabric of a civilised life, and they attract a fierce local loyalty.

I stumbled over a little of this in hearing how Spanish people talk about their home towns. Only two words kept recurring in conversations: *pueblo* (meaning anything from a small village to a medium-sized town) and *ciudad* (city). A *pueblo* might be anything from less than 100 people to upwards of 25,000—I did not hear a separate word for 'town', as the word *'ville'* is used in French (in an upwards linguistic progression from *village* to *ville* to *cité*). The phrase *'mi pueblo'* signifies affectionate pride in one's town or village, no matter how large or small. *'Mi pueblo'* is simply 'my place', the place where I and my family come from, the place which I identify as my home-town. A *ciudad* is altogether more impersonal, a large place defined by size, history, government functions, etc. Santiago (population 80,000) or Cáceres (70,000) or Mérida (50,000) are *ciudades*. But Alcalá la Real (25,000) is still a *pueblo* to its inhabitants, though it felt like a largish town to me. Spain is still a country of *pueblos*.

***

I walked on the next day, from Castuera to Campanario, still determined to keep walking till Mérida, now a mere seventy-seven kilometres away. But in Campanario my willpower faltered. It was 2.00 pm, very hot, there was no local pensión to stop off in and, with my blisters opening up again, I didn't want to walk any more that day. I succumbed to temptation, and took an afternoon bus thirty-two kilometres to the next town, Medellín, in the Río Guadiana valley, thirty-five kilometres from Mérida. On the bus, I resolved guiltily that I would get a good night's sleep in Medellín, resting my blisters, and would then definitely walk the last stretch into Mérida the next day.

But it didn't work out that way. I was tired, and I went to bed early in Medellín after spending hours laboriously composing a letter in Spanish to a dear Colombian friend from my younger days, whom I thought might enjoy getting a letter from the original Medellín in Spain.

When I got up at dawn, shouldering my heavy pack, limping downstairs with difficulty and quietly exiting the hotel, my feet led me of their own volition—not towards the Roman footbridge that would have led me across the river to the *Vía Mozárabe* pathway running westwards along the river valley towards Mérida, but back towards the village bus stop where, providentially, the first morning bus to Mérida was due in ten minutes. Less than an hour later, at 8.30 am on Friday 26 May, I was getting off a bus in the

Mérida bus station. In eighteen days since leaving Granada, I had completed 400 kilometres; though, to my shame, about 100 of these had been by bus. Later on in the walk, when I was fit and blister-free, I would regret that I had missed the experience of walking those lost 100 kilometres. By then, every step in the pilgrimage had become precious and unique to me.

But I still remember my feelings at the time: anxious to get to Mérida, to rest my blistered feet and to enjoy spending a weekend in a city again after the week of hard solitary walking from Córdoba. Most of all, I wanted to meet other Santiago-bound pilgrims, to connect with that good-fellowship and solidarity that I had been expecting but not yet found on the untravelled *Vía Mozárabe*. I was sick of feeling as if I was the only pilgrim in Spain. Mérida, I hoped, would offer pilgrim company at last, and cheer my spirit.

***

As indeed it did. Mérida is a graceful little city, deservedly on the world heritage list for its wonderful architectural monuments and museums of the Roman period. Mérida did not have quite the same urbanity as Córdoba — being much smaller, with only 50,000 people against 300,000 — but it was a sophisticated little city, and a good place to spend a rest weekend. I found a good pensión near the centre, Hostal Senero in Calle Holguin, rested there for most of the day, and went out in the early evening to explore the city.

Friday night is the most popular night out in Spain, even more so than Saturday night. The graceful city square was a busy hubbub of conversations, with every café table occupied, and the central plaza area full of people sitting, chatting in groups, and strolling. I settled down to a few hours of people-watching and postcard-writing, but first I walked around Mérida's many floodlit Roman sites. Later I enjoyed a good restaurant meal.

The Roman amphitheatre (or coliseum, for gladiatorial sports, etc.) and adjacent Roman theatre, and the nearby museum of Roman antiquities, are all set in parkland in the higher parts of the main city. They are stunning places to visit. Only in Rome could one see better-preserved Roman ruins on such a large scale. In Mérida, they look entirely in place. Not surprising, because Mérida was one of the two main administrative capitals of Roman Spain, the other being at Barcelona.

I learned interesting facts about *Hispania*, the Roman word for the Spanish peninsula (the Greeks had called it *Iberia*). The Roman conquest of Spain began in around 200 B.C. Spain, formerly a region of Greek and Carthaginian trade and influence, had been a major battleground in the Second Punic War: Hannibal's elephants had walked up through Spain on their long invasion journey to Italy. The victorious Romans liked what they saw in Spain and decided to stay, replacing the Carthaginians as the imperial power. Their conquest of Spain was officially declared complete under the Emperor Octavius Augustus in 19 B.C., according to Roman records. But I suspect that the huge task of subduing the whole peninsula went on for longer than that. From their bases at Mérida and Barcelona, the Romans pacified all of Spain and Portugal.

Romanised Spain made a huge contribution to the Empire, furnishing many generations of sturdy soldiers and three great military emperors: Trajan, Hadrian, and Marcus

Spanish Villages

Aurelius. Hispania was a major granary for the city of Rome, and its harbors also exported gold, wool, olive oil, and wine. Roman writers painted a glowing picture of Spanish loyalty to commanders and other military virtues, for example:

> The Hispanics are accustomed to abstinence and fatigue, and the mind set for death: a hard and austere soberness for all. – POMPEIUS TROGUS

> Agile, bellicose, anxious. Hispania is different from Italica in that it is more than ready for war because of the rough land and its man's nature. – LIVY

> This Hispania produces tough soldiers, very skilled captains, prolific orators, luminous bards. It's a mother of judges and princes ... – DREPANIUS PACATUS

Not much seems to have changed since. Spanish fighting men during the reconquest, the colonisation of Latin America, and even the 1935–39 Civil War showed the same kinds of qualities. Spaniards are good people to have on your side in any war.

Mérida was founded by the Roman Emperor Octavius Augustus in 25 B.C, to reward and settle retired veterans of the Fifth and Tenth Legions. He named the new city *Augusta Emerita*. Mérida had an ideal site, on a hill overlooking the fertile flats of the River Guadiana, with mountains nearby from which to quarry stone and to cut building timber, and to run fresh water down along a magnificent stone aqueduct from a dam seven kilometres away at Proserpina. The Romans were wonderful irrigation engineers, and the Spanish have inherited their skills.

With the *Pax Romana* finally established in the peninsula, Mérida on the main north-south trade-route prospered. In the late Roman period, it became the seat of the Archbishop of Spain. Its conversion to Christianity was inspired by the martyrdom of its own local patron saint, Santa Eulalia. According to the story, Eulalia was a twelve-year-old Christian girl sentenced to burn to death by a local judge in 304 A.D. because she refused to offer a sacrifice to Roman gods, as commanded by the Emperor Diocletian. There is a similar Saint Eulalia story set in the other Roman capital, Barcelona.

Mérida continued as a functioning city in the Visigothic period, and then prospered anew for five centuries as a Muslim city, with the *Vía de la Plata* now at its zenith as the major north-south trade and pilgrimage route.

I went to evening Mass in the Basilica of Santa Eulalia—a lovely, really old Romanesque church that links all these periods. Archaeologists have unearthed its interesting history, digging carefully under the church. There had been a Christian cemetery here since the fourth century. It had included a mausoleum in memory of Santa Eulalia. The first Christian basilica was constructed here between the sixth and ninth centuries under Visigothic rule. In 875, when Muslims occupied the city, the Christian community of Mérida emigrated to Badajos—it isn't clear why—abandoning their basilica, but not forgetting its memory. After the reconquest, starting in 1230, a new basilica was built on the ruins of the original one.

Mérida's importance waned after the Christian reconquest, but revived again in modern times. A few years ago, Mérida was chosen ahead of the larger provincial cities Badajoz and

Cáceres to be the capital of the new autonomous community of Extremadura, combining these two eponymous provinces. Maybe Mérida, like Washington or Canberra, was a compromise choice when larger rival cities could not concede to the other, but Mérida's rich 2000-year-old civic history must have been a major factor in the choice.

The Museum of Roman Art houses a magnificent collection, beautifully displayed, of the finest original Roman statuary and mosaics, and of pottery and household items and coins, all locally excavated. The museum basement is itself an excavated Roman city street, with house foundations and roadways clearly visible. There is also a reconstructed section of Roman road, as it would have been when newly laid: a roughly cobbled road four metres wide, with interlocked granite cobblestones the size of melons extending neatly a metre into the ground. Immensely strong, such roads look as if they were hell to march or ride along, but at the time they would have had well-maintained, smooth clay surfaces, long since washed away.

This museum is an ancient history textbook brought to life. Here are famous emperors such as Augustus flanked by his sons Drusus and the terrible Tiberius, and Trajan; divinities like Hercules and Ceres, the goddess of fertility; a massive, sacrificial stone bull, warriors, and gladiators; and huge colourful mosaics, painstakingly restored and re-cemented onto walls for clear viewing from raised galleries opposite, containing images of the River Nile, crocodiles and tigers, scenes from Greek mythology. There are also wineglasses, dinner plates, vases, perfectly carved plaques in perfect, elegant Latin. It all brings home what a technically and culturally advanced and comfortable civilisation the

Roman Empire was for so many hundreds of years—but also, it seemed to me, a civilisation with a certain coldness, a bleakness of spirit.

I think the Hollywood Biblo–Roman swords-and-sandals movies—*Ben Hur, Spartacus, Decline and Fall, Gladiator*, etc.—capture something of the kind of society that Rome must have been. Rome was an expansionist, ruthless, and cruel military civilisation, only gradually humanised by the spread of Greek philosophies and the three Abrahamic religions around the Mediterranean. For all its glories and comforts, I would not want to have lived under the Roman Empire.

Mérida has a permanent Visigothic museum too, much smaller, but unexpectedly quite endearing. The Visigothic era, roughly 400–750 A.D., that succeeded the fall of the Empire was clearly a time of disruption and cultural decline. The Visigoths were one of several waves of Germanic invading tribes who swept down from north of the Pyrenees, who converted to Christianity and settled down as a ruling aristocracy in the ruins of Roman Hispania. The quality of Visigoth-period carving and inscriptions falls away precipitously. Clumsy dog-Latin, ungrammatical and poorly carved, takes over from classically perfect Latin inscriptions. But yet, this was a young and fresh Christian civilisation. My eyes filled with tears as I read the words cut on a Visigothic tombstone: '*Arestila, servant of God, she lived 27 years, she rested in peace on 26 July 559*'. Who was Arestila, who died in peace 250 years after Eulalia's martydom? What sort of a life had she led in her brief twenty-seven years as a 'servant of God'? I felt a sharp human connection to Arestila, that I could not feel anywhere in the great Roman museum. Spanish historians call the Visigothic period a time of 'decadence', but that seems to me a misleading choice of word. I see it as a time of exciting transmigrations, of the dismantlement of a cruel and sterile imperial order, of new spiritual beginnings and of new life.

***

After Mérida, I did not want to be a tourist in Spain any more. It was time now to get on to the real business of my journey—walking the camino, to experience what it means to be a Christian pilgrim travelling to Santiago. With joy and expectation in my heart, I left my Mérida pensión just before dawn on Sunday, meeting a crowd of well-dressed young revellers drifting out of a nightclub. I recognised them: they had all been guests at a wedding the evening before in the Basilica of Santa Eulalia, which had started just after my evening Mass there. They must have been partying all night, but all of them looked surprisingly fresh still—and seemingly still sober, the young men in elegant suits and the young women in crisp party dresses and impeccable make-up. Most Spanish people I met hold their drink well—it is considered boorish and uncivilised to be seen to be drunk or disorderly. We exchanged good wishes, and I walked out of Mérida as the sky began to lighten behind the arches of the great Roman aqueduct that towered over my pathway out of the city.

Two hours later, I was standing on the stone wall of the old Roman reservoir in the mountains, the Embalse de Proserpina. A few more hours, and I was in the village of Aljucén, getting the keys from the local bar proprietor to my first pilgrim *albergue*. I walked up the hill to find it. It was a little former workmen's cottage, freshly painted, with four small rooms with bunks, a bathroom and kitchen with hot water, and cold-water washing tubs in the sunny backyard, backing onto fields. I read the *albergue* guest book, filled with the thank-you messages of preceding pilgrims. It was a perfect moment, though I was still physically alone, because at last I felt the presence of other pilgrims. I was the first to arrive that day, but I knew there would be others. And throughout the afternoon, other pilgrims came in. I had at last, twenty days after arriving in Spain, joined the community of pilgrims walking the *Vía de la Plata*. For 240 kilometres behind me, back as far as Seville, and for 760 kilometres ahead of me to Santiago, I knew that pilgrims were walking and cycling and riding on this same trail as me. I didn't feel alone any more.

chapter seven

Spanish Politics

At this moment in the story, I want to digress from the narrative to say a little about the complex and unusual contemporary politics of Spain. Those uninterested in politics might like to skip this chapter. During a long and rewarding career as an Australian diplomat, I developed skills in understanding and reporting on the differing agendas and styles of governance of various nations I was posted to. When I went to Spain on pilgrimage, I was naturally curious, probably more so than most pilgrims might be, to learn as much as I could about Spanish government and politics, about what makes this remarkable country what it is.

Deliberately, I did not do any preliminary reading. By entering the country pretty much as a blank page, I would be more open to new ideas and not bound by preconceptions. So I went with little knowledge, apart from vague recollections from books read long ago on Spanish history up to the Civil War, and a few snippets of more contemporary information from newspapers.

I knew that after Franco had died in 1975, a constitutional monarchy and parliamentary democracy had somehow been restored, and that Spain had joined the European Union. I knew—because it was world news—that in a national election held three days after Islamic terrorists had bombed Madrid train station on 11 March 2004, killing 191 people and wounding over 1700, the Spanish people had voted out a conservative government closely aligned to the United States, led by José María Aznar, in favour of a new socialist government led by José Luis Rodríguez Zapatero. Two million people in Madrid alone—and 28 per cent of the Spanish population nationally—had gone out on the streets to demonstrate against terrorism of any kind. The Aznar government initially tried falsely to blame the train attack on Basque terrorists, fearing the electoral reaction if it became known—as it immediately did through the leaking of early police findings—that the train bombing had been an act of Islamist terrorism motivated by the already controversial Spanish military presence in Iraq. By lying to its citizens on such a serious matter and being exposed so soon in the lie, the Aznar government sealed its fate. The new PSOE government shortly thereafter fulfilled its campaign promise to withdraw the Spanish contingent from the US-led coalition force occupying Iraq, despite strong pressure from Washington and its NATO coalition allies, and accusations that Spain was in a cowardly fashion cutting and running from its NATO obligations.

This Spanish response to a terrible act of Islamist terrorism interested me. Unlike the US, Britain, and Australia, which have responded to every terrorist threat or attack with ever more *machismo* and expressions of determination to confront Al Qaeda and Islamic resistance elements in Iraq with military force, Spain seemed to have chosen instead to back off from 'the war on terror', at least in its Iraqi dimension. There are still Spanish troops in Afghanistan as part of the NATO-led operation there.

I thought that it must have taken a particular kind of Spanish bravery and political maturity to respond to a traumatic terrorist act and intense pressure afterwards from major allies in such an independent way, and one that was hurtfully mocked by critics. I doubted that my country, Australia, would be capable of such political maturity, and wondered where the Spanish people had found their courage and wisdom.

I was also assuming, as I recall now, that the harsh Civil War and Franco years would have left strong psychological residues in Spain: perhaps I expected to find a country that was still quite nationalist, conservative, Catholic, authoritarian-tending, illiberal, centralist, viscerally anti-Muslim. I was wrong on all these counts.

It was all the more interesting because it took a while for me to absorb contemporary Spanish political realities. All I knew came from the Spanish newspapers I was reading daily, initially with painstaking dictionary-aided efforts to get the main gist of news stories and opinion pieces and editorials, later with increasing detail and fluency as my Spanish political vocabulary expanded; and from watching the main news and current affairs television program every evening. You can learn a great deal about a country from the way in which it selects, prioritises, and presents its national news to itself. Finally, there were valuable hints and pointers to Spanish politics picked up in many conversations, and from watching how people reacted to television news stories—for example, watching the body language of viewers in bars when Prime

Minister Zapatero or Leader of the Opposition Rajoy were speaking on the screen. With the former, I saw relaxation and familiarity, a sense of 'there is our friend again'; in the case of the latter, impatience and boredom with 'what is this man ranting on about now?'

Gradually, a consistent picture came together. But first some recent history is needed, to fill in the gaps of what happened after Franco died in 1975, over a generation ago. Franco died peacefully, though unloved and unmourned. Like Rip Van Winkle, Spain began to wake up with relief from its long-imposed political slumber to find out how far Western Europe had left it behind. The country embarked on an exciting but risky experiment in the fast-track rebuilding of a constitutional democracy.

Franco's careful succession planning had set in place a stable transitional political framework for after he left the scene. Two days after Franco's death, Prince Juan Carlos, the 37-year old grandson of the last Bourbon monarch, Alfonso XIII, who had abdicated in 1931, was reinstated as King Juan Carlos I, to preside over democratic elections and the subsequent drafting of a new constitution. Within two years, under the stabilising eye of the surprisingly wise young king, Spain in 1977 held its first democratic elections since before the Civil War. In 1978, the new parliament passed a new, democratic constitution.

These were dangerous years. Had history gone another way, Spain might have again split under the same divisive forces from the extreme Right and Left that had destroyed the Republic in 1936. There were still, it was generally assumed, many die-hard fascists and communists left in Spain, and many family scores and blood feuds to settle. What would happen now, with Franco's iron hand no longer at the helm of the ship of state, and the feared Guardia Civil (national police) de-fanged?

Fortunately, Spain by now had a large middle class with a strong interest in upholding a stable modern state. Many Spaniards would, even today, give credit to the Franco years for nurturing and building the self-confidence of this new class. It turned out that there was now a large, politically active moderate centre that was Christian Democrat in orientation, and strong enough to face down the old fascist Falange Party, which was now ideologically isolated and abandoned by history, and without effective leadership. Franco had deliberately left the Falange with no charismatic political heir, in order to steer Falangist loyalties back towards the monarch. There was not much left of the communists, either. Despite the re-launch of a destabilising Basque separatist terror campaign, which has sputtered on ever since — Spain, sadly, has had much experience of home-grown lethal political terrorism since 1975, and the Spanish people have had to live with terror bombings and hostage-taking long before Al Qaeda — the centre held in the country's first post-Franco democratic elections. This time, things did not fall apart in Spain.

Contesting these crucial 1977 elections were three newly formed national parties, all sworn to uphold the new democracy. The UCD (Union of the Democratic Centre) was a new Christian Democrat centrist coalition, modelled on similar parties that had flourished in post-war Italy and Germany. The PSOE (the Spanish Socialist Workers Party) was the direct heir to the eponymous party that led the Centre-Left Republican coalition government at the start of the Civil War in 1936. The AP (Popular Alliance) represented post-Francoist conservative elements on the far Right—the Falange had collapsed. Finally, there were the Communists.

The election results were: UCD, 31.1 per cent; PSOE, 28.6 per cent; Communists, 9.4 per cent; and AP, 8.5 per cent. Smaller voting shares went to regional–nationalist parties, especially in the Basque and Catalonian regions, with their strong local tradition of separatism. This was a very reassuring outcome. The electorate had rejected both the extreme Left and Right (for both the AP's and the Communists' credentials as democratic parties were widely mistrusted). The two centrist parties, the UCD and PSOE, had won sufficient parliamentary dominance, 60 per cent between them, to cooperate in the drafting of a democratic constitution.

This constitution, passed in 1978 and the third key hurdle, established Spain as a 'parliamentary monarchy'. This is the first of many semantic contradictions I encountered in Spanish political language. In English, the phrase makes little sense, but I think it means a parliamentary democracy under a constitutional monarchy that retains strong reserve powers. Spain chose to be a kingdom once again—no longer a republic—with a strong hereditary constitutional monarch and an elected prime minister whose formal title, confusingly for Anglophones, is 'President of the Council of Ministers'.

The preamble of the constitution sets out the aspirations of the new Spanish democracy:

> The Spanish Nation, wishing to establish justice, liberty and
> security, and to promote the welfare of all who make part
> of it, in use of her sovereignty, proclaims its will to:

Guarantee democratic life within the Constitution and the laws according to a just economic and social order;

Consolidate a State ensuring the rule of law as an expression of the will of the people;

Protect all Spaniards and all the peoples of Spain in the exercise of human rights, their cultures and traditions, languages and institutions.

Promote the progress of culture and the economy to ensure a dignified quality of life for all;

Establish an advanced democratic society; and

Collaborate in the strengthening of peaceful and efficient cooperation among all the peoples of the Earth.

All the familiar democratic building blocks are here: justice, liberty, security, sovereignty, economic and social justice, rule of law, human rights, culture, quality of life, and international good citizenship. What stands out as specifically Spanish, and problematical, is this clause: 'Protect all Spaniards and all the peoples of Spain in the exercise of human rights, their cultures and traditions, languages and institutions'. The puzzling phrase 'all Spaniards and all the peoples of Spain' goes to the heart of the existential Spanish question: is Spain one people, many peoples, or both at the same time? Another key article in the Constitution, Section 2, is again a brave straddle of this same semantic contradiction:

The Constitution is based on the indissoluble unity of the Spanish Nation, the common and indivisible homeland of all Spaniards; it recognises and guarantees the right to self-government of the nationalities and regions of which it is composed and the solidarity among them all.

This wording acknowledges the fact that Spain is composed of nationalities and regions, and affirms their right to self-government; but it frames this assertion within an even stronger statement affirming the unity of the 'Spanish Nation' (note the significance of the upper case letters here), and the solidarity of all the nationalities and regions. Spain is to be at the same time both one united nation, and composed of self-governing peoples, nationalities, and regions.

It is all a bit like the mystery of the Holy Trinity: Three Persons in One God, incomprehensible by pure reason alone and requiring a great leap of faith.

Originally, the framers of the 1978 Constitution had envisaged Spain would be a largely unitary State, except for three self-governing *comunidades autónomas* (autonomous communities) in those regions in Spain that were understood to be the most historically and culturally distinct from the rest of the country: Catalonia, the Basque Country, and Galicia. The evident contradictions in the text were intended to accommodate these three particular national aspirations within Spain. Such autonomous communities were authorised by Article 143(1):

> In the exercise of the right to self-government recognised in Article 2 of the Constitution, bordering provinces with common historic, cultural and economic characteristics, island territories and provinces with historic regional status may accede to self-government and form Autonomous Communities in conformity with the provisions contained in this Title and in the respective Statutes.

However, this Article did not prevent other regions from

choosing to form autonomous communities, too. Interestingly and unexpectedly, over the four years from 1979 to 1983, all the provinces of Spain did so, combining themselves into seventeen autonomous regions: Andalucia, Aragon, Asturias, Balearic Islands, Basque Country, Canary Islands, Cantabria, Castilla-La Mancha, Castilla y León, Catalonia, Extremadura, Galicia, Madrid, Murcia, Navarre, La Ríoja, and Valencia. Spain became, de facto if not in original intent, a federal system.

Motives varied. Regions with their own strong latent identity, like Andalucia and Valencia, were keen to test new possibilities for their expanded autonomy. Other more conservative regions that initially simply saw themselves as simply Spanish (for example, Extremadura and the two Castiles) might have decided they had to follow suit if they were to avoid the risk of being left behind in a centralist rump Spain, while wealthier regions opted for autonomy, draining political and economic weight and the tax base away from an increasingly weak and impoverished centre. It became a case of 'one in, all in'.

Each of these seventeen autonomous communities has a different degree and form of autonomy. There has been an asymmetric devolution of power from the centre to the periphery, with some autonomous community governments wanting a more federalist relationship with the centre, and others remaining closer to the original national-central model. It is all quite confusing. For instance, some regions have set up their own law codes, educational and health systems (albeit loosely coordinated by the central government), and their own co-official language alongside Spanish (Catalan, Basque, Galician). Others accept Castilian Spanish as their language of governance and stick pretty closely to 'national' models of law, education, and health.

This devolution of power in Spain from the centre to regional governments is still an unfinished dynamic process, whose end-point cannot be known. Conservative pessimists regularly complain in newspaper opinion columns and letters that it could lead to the dissolution of Spain. Others argue that Spain will be all the stronger if it allows free expression to democratic regionalist aspirations. Acts of devolution might in theory be revoked by a future national government in Madrid, but most Spaniards see the process as a one-way street. While I was in Spain, Andalusians joyfully celebrated a further advance in their region's autonomy that was approved by the national parliament. But Castilian and Extremaduran newspapers expressed concern that Andalucia was going too far, too fast. Politics is never dull in Spain.

***

Over the two decades after the first 1977 election, the Rightist parties re-organised. Most of the UCD merged with the AP, and the new party in 1989 renamed itself the People's Party (PP). The PP thus became the party of the Centre-Right. It has been described as a broad umbrella coalition of Centre-Right, conservative, Christian Democrat, liberal, and popularist elements. Spain now has a stable two-party system, with voters offered a choice of two strong Centrist parties, the PP or PSOE, representing Centre-Right and Centre-Left orientations respectively. Essentially, these two parties set the terms of the national debate.

In the second national election in 1982, the PSOE won an

absolute majority—an event which many saw as the final defeat of Spanish fascism, because it proved that the party which Franco had destroyed by force in his 1936 rebellion had democratically regained power in Spain forty-six years later. The PSOE governed Spain for the next thirteen years to 1995—years that defined the political shape of modern Spain. Spain joined NATO in 1982, and the European Community (Union) in 1986. These were also the years of greatest activity in devolving powers to the regions.

Then the PP, led by José María Aznar, gained power in the 1996 election. Aznar moved to liberalise and privatise the economy. Spain greatly strengthened its military cooperation with NATO and the US, taking part in military operations in the former Yugoslavia. After the PP was re-elected in 2000, Aznar consolidated Spain's international role as the US's staunchest ally (with Britain) in Europe in the new US-led war on terror. In May 2003, defying majority public opinion, Aznar sent 1500 Spanish troops to take part in the US-led Iraq occupation. For the 2004 election, Aznar's deputy, Maríano Rajoy, replaced him as the People's Party candidate.

In the aftermath of the 11 March terrorist bomb attacks in Madrid, the PP lost the 2004 election. The PSOE, led by José Luis Rodríguez Zapatero, got 43.3 per cent—a decisive 5 per cent margin over the PP's 38.3 per cent. Voters, angered by the PP's attempt to falsely lay the blame for the train bombings on Basque separatists, in spite of police evidence already known to the government (which was trying to deny any link to the war on terror), embraced with relief Zapatero's long-standing election promise to bring Spanish troops home from Iraq: the PSOE had from the start condemned the invasion and military occupation as internationally illegal.

Zapatero faces a new election in 2008. He will probably win again: he has established himself as a quietly charismatic, cautious leader with an attractively low-key style and great skill in navigating the treacherous shoals of devolution politics, who is seeking a lasting settlement of the Basque separatist problem. Zapatero was born in 1960 to a well-off family with a long history of left-wing politics. His father, Juan Rodríguez García-Lozano, was a prominent lawyer. His paternal grandfather, Juan Rodríguez Lozano, was a Republican Army captain, killed by Nationalists during the Civil War. Philip Pettit, an Irish political philosopher, praises Zapatero as Europe's most successful 'Third Way' politician, well balanced philosophically between Right and Left. From what I saw of Zapatero, that is a fair judgement.

The PP under Rajoy seems still to be floundering, discredited and confused by the events of 2004 and yet to offer a credible, alternative, forward-looking agenda. Rajoy comes across negatively as a stiff, rather peevish politician. On devolution and the Basque issue, the PP's platform is essentially nay-saying and fear-mongering, appealing to more conservative views that devolution risks destroying Spain as a nation, and that Basque terrorists have been rewarded by being invited to negotiate with the national government. The PP has similarly conservative views on immigration and on the need to improve relations with the Bush administration in the US. I did not detect much public sympathy for such views—the PP seems, at least for the time being, to have lost touch with the majority mood of the electorate.

Controversially, Rupert Murdoch's News Corporation has employed José María Aznar as a lobbyist since 2004, paying him a consultancy fee of 120,000 euros per annum.

Aznar continues to serve (*ex officio* as a former prime minister) as a member of the Council of State, the highest consultative organ of the Spanish government. This council has no executive functions or powers—it performs as a constitutional advisory panel of experts.

Under both Centre-Right and Centre-Left governments, the Crown remains a much-loved and respected national institution, now effectively above politics and valued for its reassuring stability. I never met anyone in Spain calling for a Republic. No doubt republicans do still exist, but not in politically significant numbers any more. The style of the Spanish monarchy is more formal and akin to the British style than the homely Scandinavian–Low Countries 'bicycle' monarchies. But it is not beset by the kinds of family scandals that have wreaked havoc in the British royal family. King Juan Carlos never identified himself with the far Right. He has always behaved scrupulously in accordance with the constitution, and his family life is scandal-free. He married in 1962 to Princess Sophia of Greece and Denmark, daughter of King Paul. She was Greek Orthodox, but converted to Catholicism to become Spain's Queen. They had two daughters, Elena and Christina; and a son, the heir apparent, Prince Felipe, born in 1968. The Spanish royal family is a success story in every way: the British royal family must wish it was so lucky.

***

Spain's history prior to 1975 offers ample proof of Lord Acton's maxim that 'power corrupts, and absolute power corrupts absolutely'. After Franco, there is a determination in Spain that political power must be structurally distributed among many players and levels of government. A key characteristic of Spanish fascism was its extreme centralisation of power, all flowing upwards to one leader, Franco. In sharp contrast, the key concepts of modern Spanish democratic politics seem to be, first, maximum separation of powers through devolution of power to the autonomous communities and on down to provinces and local districts; and second, adherence to a political style of scrupulous civility, including towards opponents. Underpinning these concepts is a strong community value that ultimately, politics is local. National politics comes a long way down the list of importance, after the politics of your *pueblo,* district, province, and region. The devolved structures that have been established in Spain make it hard to conceive of any national leader, no matter how ruthless or well-resourced or charismatic, ever acquiring such power as Franco once had again.

I saw a work of public art in front of Salamanca's main post office that strikingly symbolised these kinds of political ideas: a large bronze sculpture called 'The Spanish Constitution'. It is a framework of four open-ribbed quadripedal pyramids, one sitting inside the other, like a Russian *matryoschka* doll. All the pyramids are free-standing—they are not connected, except by a web of joining rods at the base. The political message was clear—these are the four levels of Spanish government (local, provincial, regional, national), all independent of one another, but all resting on a united Spanish people at the base.

The Spanish newspaper industry reflects and reinforces this decentralised and power-sharing political culture. There is a healthy diversity of national newspapers in Spain, with editorial slants inclined to either Centre-Left or Centre-Right. National newspapers come out in separate regional or provincial editions. I could buy the same-name national newspapers in Andalucia, Extremadura, Castile, or Galicia. In Extremadura, there were even different editions for the cities of Mérida, Cáceres, and Plasencia (in the north). There is not a separate tier of regional, provincial, or local newspapers: the national newspaper in its local edition covers all levels of news and advertising. And here is another interesting thing: to get to national, international, and business news, one has to turn to the middle pages of these thick newspapers. The front and back sets of pages are packed with local and regional news, local cultural events, local business and advertising, and local sport. The front-page headlines are usually to do with regional news, unless there is a major national event such as the Valencia train-crash disaster in July 2006. Political reporting is mostly local-centred and human-centred.

Another thing—there is nowhere near the same media fascination with the sayings and doings of national political leaders, nothing like the personalisation of leadership politics that many Western countries now regard as normal reporting. I had to hunt for stories about the prime minister or the opposition leader in Spanish newspapers.

There is much less national opinion polling, much less sense of a national electorate obsessively taking its own temperature all the time. Spanish voters seem more interested in the substance of political debates than in process, personalities, and spin. There is plenty of political opinion commentary, but it seems more serious than much of what passes as political commentary in Anglophone countries, which is often more about looking for 'an angle' on news rather than discussing the news as such.

Spanish politics is scrupulously courteous. I hope Spain can hold on to this. Spanish politicians know why civility in politics is essential. There was great verbal violence, name-calling, and angry words in the bitter years leading up to the Civil War. Spaniards saw then how verbal violence blunts inhibitions against physical violence, and how the way politicians speak to and about their opponents really does matter.

It seems to me that these are the political characteristics of a successful and mature civil society, from which Anglophone countries might learn sómething. Spain went through huge bloodshed and cruelty to reach the political place where it is now: it seems a good place to be.

If the Civil War was, as Antony Beevor suggests, about three ideological conflicts—Left versus Right, centralism versus regionalism, and liberalism versus military-clerical authoritarianism—Franco's victory was in the end a hollow one. Modern Spain, under PSOE rule, is 'Third Way' Centre-Left, regionalist, and liberal-pluralist. When the chronic Basque autonomy issue is finally settled by a historic compromise—and it seems to be moving that way now—the last traces of the bitter enmities that provoked the Civil War will be gone. And Spain has sensibly withdrawn from the excesses of Bush's war on terror. It is a country, blessedly, at peace with itself and with the world.

* * *

In Mérida, on a large patio in front of the Extremadura Autonomous Community regional parliament building, surrounded by potted cumquat trees with glistening green leaves and laden with ripe orange fruit, I saw a remarkably powerful sculpture, *23 Años*, celebrating the twenty-three years of 1983–2006 since the Assembly of Extremadura, the autonomous region's parliament, was set up. It was an array of twenty-three freestanding white louvre doors, all hinged and open, with one word painted on each side of each door. The first door had two sculpted hands on it, one opening the doorknob from each side—the symbolism being that both Left and Right parties must work together to keep the doors of Spanish democracy open. Here are the words on the twenty-three doors:

Reconciliación	reconciliation
Integración	integration
Impreso	form, due process
Igualdad	equality
Educación	education
Cultura	culture
Realidad	reality
Prosperidad	prosperity
Esfuerzo	effort
Dedicación	dedication
Autonomía	autonomy
Estabilidad	stability
Eficacia	effectiveness
Amistad	friendship
Consideración	consideration
Ayuda	help
Objetividad	objectivity
Concordia	concord

Transparencia	transparency
Claridad	clarity
Responsabilidad	responsibility
Exigencia	demand
Equidad	fairness
Eficiencia	efficiency
Trabajo	work
Etica	ethics
Entendimiento	understanding
Respeto	respect
Paz	peace
Libertad	freedom
Democracia	democracy
Dialogo	dialogue
Pacto	agreement
Justicia	justice
Oportunidad	opportunity
Solidaridad	solidarity
Negociación	negotiation
Apoyo	support
Unidad	unity
Lealtad	loyalty
Identidad	identity
Gestion	management
Fidelidad	fidelity
Experiencia	experience

The meaning is clear—this is an exhaustive list of Spanish democratic values. But it was the contextual symbolism of the doors that impressed me. These are doors that people are being invited to walk through, as I did, not to look at from a respectful or uninvolved distance. The work thus suggests that healthy democratic politics involves active participation by citizens, and that citizens must know what the values of the state are. The doors are all open, not locked. They are light and fragile, easily overturned by clumsy or violent movements. They follow each other in an orderly progression—values complementing and reinforcing other related values. The words are written on both sides of the doors—there is no Right or Left side, no right or wrong side, to these doors.

I saw this work as a brilliant exercise in symbolist art, setting out the values of the contemporary democratic pluralist Spain that I found. But nowhere in Mérida or anywhere else in Spain did I come across the loaded, over-arching phrase 'Spanish values'. Those words, tainted by their misuse by Spanish fascists, are not part of mainstream Spanish political language any more.

chapter eight

Walking through Extremadura

From Mérida to Baños de Montemayor, a health-resort spa village built over Roman thermal baths, just south of the regional border between Extremadura and Castile-León, is a walk of 210 kilometres. There are two cities on the way: Cáceres, eighty kilometres north of Mérida, and Plasencia, about fifty kilometres south of Baños, a little to the east of the waymarked *Vía de la Plata*, but an easy side-trip by bus. After Cáceres, the camino skirts a very large reservoir, the Embalse de Alcantara, fed by two major rivers, the Río Almonte and the Río Tajo.

The camino then crosses some low mountains, just north of a village called Cañaveral, after which it enters marginally higher and better-watered country. After passing through a large irrigated valley, the Valle del Jerte, it returns to dry *encina* grasslands, climbing gradually towards greener hill country surrounding Baños de Montemayor, and on through the mountain pass of Puerto de Béjar on to the high Castilian *meseta*. It took me twelve days to walk from Mérida to Baños, including two rest-days in Cáceres and Plasencia, averaging around twenty kilometres per day.

I had expected this be a fairly boring part of the journey, to be endured and completed as quickly as possible before enjoying the anticipated greener country further north in Castile. But walking across these harsh dry plains of Extremadura started to unblock my memories and my spirituality. In these two weeks, doors into my soul started to open. Though I did not recognise it at the time, these were probably the most life-changing days of my walk, days that re-shaped it as a real pilgrimage and something more than just an interesting, long walk through Spain. Spiritual growth can steal up on you: it does not have to be a moment of blinding, dramatic revelation, of Saul becoming Paul on the road to Damascus; it can also take the form of a slow recognition of good things, the slow spreading of a sense of peace, and the inner healing of an unsettled soul. It was more like that for me.

Still, there must have been some resistance and inner turmoil as the old Adam in me, my controlling and over-controlled personality, obstinately resisted the strengthening spirit of pilgrimage in me. Does this sound like a sort of process of exorcism, of good driving out bad? Perhaps it was, but I did not experience anything like that. It was more of a quiet and slow healing process, re-discovering a calm after the storm that had been my life for the past few years. When I look back at John Eddy's wise words in his blessing, predicting good things I might find on my pilgrimage—words whose significance I did not fully appreciate at the time—I think now that these were the days when I began to experience such things. But it is hard to relate this in writing, for how does one report a personal miracle? I must just go on telling the story of the journey as it happened, and let interested readers join the dots as they will.

After the generous hospitality of the brothers at Alcuéscar (see Chapter 1), it was a very long day's walk, forty-odd kilometres, to Cáceres. Again, I did not quite make it, getting only as far as Valdesalor, a small village that had grown into a rather soulless modern dormitory town of Cáceres. I caught a local bus the few remaining kilometres into the city centre, and this was the last time I took a bus on the camino.

Cáceres, a city of 70,000, with rich links with the Spanish conquest of Latin America, was a much more attractive and interesting city than I had expected. It sits in the foothills of uplands—bare now, but they would have been forested once—overlooking vast dry plains. It had been founded by the Romans in the first century and the whole area would have been heavily settled by Roman former legionaries moving up from Mérida. Many of the original *conquistadores* and soldier–colonists came out of this south-western region of Spain; for example, Hernán Cortés and Francisco Pizarro both came from this area. The Roman military genes, and fourteen centuries of surviving in the harsh Extremaduran environment, bred tough, resourceful people here, well up to the huge challenge of conquering Latin America. Many *conquistadores*, having returned to Spain with their acquired American fortunes, settled in Cáceres, a city to their taste that had had a notorious reputation as a violent, free-wheeling frontier town since its reconquest from the Moors in 1229. In the sixteenth century, Cáceres was still a strange place: an urban jungle of rival great families jostling for power, a violent city of strongly built fortified palaces. It took many years for the Spanish monarchy to bring the fractious and fiercely independent great families of Cáceres to order.

The old city—a UNESCO heritage site—is an impressive

collection of austerely beautiful palaces and churches in golden sandstone, running along the crest of a walled hill. I wandered around early in the morning, soaking up the atmosphere of this unusual city, which still has a strong *macho* mood about it. I was remembering scenes from *Romeo and Juliet* and, indeed, Shakespeare might have recognised this city as the Verona of his imagination. It was easy, walking through the now-silent narrow streets of this city, overtopped by its brooding, windowless fortress-palaces, to imagine the bodyguards of the Montague and Capulet families brawling their way through these same streets, to hear their shouted threats and boasts, and the clashing of their swords and the cries of the wounded.

Around the old aristocratic city is an equally old residential and market city centred on the large Plaza Mayor, where I found a rundown but friendly place to stay, the Pensión Carretero. There were good, inexpensive restaurants tucked away in side streets, once you got out of the rather touristy main square. Walking uphill along the main shopping street, a pedestrian mall now, I entered a third Cáceres, a dignified and green nineteenth-century city of broad, treed avenues, parks, and refreshing fountains—a miniature Paris. This part of Cáceres was all the more beautiful, knowing as I did at first hand how dry and harsh the countryside was just outside the city. This Cáceres was a welcome oasis. On a quiet bench in the main city park, I called home and had a joyful, long conversation with my wife.

Walking out of Cáceres the next day, I had my first taste of highway walking along the N630, the main national trunk road that runs from Seville in the south to León in the north. The N630 is the modern-day successor to the *Vía de la Plata*, but is itself in course of being superseded by a north-south motorway under construction. I would grow to hate this busy and overcrowded road in my encounters with it over the next 300-odd kilometres. The camino runs roughly parallel to it, but is mostly mercifully out of sight and hearing of it. But sometimes you have to walk alongside it or, at worst, as here, on its very verge. It was a narrow and busy two-lane highway, on a high road embankment with impassable wheatfields below it on either side. It felt, and was, dangerous to walk here. I was at risk of being blown off my feet by the airwash from huge trucks and buses roaring past me only a metre away at speeds of 130 kilometres per hour. After ten kilometres of this, it was a relief to get off the highway onto a parallel dirt road.

Soon I was in Casar de Cáceres, a pretty village with a pilgrim *albergue* in the main square, opposite a loud, electric town clock that chimed all night on every hour. Earplugs helped a little. I met interesting fellow pilgrims that night, including José, an assertive but cheerful retired waiter from Seville, forty-ish and on an invalidity pension (back troubles, he said), but seemingly pretty fit to me—fit enough to bicycle from Seville to Santiago. He first demanded that I help him carry his heavy mountain bike up the steep stairs to the second-floor *albergue* rooms, because he was sure it would be stripped of parts if he left it downstairs in the street overnight. He would not hear of one of the two dormitories being reserved as a courtesy for women, insisting that unisex sleeping was a firm camino rule. But he was a friendly dinner companion, like many Spaniards, with a highly vivid and dramatic style of conversation.

There were also Tim and Liz, a quietly charming young

walking couple from Wales, whom I was to meet several times on the way until finally—improbably—crossing paths again at the very end in Finisterre. And there were Marit and Karin, two cheery Swedish women walkers; Karin was combating a sprained knee, which was forcing her to use buses and taxis for much of the way. They soon became famous along the camino as *las chicas suecas*, 'the Swedish chicks', merrily losing their way from time to time, only to be put back on the right road by helpful Spanish police and taxi-drivers. Marit is a social worker who works with refugees; Karin is a journalist. Both had grown-up children but, as far as I could gather, were currently partnerless. They had done pilgrimages to Santiago together before, on the *Vía Frances*. But this was their first time on the *Vía de la Plata*, and the heat and aridity of the route was still a bit shocking to them.

The next day, Marit and I set off together on the camino along a high ridge, with stunning views westwards towards Portugal and eastwards across dry plains to the central uplands. We were walking on the old Roman/Moorish *Vía de la Plata* now, marked by the worn-down stumps of huge Roman granite *millario*s (milestones). It was exciting to imagine the Roman legions or the al-Andalus trading caravans moving along this very same road.

We were headed for a remote country train stop called Río Tajo, overlooking the huge Embalse de Alcantara, where, according to the guidebook, we should have been able to catch an afternoon train to the village of Cañaveral, further on up the N630 highway. But when we reached Río Tajo we found Karin, who had come up by taxi, bearing bad news that the train no longer stopped here. It was a frustratingly surreal moment: there was the tidy but locked station, with shade and green pot-plants inside, a ticket office, signs, boxes of timetable leaflets … I just couldn't believe it was closed. I rang RENFE (Spanish Railways) on my mobile and, sadly, it was indeed true—trains had ceased to stop at Río Tajo a few months earlier. In a bad temper, we climbed back up to the N630 and endured another several kilometres of walking in blazing afternoon heat. Someone in a passing vehicle threw a raw egg at the girls—the only incident of bad behaviour towards pilgrims I ever encountered in Spain. The egg fortunately missed them.

Then we arrived at an improbable oasis: the Villa Lindamar, a palatial, modern-style country bungalow, now a tourist centre specialising in 4WD bird-watching tours into nearby national parks, run by an enterprising, young Netherlands-based couple, Martin and Linda. It was bizarre to walk off the awful N630 into this little boutique hotel, with a long bamboo bar, nice bedrooms, and even a swimming pool. As the sun finally set over the lake below, I went for a cooling dip in the pool. The intense heat and glare of the day had at last turned into a pleasantly warm evening, with the rock walls around the pool terrace holding onto the day's warmth as the evening set in. The lake below was no longer the hard, glittering metallic sheet it had been all day. Now it was recognisable as blue water.

I was drinking cold beers, luxuriating in my swimming trunks in the cool pool, while a middle-aged, badly sunburned Englishman, with a white towel round his ample belly and a mobile phone glued to his ear, sat nearby in a deckchair, irascibly trying to sort out last-minute hitches in a complicated Spanish land-purchase. It was an entertaining but jarringly incongruous moment. What was I doing here in this swimming pool listening to an English property developer haggling over a deal? This was supposed to be a pilgrimage, not a business holiday in a resort that felt like California or Mexico. I felt uneasy, disconnected. It went on that way later, as I sat sipping gin and tonics over the bar, chatting in English with Martin and *las chicas suecas* about the eccentricities of the locals. It was fun, but I knew I had fallen into the world of Anglophone tourist Spain. In just these few hours, the precious pilgrim's Spain, which I had just been starting to connect with in recent days, had again drifted out of reach.

The next day, a Saturday, I was anxious to be off early and alone with my thoughts. I wanted to cross the mountains at Cañaveral, and get out of these arid plains, to reach the city of Plasencia—which I sensed would be soothing for my uneasy soul—in time for my daughters' confirmation Mass in Canberra the next day, Sunday. So in the first light of dawn I was climbing back up onto the high plateau, back to the old Roman road high above the N630. It was red-earth country with very little grass, the main vegetation being a sort of wild fennel bush. There were cows, a few windmill pumps feeding stockwater tanks, and nothing else. It looked and felt like Texas or outback Australia. Far over to the east was the huge, new north-south motorway under construction.

I by-passed Cañaveral without stopping, and the yellow arrows then took me up a steep pine-forested slope to a mountain pass. I was glad to leave the dry plains behind. What lay ahead looked marginally greener and softer. I walked down into a tiny village called Grimaldo, on a north-facing slope under high hills that sheltered it from the parching southern winds and sun. There were almond and peach trees, vegetable plots, grapevines, running streams from a mountain spring. My spirits lifted at last. I had a snack and chat at the local bar and then caught the late afternoon bus into Plasencia, promising the friendly bar lady that I would come back the next night to Grimaldo to sleep in the pilgrim *refugio* attached to her bar.

Plasencia was all I had hoped for, and more: an elegant little city with a strong local pride and culture, nestling at the foot of high mountains, the Sierra de Gredos, which are snow-covered in winter and still with snowdrifts on the peaks. It is well-watered country, with the cool, clear waters of the Río Jerte running down from the mountains through pleasant parklands set out below the old hillside town. Plasencia has an important place in the history of the *Reconquista*. It was founded in 1186 by King Alfonso VIII of Castile as a fortress city, with the double purpose of colonising and guarding Castile's recent conquest of the strategic northern borderlands of Extremadura. It was recaptured briefly by the Moors in 1196, but was retaken and held by Castile the following year. It was interesting how my walk was tracing in reverse chronological order the Castilian conquest of most of the great Moorish cities of Spain: Granada, Córdoba, Mérida, Cáceres, and now Plasencia ... with Salamanca and Zamora, the most northerly Moorish city on my route, yet to come.

I hastened to find the Plasencia cathedral. I wanted to go in there and pray for my daughters, Vanny and Raingsey, at the same hour that they were being confirmed in Canberra's Catholic cathedral, Saint Christopher's. Their coming confirmation had been very much on my mind these past weeks. They had prepared for it in my absence, but my prayers had been with them. Confirmation, one of the seven Catholic sacraments, is an important moment in Catholic life because it

is the sacrament whereby a Catholic begins to leave childhood
behind to become a full adult member of the church.

The cathedral was a magnificent building, begun in the
thirteenth century and finally completed in the sixteenth
century. It was a hybrid of styles, blending a small early
Romanesque part with a much grander sixteenth-century
completion, the latter in gloriously ornate High Gothic style
(the 'plateresque' style). It was a cathedral out of a fairytale,
with romantic carvings around the doorways and spires, and
a magnificent huge painted and woodcarved *retablo* (altar
screen) behind the main altar. Recently cleaned, the almost
white sandstone glowed in the late afternoon sun.

As I walked into the cathedral, I stopped, entranced, as the
glorious first notes of the *Magnificat* of the Italian Renaissance
composer Francesco Durante rang out through the towering
naves. This wonderfully triumphant choral music, in final
rehearsal by a choir from Salamanca University for a free
concert later that evening, sounded absolutely right in this
setting. I stayed to hear the full rehearsal and came back later
for the evening concert, which also included Mozart's *Missa
Brevis*.

After the concert, I dined in a good restaurant nearby on
a roof terrace overlooking the floodlit cathedral plaza. I was
having the *menú del dia* (the economical, set-price menu of
the day that most Spanish restaurants offer), and so expected
to be seated modestly in the dining room downstairs; but the
patron, in a special moment of kindness on seeing I was a
pilgrim, graciously insisted I sit on the special upstairs terrace
under the grapevine pergolas. I was in such a good mood
afterwards that I stopped into a bar on the main city square
to treat myself to a nightcap, which turned into three leisurely

malt whiskies, two Scotches and an Irish. This little luxury cost me considerably more than the whole earlier dinner had. I found that the best rule in Spain is always to drink local Spanish alcohol, avoiding imported drinks. Spain makes good gins and cognacs, but I never tried Spanish whisky.

Plasencia, like Cáceres, had some grand old palaces, a former Jewish quarter, and many good clothing boutiques and gift shops tucked away in the cobbled walking streets for well-off Spanish tourists—of whom there were many, presumably from Madrid, an easy few hours' drive eastwards from here. There wasn't much cheap accommodation, but again I was lucky: I found a traditional *hostal*, the Rincón Extremeno, hidden in a tiny lane just off the main square. By now I felt quite comfortable walking into such places and saying politely, '*Soy peregrino andando a Santiago, quiero un dormitorio individual por favor, no muy caro si es posible.*' ('I am a pilgrim walking to Santiago; can I please have an inexpensive single room?'), and getting what I am sure was a generous discount (I never asked) on a simple basic room, and a friendly welcome in the bar and restaurant later. I loved the courtesy and friendship in these little family-run *hostals* where, if the wife of the *patron* was running the kitchen, you could always rely on getting a good, honest meal.

Back to Grimaldo by the bus the next afternoon, I found a bunk in the pilgrim *refugio*—a spartan, minimally renovated workman's cottage. There were quite a few other pilgrims there. Alex, a pleasant, retired Englishman who had lived on the Costa del Sol for many years, filled me in on the local history. He stressed that I could not imagine how poor and deprived these now picturesque and comfortable villages had been twenty years ago.

The next day was a magical walk through rolling hills down into the Valle del Jerte irrigation area, a broad, gently dished green valley, with two long, concrete aqueducts circling high around it, diverting the main flow of the Río Jerte and channelling its precious water around the valley's side contours. From these aqueducts, smaller concrete water channels meandered down well-graded slopes into the river valley, feeding croplands and feedlots and orchards and tree plantations on the way, the left-over and run-off water eventually rejoining the original riverbed.

As I walked across the aqueduct and then down the hill into the valley, the cheery, bubbling sound of flowing water was all around me. The whole system was gravity-fed, simply and ingeniously engineered, and it nourished a rich variety of intensive, small-scale agriculture and animal husbandry. It filled me with a sense of wonder to see how dry hill country had been made to bloom through hard work and careful irrigation engineering, using the simple gifts of nature—gravity, ample water, good soil, and a lot of human toil. I suppose it is unfashionable to feel joy and pride in the works of man, and some of us these days are inclined to put more value on wilderness than cultivated agricultural land, but I have to admit that the good husbandry of this thriving irrigated valley delighted my spirit.

In the middle of the valley was Galisteo, a remarkable hilltop village completely encircled by massive stone walls. It was, mercifully, still an unspoiled village, all the more charming for being so taken for granted by its inhabitants as simply their *pueblo*. I could not even find a postcard of this beautiful little place to send home. I climbed the walls, and almost circumnavigated the village by walking around them.

After Galisteo it was another long walk, through two nearby valley villages and then gradually up out of the green valley of the Río Jerte, across the northern aqueduct and into more rough, dry hill country, until finally reaching a large, Roman triumphal arch sitting improbably in the middle of nowhere—the Arco de Cáparra. No one yet knows what this arch signified in Roman Spain. Archaeologists are still excavating a small adjoining Roman settlement. Was it a crossroads town of north-south and east-west Roman roads, a staging post on the south-to-north road, or the scene of a great battle victory or peace treaty signing?

I detoured off the camino here to stay in a roadside hotel on the N630 a few kilometres to the east. By prior arrangement, the hotel owner came across on a connecting road to pick me up at the arch in his beaten-up car. At the hotel, I ran into Marit again. The camino is like that—people move at different speeds, taking rests at different times in different places, and there is the pleasure of meeting friends again unexpectedly. We swapped travel notes over dinner. The next day, we walked on together, through greener slopes now, to meet Karin in Aldeanueva del Camino, a pretty village at the foot of the Sierra de Gredos.

Here in the village park I came across an unexpected little memorial, an inobtrusive stone plaque whose inscription under a carved Jewish candlestick and olive branches simply read: *1492–1997. En homenaje a los judios de Aldeanueva expulsados por los reyes catolicos. Aldeanueva del Camino, agosto—1997.* (In honour of the Jews of Aldeanueva, expelled by the Catholic monarchs. Aldeanueva del Camino, August 1997). My eyes filled with tears at the simple humanity of this inscription. I did not know that Jews had

lived here, and I was strangely moved by this sign of love
and respect for neighbours long since departed. Reading it,
I could believe that the modern-day villagers of Aldeanueva
really did mourn the loss of their former Jewish co-villagers,
and would have liked them still to be living here. I thought of
Tevye and his family in *Fiddler on the Roof*, walking sadly out
of their beloved Russian–Jewish village into exile, away from
the country in which they had lived in peace for centuries
alongside their Orthodox Christian neighbours, until cruel,
state-encouraged *pogroms* forced them to abandon their
homes and scatter all over the world. I thought of the
suffering of refugees everywhere, pushed out of their homes
by state policies and stirred-up religious or ethnic hatreds.
And I remembered that in all my travels in Russia, Poland,
Czech Republic, or Slovakia, I had never seen anything like
this modest little memorial to lost Jewish neighbours: only
the cold silence of conveniently lapsed memories.

The next day I walked a little off the route, to Hervás,
a picture-postcard hill town surrounded by vineyards and
orchards. Here I found more rich Jewish memories, but not
the same uncomplicated warmth as in Aldeanueva. There
was a large tourist-information plaque in the picturesque
and well-signed Jewish quarter, an area of narrow winding
lanes and pretty, half-timbered houses. The plaque contained
a wealth of architectural detail on the building styles, framed
by a brief sanitised history:

Northeast of here, on a steeply sloping hillside, there was
a Jewish population in Hervás, especially in the fifteenth
century. Famous family names included Cohen, Haben
Haxis, Rabi Samuel and Bellida la Rica. It is a fact that

after the expulsion decree, Hervás lost much of its Jewish population through movement away to the Portuguese frontier, to which the majority departed ... When in 1492 the Catholic monarchs decreed the expulsion of the Jews, about 25 families left from the Jewish quarter of Hervás, moving to Portugal through Ciudad Rodrigo. Others became Christian converts.

It all sounded painless, a minor movement of a few families to nearby Portugal. I could not believe it was really like that, and I felt a stab of anger at this smooth passing over of the truth of what must really have happened in Hervás in 1492. I surmise that the Jewish community of Hervás had been large—it was well situated on the north-south *Vía de la Plata* trade route in the remote borderlands between Castile and the south, and may have been a Jewish-majority town—and that their expulsions and forced conversions would have been of a much larger scale and more painful than this account suggests. No one could tell me where the synagogue had been: my guess was that it might have been on the hill directly above the 'Jewish quarter'—more likely, the original medieval town—on the site where the large church now stood. I felt more silences around me in Hervás than truth.

But then, later, not far from a grand, old baroque convent that is now a museum, I came across a new bed and breakfast guesthouse, Hostal Sinagoga, with Jewish Sabbath candlesticks proudly displayed in the front windows. I introduced myself to the owner, Abigail, a charming, auburn-haired Israeli woman, originally from Prague and now living here, married to a local Spaniard. They were setting up this new tourist venture together. Abigail told me Hervás was a friendly and good town, where she was being made to feel welcome. Her guesthouse was doing well, with lots of tourists—including from Israel—coming to see Hervás. I said goodbye, blinking back tears.

Onwards now, I walked down through cherry orchards and on to Baños de Montemayor, with the high Gredos mountains looming all around. I found a family-run pensión in Baños, two flats joined together in a modern apartment complex, simple and homely, and then it was off to the famous, restored Roman baths where I ran into Tim and Liz again, floating in a princely, hot spa pool. What a luxury! I went down a stairway to a warm and steamy basement pool area, smelling of sulphur and other minerals. On one side was the original Roman bathhouse museum area, excavated out of the soft, calcified mudstone—there were Roman stone baths, lounging benches, columns, bits of metal pipes and taps, broken statuary ... and on the other side there were two modern thermal pools, all in gleaming white marble—a delightful modern interpretation of a Roman public bath. The two large pools were flanked by reproduction classical statues in white marble. The water was just short of too hot, with a cascading waterfall to luxuriate under, and underwater side-jets to caress sore backs. I stretched and arched my body in the warm water like a cat under a hot sun. It was all too much, but it was glorious.

That night, unexpectedly and with no obvious physical cause, I was hit with the worst attack of diarrhoea I have ever suffered in my life. I was not sick—there was no headache or nausea—but over a few hours all my insides dissolved and turned to water. In one unsettled night, I lost four kilograms of body weight. I know this, because by coincidence I had weighed myself in a pharmacy the day before, and I checked it again the next day. In the morning, with hollow stomach and trembling limbs, I dragged myself weakly to the village medical clinic, where a kindly doctor prescribed rehydration salts and tablets to glue my insides up again. I went back to bed for the whole day, eating nothing but boiled fish and white rice, and drinking weak tea. The next day, with some apprehension, I set off on the road again, walking slowly the few kilometres over a mountain pass and into Castile.

I realised later that this unexpected bout of illness marked a physical and mental turning point in my pilgrimage. I don't know what brought it on—probably a combination of things: the accumulated tiredness and physical stress from pushing myself too hard for the past month, too much sun, the cumulative emotional impact of the pilgrimage so far, the unaccustomed heat and luxury of the baths finally triggering it off—who knows? Whatever the cause, my digestive system just gave up and went on strike.

Until that day, I had been eating and drinking as if I were at home, not admitting that as a distance walker I might need to cut back on food intake, to take in no more food and drink than what I needed as daily walking fuel. We tend to eat and drink too much at home out of social habit or sheer boredom, as a distraction or relief from stress, or because we hope it might make us sleep better. Many of us become progressively more overweight as a result.

It is a fallacy that you need more food when working hard physically—most of us work better and have more energy when we eat less. People who can cope comfortably with long-distance walks tend to be lean and wiry. I had thought the leanness came as a consequence of the walking, but it might be more the other way around. To walk long distances enjoyably requires the self-discipline of reducing your food and alcohol intake to no more than you need. If you make your body work on digesting excess amounts of rich food and drink, this takes energy away from the energy you need to walk. Why make your body do all that extra work of digestion, when you can walk comfortably on much less food? Ruefully, I recalled that, despite 500 kilometres of strenuous walking, I had not lost a single kilogram of weight between Granada and Baños de Montemayor. The illness in Baños was a blessing in disguise: it was telling me it was time to try a different approach.

I gradually rebuilt my strength over the next few days, increasing my walking distance each day, and the diarrhoea never returned. I took care now to eat no more food than I needed. I drank a lot more water, and less tea and coffee. I no longer carried around with me great wedges of cheese, ham and salami, and 'energy' bars. I ate a bit of fruit and plain bread in the morning, and usually had just one main meal a day in the evening. I kept my alcohol down to two glasses a day. Doing this, I found that I was now shedding weight steadily and painlessly—about one kilogram a week. By the time I got to Santiago, I was eight kilograms lighter than when I left home. My belt was three notches narrower. There was a spring in my step and I felt fifteen years younger.

With the weight loss came greater clarity of mind. It was as if a fog was clearing from my brain. I found I could think more calmly and productively—my brain was not clogged and dulled by the work of digesting so much food and drink. I think my emotional intelligence, my ability to confront uncomfortable thoughts and take a harder and more honest look at my own life, was greatly enhanced by the change of diet. It is no accident that in the history of the Church, mysticism and physical asceticism have tended to go together. I don't think there have been many fat saints.

In these ways, Baños de Montemayor marked a turning point. The remarkable thing was it had taken me so long to get to this point. I was thirty-one days into my journey, and had already walked nearly halfway to Santiago. It had taken the stubborn old Adam a month to admit that he might need a lifestyle change.

chapter nine

Across Castile to Salamanca

My walking now settled into a generally predictable and pleasurable routine. Baños was about halfway from Granada to Santiago in terms of distance; Santiago was 570 kilometres ahead. There were no more dramas, but rather the quiet satisfactions of meditation on the move, letting the mind and spirit relax completely. I was just under halfway though the ten weeks I had planned to stay in Spain. With thirty-six days in Spain to go till my booked flight home, I was confident that, barring accidents or serious illness, I could now complete the journey. I was now regularly walking up to thirty kilometres a day without strain, and I only needed to maintain a daily average of sixteen kilometres to get to Santiago in time. As my weight came down, as the weather started to get cooler moving north, and as my walking technique improved, it all became easier.

I was not thinking about getting to Santiago, but rather enjoying each day as it came. The blisters had been finally left behind in Extremadura, the soles and heels of my feet had hardened, my legs and thighs had trimmed down to an athlete's physique, and the flabby folds of surplus skin left around my thighs from my lost fat were disappearing as skin elasticity returned. My buttocks had tightened, and even my belly—the middle-aged man's last stubborn reserve of fat—had started to shrink. My cotton trousers felt pleasurably loose. I was sleeping well, no longer waking myself up with my own snoring, and not needing asthma relievers any more. I was happy with this new body.

The benign endorphins of long-distance walking had at last kicked in, relaxing the mind, and walking had at last become less a matter of harsh will power, the exercise of 'mind over matter', than of just letting it happen. I was now truly riding on 'Shanks' pony', a phrase whose meaning I now pleasurably understood. For my legs were now striding forward automatically and effortlessly, while I enjoyed an unparalleled relaxation and liberation from daily cares.

The huge, rolling landscapes of the Castilian *meseta* unfolded like a slowly moving Circorama film around me as my mind ranged freely over my life. There was unlimited time to muse; to try to remember old snatches of poetry or music learned at school; to reflect on old loves, friendships, estrangements, enmities—all the knots and tangles of a complicated personal history. I found myself thinking more unselfishly and compassionately than ever before about important relationships and events that had happened in my life, whether spiritual, interpersonal, or political. It was a steadily developing process of mental relaxation and discovery of truth about myself. Talking afterwards to Father Frank Brennan, another Jesuit friend, about this, he agreed, saying that he had found his Santiago pilgrimage to be 'taking your life for a walk'. And that is indeed what it had become now, in these happiest days of the pilgrimage.

Let me say a little more about the physical character of this walking. In my life I have been lucky to enjoy several kinds of natural sporting motion—small boat sailing, cross-country skiing, horse riding, long-distance running. Once the specific skills had been mastered, all these sports involved the joy of movement with little sense of bodily effort, the same joy and excitement a small child gets out of being on a swing or rocking horse. In sailing, you have those wonderful moments as the boat comes about and your sails catch a new wind, the boat springing forward willingly as the helmsman is pressed back into his seat by its gentle acceleration. In cross-country skiing, you feel the easy slide of well-waxed skis in smooth tracks across a snowy plain, just the slightest push of your leg muscles sending the skis forward in a push-and-glide movement, so gloriously effortless once you have fully acquired the knack of it. In riding, you enjoy the gentle pressure of your shanks on the horse's sides, sending him forward into a willing trot or canter. And even in long-distance running, there is that terrific feeling twenty minutes or so into the run (if you are fit) when your endorphins have started flowing, your muscles have relaxed, your breathing has settled down, your heartbeat is steady, and you are just letting the countryside slide by with hardly any effort at all …

I had not expected long-distance walking could give me anything like those pleasurable sensations. My practice walks around home had certainly not been like that: they had been hard slogs, lung and muscle conditioning, dutiful exercise. And yet now, my walking in Spain, once I was fully fit, had became enjoyable in just these ways. I felt sorry for the nice but unfit and physically exhausted Englishman, Alex, whom

I met briefly in Grimaldo, who complained sadly to me of how he was finding his camino: 'It's just a plod, really'. To me now, miraculously, it was no longer a plod. It had become a ride, a glide, a sail ...

How can I convey how walking these kinds of long, steady distances day after day can nourish the human spirit? It is not so easy to put this into words, but I will try. It was quite different from shorter exercise-walks around home, because there I never really left my daily concerns and worries fully behind. But once I was fully acclimatised mentally and physically into the walk in Spain, once I had left my home cares behind me, my soul entered a gloriously private and peaceful world as my 'Shanks' pony' strode on reliably beneath me, walking me across the map of Spain.

I was certainly still aware of the countryside, and I was appreciating and enjoying it, but in a strange way it didn't really matter so much any more to identify where I was on any particular day or hour. I was now free-wheeling through a benign, ambient space. I felt safe, untroubled, joyous.

The thought often came to me that I was a little capsule of life crawling forward across a vast landscape, where only the here and now had any meaning for me. Time had expanded enormously: yesterday was already a fading memory, and tomorrow was just a distant prospect. Today as I write this from home some weeks later, I could not tell you where I was or what I saw each day, without the memory-prop of the guidebook and my pocket diary to fix those geographical facts in retrospect. Were it left to me, the walk across Castile would just be a pleasurable blur now, jumbled memories of dirt tracks undulating up and down gentle hills around me, grasslands with scattered *encina* trees, golden wheatfields, dark storm clouds that massed but never brought rain, the strange Martian shapes of huge mobile irrigation rigs sprawled across the wheatfields, vineyards, gentle hills, dogs that came out to growl or bark greetings at me, neat white villages ...

So if I were to go on giving you a precise, day-by-day account — about villages passed, of interesting buildings and other things seen, of good people met — it would be true in one sense but less relevant in another, because my walk had now become a different kind of observed reality. It didn't really matter so much anymore where I was each day, no more than it matters to a sailor scudding across the waves on the sea, or a wild horse cantering across an open prairie. I was a free spirit now. Of course, I still had to navigate; I still had to know roughly where I was, and take in the markers of a day's journey from A to B. I had to remain, to that limited extent, planted in physical reality. But to let my mind slide into a different rhythm of existence — that was a rare and lovely feeling.

In one way it became mindless, but in another way it had became an intensely spiritual experience of extended and focused meditation on my life. My walking was now a smooth flow of energy, rather than a chain of discrete events. My body and mind were engaging together in a different way than they do in normal life. There was a great simplification, a sense of leaving behind bodily cares, of forgetting the body. For when the body is just the vehicle, the conveyance that is taking you along the camino, the soul becomes truly free. I think this must be a little like how an animal might feel as it moves across terrain. How a wild horse, a free-ranging wolf, might experience its passage through open country.

* * *

It also occurred to me that a long pilgrimage is more than just a metaphor for a life. It is a separate little life within the larger life, a life experience that takes you so completely out of your 'real' life back home that you enter an altered state of perception of being. The camino to Santiago, like a life, has a beginning, a middle, and an end. Getting to Santiago marks the fulfilment of the goal of this 'little life'—it is what you have been aiming for. But, in another important sense, you dread the journey's end in Santiago, because it is a kind of death. Arrival in Santiago, the end of the camino, is the end of your little pilgrim life. And just as one clings to the joy of life even if one believes in the hope of Heaven, one clings to the joy of every day's experience on the camino—because it has become one's life. As most of us live most of our lives in the present, without thinking about the death that awaits us all, so it had now became for me on the camino—the journey was now more real than the inevitable destination. The joy was in the doing, more so than in the anticipated arrival.

While on pilgrimage, you are experiencing the 'real' world from a different place, and looking at it through a different lens that refracts the things you see and offers a different perception of them.

* * *

I mentioned earlier a matter I called 'walking technique'. This was the final ingredient—after getting fit, getting my weight down, and adopting good dietary habits—in making my long walking pilgrimage most pleasurable. 'Walking technique' is really an inappropriate term to describe something that is mostly a matter of simply listening to your body and trusting what it tells you. I gradually discovered the main elements of this. They will be obvious to experienced long-distance walkers, but may help others who are newer to it.

First and foremost, it is a matter of how you use your legs and feet, and how you use your staff efficiently to help as a third leg. I have already talked about the staff, and here are some thoughts on legs and feet. Above all, you must learn to walk the way an animal does: lightly, never stamping. Think of how a cat or a dog walks. They don't march. Marching is a thoroughly unnatural and tiring, learned human gait; an animal's natural gait is a light, relaxed pad. As the Irish traditional traveller's blessing says, 'Let the road rise to meet you'. Don't try to stamp the road down into submission. Many female walkers know this instinctively—perhaps that is why women take to long-distance walking so well, as they do to endurance horse-riding. Male walkers have to unlearn the competitive conditioning of a lifetime—the idea that sport is about beating the challenge, driving yourself on, forcing the pace, staying the course, climbing that mountain even if it kills you, pushing your limits ... all those misleading, inspirational metaphors that were drilled into us in competitive school sport.

If you approach your walking in that way, your body inevitably tenses up, your legs stiffen and so have to work harder to transmit the energy from your heart and lungs, your feet bruise and your soles blister more easily, and sprains and pulled muscles are more likely. And it is just like riding a horse—if the rider is stressed and anxious, the horse will feel it through the rider's body, and become tight and stressed in response. Shanks' pony reacts similarly. Good, safe walking, like good, safe riding or cross-country skiing, is all about mental relaxation, putting your feet down gently, breathing evenly and easily, and helping your body to relax and de-stress. It is in no way about 'winning', about 'triumphing over yourself' or over nature. Indeed, the secret of good walking once you are fit is to let your body take charge. Like an animal, it knows exactly what it can do. You must simply trust it.

Micro-navigation, watching where you plant your feet, keeping an eye on the terrain immediately in front of you, is something that, initially, you need to do consciously; but after a while it becomes as instinctive and automatic as steering a car. You don't want to step in ruts or holes, obviously, but you also want to avoid stepping on sharp protruding stones because they can unbalance you and cause ankle injuries. I found myself looking for softer, sandier ground or turf surfaces to walk on in preference to bitumen or hard-baked clay, because soft ground is easier on soles and heels, which can bruise even through thick, rubber-soled shoes.

If you are walking on the sloping shoulders of a main road that's not busy, it is good to walk alternately on either side, to balance the sideways pressures on your feet. On a busy road, on the other hand you should always, for safety's sake, face the oncoming traffic.

It is important to start the walking day gently. You may be stiff and sore with seized-up muscles from an uncomfortable sleep or a hard previous day. Do a few leg- and back-stretching exercises before you start. Then let your legs warm gradually into the walk. If you force the pace at the beginning you are more likely to pull or strain something. As a horse does, let your legs warm up, and don't rush to get into your full walking stride: it is going to be a long day, and you don't have to gallop in the first half-hour. As your legs warm up and relax, your pace will naturally quicken and your stride will lengthen, in their own good time.

Everyone has their own natural, long-distance optimal walking speed, depending on their physique, metabolism, and fitness level. For me, when fit, it was about four or five kilometres per hour on level ground in the morning, slowing back towards three as the day got hotter and I became more tired. Back in Australia afterwards, still fit from Spain, I walked one day with a young distance walker from Canberra, Amy Banson, who was just finishing an epic 1400-kilometre, solo charity walk from Brisbane to Canberra. A tall, slim young woman with a body like a gazelle, Amy's thigh joints sat up somewhere above my waist, and her natural speed was a long, fluid lope of around six or seven kilometres per hour. It was fun walking with her on that day; but in trying to keep up with her I tensed up, in spite of my fitness, and after a few hours my legs were stiff and aching. If you try to walk faster than your natural speed, you will pay for it. And so in a group it is physically important — not just a courtesy — for all to go at the speed of the slowest walker, or for the naturally faster people, if they want to move faster, to go ahead and meet up at the next agreed stop.

How many rest stops to have through the day are an individual preference. Some people like to stop more often; others like to keep going. Too many stops become energy-draining and morale-sapping. It is always harder to start again after a stop: your leg muscles seize up quickly, and any bruises in soles and heels certainly remind you of their presence when you start off again. Thus some people prefer to keep going steadily for hours, snacking or drinking on the move, out of a convenient hand bag or a rucksack-fitted drinking tube. On the other hand, after a pre-dawn start, an early or mid-morning coffee and toast with jam if you pass an open bar can be sheer bliss! Taking photos need not slow you down too much, if you keep your camera in an accessible front belt-pouch. Towards the end of the day, as you approach your destination, your body tends to speed up, as a horse does in anticipation of the end of a ride.

The sun on the *meseta* is potentially debilitating and dangerous. I always kept my head and neck and arms well covered: Australians are taught to respect and fear the ultraviolet rays of the sun. Northern Europeans understandably love to strip off to bare skin after their long cold grey winters, but I was not taking any chances. Even after six weeks back home, my arms were all white while the backs of my uncovered hands were still deeply tanned and freckled from the sun.

I wore comfortable, loose-fitting, long-sleeved clothing. I took care of my skin, watching for any chafings or insect bites that could turn into something nastier, and medicated them appropriately, either simply with talcum powder and Vaseline-type creams or, if they were more inflamed, with a hydrocortisone cream such as Dermacort.

You can usually walk out minor foot, leg, or body aches, because a slightly pulled muscle will usually loosen up and fix itself on the move and with a bit of liniment cream. If real pain doesn't go away after an hour's walking, though, you know it's more serious. Then it's time to stop, have a rest, take some Nurofen, and take it gently until you get to somewhere to rest up properly and evaluate the problem.

For most people it is a mistake to try to walk non-stop, day after day, without breaks. Rest days are necessary for most of us, especially in the early stages of a long walk when you are still conditioning your body. Once again, it makes sense to trust your body. If, as happened to me several times during the initial three weeks from Granada to Mérida, your body tells you that it needs a rest day after only three or four days of walking, trust it. Stop. By the end, you'll be going six, seven, and maybe more days without your body feeling the need for a rest day. Alison Raju suggests—and my experience supports this—that rest days in little villages are more beneficial than rest days in cities, which all too easily can become sightseeing marathons. (Visiting museums, for me, is the most exhausting exercise of all.) My best rest day was in Alcaracejos, where I did almost nothing all day beyond a gentle morning stroll around the village, hearing Mass, listening to music on the radio, having a long afternoon siesta, enjoying a leisurely dinner, and then taking in some television.

Finally, it is important to decide, before you head off each day, where you intend to stop and sleep at the end of the day. Your body and mind need this information to pace themselves through the day. There is almost nothing more stressful than arriving somewhere and then deciding, or being forced, to go on further. It is like a time change—it disrupts the rhythm of your whole day.

That is all I have to say about 'walking technique'!

***

From the border of Castile to Salamanca was seventy-three kilometres, a relaxed four-day walk for me, all blessedly far away from the N630 through quiet back-country roads and walking paths. I stayed in three villages: Calzada de Béjar, in a charming, new, commercial *albergue;* Fuenterroble, in a quaintly eccentric *refugio* set up by the famous and tireless parish priest Don Blas, who sadly was away—I would have liked to meet him, as I was told he loves pilgrims and is the kind of Spanish priest I would have really enjoyed talking with and getting to know; and, finally, in a comfortable little *refugio* in San Pedro de Rozados, which I remember as the most perfect little village I encountered in Spain. I had plenty of fellow-pilgrim company on the three nights in these villages. Although I was still choosing to walk alone by day, I was meeting pretty much the same people each night, forming friendships.

The short day from Baños to Calzada was mostly downhill after crossing the pass. It was initially very green and mountainous, with the sound of streams never far away, but dried out as I got further away from the rain catchment of the Béjar pass—with wonderful views opening up as I looked back at the still-snowy high peaks of the Gredos mountains. The first day, I met a bunch of school-kids and parents and teachers out on a local walk; it was a good meeting, and it was nice to be looked at in awe by the children when they heard I had walked all the way from Granada! Calzada, a tiny village, had a sweet *albergue*, a converted barn at the entrance to the village, with a charming *casita* (house warden), who cooked a good and reasonably priced, simple dinner for us. These sorts of pilgrim accommodation facilities, provided by local village councils with financial help from the Spanish government or EU funds, help keep travel costs down, are a good way to meet other pilgrims, and are good for the village economies as well.

The next day, from Calzada to Fuenterroble, is not a day which I remember much about, except that it seemed harder going than the day before. Don Blas' *refugio* was a lovely place, with a library and a fireplace (we did not need to light it — far too warm), and gifts and mementoes everywhere. Without meeting him, I could see that Don Blas was a priest with a romantic imagination and a love of humanity that led him to to understand the wonderful potential synergies of the faithful pilgrims passing through his remote village, and the life of his regular local parish ministry.

Fuenterobble to San Pedro was a tough day: twenty-nine kilometres, including crossing the Pico de la Duena hills, at 1140 metres the highest point between Seville and the mountains on the Castile–Galicia border. The peak wasn't much of a climb: more of a steady, long walk up a ridge, past a long array of about sixty, softly whirring electricity-generating wind-towers. They were the first wind-towers I had seen, and they had a beauty of their own. Ranged along the crest of the ridge, they looked like big, white, friendly giants. Some were resting, motionless — I was told these were the times when they switched themselves off to download stored power into the grid — and others were in action, their huge, white blades lazily turning under a gentle breeze from the west.

Later that day came a long, hot, roadside walk through dry *encina* fields, and past a huge pig farm where I was generously welcomed and given ice-cold water from the refrigerator; I had run out again. Then came more road-walking, over an endless plain ... this part of the walk was the closest thing I could imagine to walking in inland Australia. I remember cresting a low rise soon after the Pico de la Duena, and looking forward in horror at a long, straight, dipping stretch of road in front of me that must have been seven or eight kilometres long without shade or turning. In its own way, this Castilian *meseta* country was as harsh and sun-baked as Extremadura had been, and it was almost as hard going. I was pretty exhausted when I finally crested the last rise and saw, in the middle of golden, ripening wheatfields, the white walls and terracotta roofs of the little village of San Pedro de Rozados in a gentle valley before me.

Going down into the village, I soon found the bar ... and walked in to see the televised second half of Australia versus Japan, Australia's first World Cup football game. Japan was ahead 1–0, but Australia miraculously came from behind in the final minutes to win 2–1. It was my first 2006 World Cup match; I was to see many more while in Spain. San Pedro was a most attractive village, with a lovely old church, a bar, a small, hidden-away *supermercado*, nice village gardens, an adequate little *refugio* ... and not much else.

If I remember the next day well, a twenty-five-kilometre hike to Salamanca, it is because of an inspirational moment about halfway through the day's walking. Coming over a low rise, I saw across the low, rolling brown hills ahead of me, in the distance, what looked like two tiny church spires poking up from a flattish horizon. Could they possibly be the spires of Salamanca's cathedral, now some fifteen kilometres away? They kept reappearing as I crested rises, a little bigger every time. Yes, they were! The spires continued to grow as I drew closer to the city. The wonderful thing was that there was nothing to block my view of them, no intervening modern buildings. I was seeing Salamanca's mighty cathedral from afar, exactly as medieval pilgrims coming up the *Vía de la*

Plata from the south would have seen it, and I shared that same excitement and tingling anticipation of the city that they would have felt. How wise of the modern city authorities in Salamanca to have protected this glorious view from the south—all the modern suburban and industrial development of the city is away to the east and west. I thought of our cities, with their proud glass towers to commerce, and their church spires and cathedrals now buried in their shadows. How wonderful it was to see the cathedral, still the highest landmark building on the horizon of a modern city.

That afternoon I walked into Salamanca through an attractive modern suburb of apartment buildings set in a riverside park, eventually arriving at an old, stone bridge just below the magnificent cathedral and university-precinct buildings, all glowing golden sandstone in the afternoon sun. I crossed the bridge, walked up a short hill into the cathedral quarter, and soon found myself in a comfortable large pilgrim *refugio*, built into an old palace next to an exquisite little city park. A charming *casita* offered us fresh apples, ice water from the fridge, and tourist maps of the city. In the best *refugios*—and this was one of the best—arriving pilgrims are greeted with such quiet affection and hospitality, a memory that I still treasure. In the dormitory, I again found my friends from the past few days, showering and getting ready for the evening in Salamanca.

Salamanca, population 167,000, was the largest city on my route after Córdoba. A dignified city of sandstone churches and colleges, it is quintessentially Spanish, the heart of proudly conservative Castile—the region that, more than any other, has shaped and defined Spain. But Salamanca left me with mixed feelings, all those great buildings somehow intimidating me a little. The university had been, in medieval times, one of Europe's greatest centres of learning, but it shrivelled intellectually under the destructive interference of the Inquisition, and then quietly stagnated through the decadent eighteenth and nineteenth centuries, almost untouched by the European Enlightenment. In the twentieth century and now in the twenty-first, it is enjoying a revival of real scholarship. It is now one of Spain's great universities again, and certainly the most beautiful.

I arrived just as the summer-school season was starting, with thousands of foreign students coming to stay for Spanish residential language and acculturation courses. The city streets were full of groups of excited and happy young Americans and Latin Americans, many already talking fluent Spanish as well as English. The city had all the signs of a university town—good bookshops, art and music shops, internet cafés, photo shops where one could burn CDs of one's photos and send them home ... and Salamanca has the largest city plaza in Spain, the size of a city block and an almost perfect square. Banned to traffic, the plaza would have been a great sight had it not been for the huge, ugly, temporary stage erected in the middle for a series of pop concerts.

I met with pilgrimage friends Richard, Aldo, and Nigel in the plaza for a drink, and we went on together for dinner. Nigel, an Englishman, was charming company, thoughtful, and well-informed on many things to do with the pilgrimage and Spain. Like me, he seemed to be looking for some sort of healing through the pilgrimage, and was taking it at a leisurely pace; I did not press him as to why or wherefore.

Salamanca today is a happy and youthful city, but it has a

dark past. It was a major site of the Inquisition, and cruelty returned to the city in the Civil War years. Antony Beevor's Civil War history tells the unforgettable story of a dramatic confrontation in the early stages of the war between Franco's victorious Nationalists and Salamanca University's liberal-minded rector, the famous Basque philosopher Miguel de Unamuno, then at the peak of his career. Castile had fallen early in the war to the Nationalists. Unamuno had originally sympathised with their cause, but had then been appalled by their vengeful slaughter of Republican supporters after Salamanca was occupied.

The confrontation took place at a celebratory 'Festival of the Spanish Race' at the university, where the audience consisted of prominent local Nationalists, including many local members of the fascist party, the Falange. On the dais sat four people: Franco's wife; the one-eyed and one-armed General Millán Astray, founder of the Spanish Foreign Legion; the bishop of Salamanca; and Unamuno.

Astray gave a violently provocative speech, attacking Basques and Catalans as 'criminals guilty of high treason' and 'cancers in the body of the nation'. He went on: 'Fascism, which is Spain's health-giver, will know how to exterminate both, cutting into the live, healthy flesh like a resolute surgeon free from false sentimentality'. In response, an excited Falangist in the audience yelled out Astray's Spanish Legion battle cry, '*Viva la Muerte!*' ('Long live death') The audience leapt to their feet, screaming Falangist slogans, their blue-shirted right arms raised in fascist salutes to the portrait of Franco hanging above the dais. The noise died as Unamuno stood up slowly and began to speak quietly:

All of you are hanging on my words. You all know me and are aware that I am unable to remain silent. At times, to be silent is to lie. For silence can be interpreted as acquiescence. I want to comment on the speech, to give it that name, of General Millán Astray, who is here among us. Let us waive the personal affront implied in the sudden outburst of vituperation against the Basques and Catalans. I was myself, of course, born in Bilbao. The bishop, whether he likes it or not, is a Catalan from Barcelona.

The bishop of Salamanca seemed embarrassed at the public reminder of his birthplace, which was almost in itself an implication of disloyalty to the Nationalist crusade. Everyone stood in numbed silence as Unamuno went on:

Just now I heard a necrophiliac and senseless cry: 'Long live death'. And I, who have spent my life shaping paradoxes, must tell you, as an expert authority, that this outlandish paradox is repellent to me. General Millán Astray is a cripple. Let it be said without any slighting undertone. He is a war invalid. So was Cervantes. Unfortunately, there are all too many cripples in Spain now. And soon there will be even more of them if God does not come to our aid. It pains me to think that General Millán Astray should dictate the pattern of mass psychology. A cripple who lacks the greatness of Cervantes is wont to seek ominous relief in causing mutilation around him. General Millán Astray would like to create Spain anew, a negative creation in his own image and likeness: for that reason he wishes to see Spain crippled, as he unwittingly made clear.

The general was unable to contain his fury any longer. He could only scream, *'Muera la inteligencia! Viva la muerte!'* ('Death to intellectuals! Long live death!'). The Falangists took up his cry, and army officers took out their pistols. The general's bodyguard even levelled his sub-machine gun at Unamuno's head, but this did not deter Unamuno from continuing:

> This is a temple of the intellect, and I am its high priest. It is you who profane its sacred precincts. You will win, because you have more than enough brute force. But you will not convince. For to persuade you would need what you lack: reason and right in your struggle. I consider it futile to exhort you to think of Spain.

Unamuno paused and his arms fell to his sides. He finished in a quiet, resigned tone, 'I have done'. It would seem that Franco's wife saved him from being lynched on the spot, though when her husband was informed of what had happened he apparently wanted Unamuno to be shot. This course was not followed because of the philosopher's international reputation and the shocked reaction abroad to the poet Lorca's state-supported murder that had taken place a few weeks before. Unamuno died six weeks later, broken-hearted, and cursed as a communist and a traitor by those he had thought were his friends.

This dramatic confrontation illustrates important truths about the Spanish people: their intense pride in their country, their dignity and grace under pressure, their capacity for incredible and glorious bravery, but also the depths of fanaticism and cruelty into which they can sink under the spell of evil leaders. How could Unamuno speak in such wonderfully clear sentences at such a terrifying moment, perhaps the last moment of his life? How did he find the courage to go on speaking to a roomful of hostile armed people thirsting to kill him? And what a magnificent memory his last public words have left to his beloved University of Salamanca and to his nation.

chapter ten

Doing Without

I left Salamanca under a rare rain shower. It wasn't cold, and my cotton clothes soon dried again. Salamanca to Zamora was only seventy-eight kilometres, an easy three-day walk. Again, as from Cáceres, the walk started with a few unpleasant kilometres along the N630 highway, but eventually the yellow arrows mercifully led me away into quiet countryside. It was sixteen kilometres from Salamanca to Calzada de Valdunciel, a village about which I now remember little, though I spent a night there. I can't even remember now whether I slept in an inn or a *refugio*, because I missed getting my *credencial* stamped that night: I think I was already on pilgrim's automatic pilot.

I do remember thinking a lot, struggling along the N630 highway, about time and space and energy. I was walking at the interface of two radically different human worlds, separated by technology and hundreds of years: through two overlaid maps of Spain, the medieval and the modern. It was one of those piercing moments of altered perception that pilgrimage brings about.

Walking along the edges of the roaring N630, I

experienced intense physical distress. The motor traffic on the highway assailed my ears, lungs, nose, eyes. As huge mechanical monsters screamed along the highway, brushing aside my frail human body, I felt and smelt huge blasts of heat and carbon dioxide gas they were pumping out into the highwayside air. I experienced with almost physical pain the fact of how fast humankind is burning up its precious stored-energy resources. I thought of this scene infinitely multiplied on every highway in every rich industrial country in the world, and an overwhelming sense of profligate waste overwhelmed me. I thought: this cannot go on, it is totally irresponsible.

Where on earth were all these laden trucks coming from? Where were they going? What were they carrying that was so important to have to be moved hundreds of kilometres across Europe? Why did mankind have to cart so much stuff all over the planet, to the point where old-fashioned trade concepts like 'luxury imports' no longer have meaning? All year round I can buy grapes in Australia flown out in winter from Europe or California, and vice versa. The anticipation, the thrill of waiting to enjoy fresh fruit in its season, is gone. Why can't we eat what we grow locally in season? We have lost the pleasure of waiting for different fruits and vegetables to come into season at different times of the year, and the thrill of exotic tropical fruits such as bananas or pineapples or mangoes being kept for special occasions. We are burning up the planet, but for what? A dreary sameness and levelling-out of consumption.

My sense of wasted resources for no real gain in human happiness was all the sharper because my pilgrimage was defying the tenet of industrial civilisation that we need our transport machines. It was proving to me that I could move myself efficiently, albeit slowly, over long distances, without needing the petro-economy to get me there. I knew now that if I wanted to and had time, I could walk around the world like this.

It led me to wonder how our world had managed before the petro-economy transformed the way we think about production and exchange and consumption and travel. Had our quality of life really been so much worse before the petro-economy? Or alternatively, has the petro-economy—which really only got underway in the West in the early 1900s, and in the developing world only in the past forty years—now taken our civilisation to a stage that is terrifyingly beyond what our poor little planet can handle for much longer?

Battling up the N630, I knew with absolute certainty, as I had never fully understood and accepted before, that this kind of life could not go on—that we are living through a moment of economic and technological madness, of gross dysfunctionality. There is something insanely out of balance in the way we are burning up our energy capital for no benefits of lasting value. Sadly, our children will pay for our society's greed and thoughtlessness if we do not get a grip on this problem very soon.

I thought about how Europe's and North America's industrial revolutions had been made possible over the past 300 years—a mere moment in human history—by our profligate exploitation of stored deposits of non-renewable, hydrocarbon-based energy: initially clear-felling old-growth forests, then coal, now oil. There is nothing else to come. We have spent these 300 years like Ali Baba's reckless brother, going more and more often to the fossil-fuels treasure cave as our appetite for easy energy has increased. The world has probably already passed the point of 'peak oil': from now on, there will be less new oil discovered in the world each year, and what there is will steadily become more costly to access. Oil scarcity will come on very quickly in our lifetimes, as the exploding mega-economies of China and India compete with Europe and North America for what is left of the world's readily accessible oil.

We were taught to scoff at the Club of Rome's warnings thirty years ago, but now we know they were essentially right. Inevitably, as the knowledge of looming scarcity finally hits home in the international marketplace, oil will get exponentially more expensive. We are looking, not too many years ahead, at crude oil prices that are ten, twenty times what they are now. And they will never come down again, because the new oil just won't be there to find again. We won't be flying bulk grapes across the world for too much longer.

I realised also that economic rationalism has nothing useful to teach us about how to conserve a finite, exhaustible energy resource on which the world has come to depend. The price mechanism of the world oil market is like a simple oil lamp. The wick will suck up oil, and the flame will burn no less brightly, so long as there is some oil left in the bowl. Even though we will see the level falling rapidly, the wick will not burn more slowly in order to save fuel. As soon as the wick sucks up the last drop of oil, the lamp will go out—phut.

While I was in Spain, one of Australia's state governments floated the idea of setting aside a proportion of its known large coal reserves as a bank for Australia's anticipated needs in predicted energy-scarce times ahead. The idea was

laughed to scorn by our economic experts and the federal
government; they said that, as long as there was cheap coal
to sell and world buyers ready to buy it at a price that made
profits for the seller, Australia had no 'rational' alternative
but to go on mining its coal as fast as possible, shovelling the
stuff out of the ground and off to China to be turned into
more Wal-Mart junk, at the same time continuing to pump
more global-warming gases into the air. 'Have coal, will sell',
is Australia's operating rule.

The market mechanism has no way of putting a value on
the future, on the world our children will have to live in. An
ethical society, a society able to think beyond a time horizon
of four or five years, would be husbanding what is left of
our fossil-fuel resources, setting tax mechanisms in place to
slow down their now entirely foreseeable exhaustion, and
using them productively as investment capital to convert to a
renewable-energy-based economy, to build the expensive new
infrastructure that such an economy will need and that we do
not yet have in place.

I know, as an engineer, that building a bank of renewable-
energy infrastructure will require very large initial capital
investments of energy and of materials whose manufacture
itself consumes energy. It takes a lot of metals, concrete, fuels,
plastics, and silicon wafers to build tidal, geothermal, solar, or
wind-energy power plants and the new reticulation networks
to distribute power from those new plants. The longer we
delay building the renewable energy infrastructures that we
already know our children will need, the more painfully
expensive they will be to build. We will regret then that we
did not build them now, while energy and materials are still
cheap, instead of flooding the world with unwanted plastic

junk, and cooking our planet with excess carbon dioxide gas. We will regret that we did not use these lotus years, the late-afternoon warm sun before the long, cold night falls, more wisely.

I wondered, what will happen to our world economy when we have no more cheaply accessed hydrocarbons, when oil and coal have become luxury producer goods? We might try to stagger on with a few stop-gap solutions: squeezing more expensive oil out of shale rock, and growing more biomass to make alternative fuels like ethanol. But growing biomass fuels will eat into scarce water and land, and the soil fertility needed to grow humanity's food and fibre.

We will have to move towards fully exploiting global technical potentials for safe, renewable sources of energy. It is likely that all of those sources, even when fully developed, will together produce only a part of the energy we in the West have got used to consuming. So there will have to be major cutbacks in energy usage in coming decades. It will inevitably be a very different world.

Nuclear energy won't be any long-term solution, either. Even if we accept the added risks of weapons proliferation, catastrophic power-plant accidents, and disposal of poisonous, long-life radioactive residues, it would only postpone the inevitable energy-crunch for a few years. Like fossil fuels, uranium is itself a limited, non-renewable resource. Even on best-case scenarios, accessible high-grade uranium will run out within a generation or two. Moving to a uranium economy would involve living off our capital, too.

What about fusion—the science-fiction, comic-book dream of a hydrogen-powered economy, turning unlimited seawater into hydrogen and oxygen to run new kinds of machines? I have to say that, as an engineer with some knowledge of physics and chemistry, and as a student of human history who sees how often humanity has misread its optimistic scientific dreams for real goal-setting, such a hydrogen economy is unlikely to help us. It comes down to the second law of thermodynamics, the iron law of entropy: unless you have new energy coming in from somewhere else, everything eventually runs down to the lowest level of energy equilibrium. The reason there is so much water (H_2O) in the world is that the H_2O molecule exists at a lower energy level than do free atoms of hydrogen and oxygen. While we could no doubt create ingenious new technologies (perhaps we already have done so) to split off and store huge quantities of oxygen and hydrogen, and then power our cars and heat our houses in little reactors that burn them, such serial conversion processes will be net consumers of energy as a whole. It is why humanity was unable to turn lead into gold, or to fly by muscle power with artificial wings, or to invent a perpetual-motion machine, despite the world's best scientific and engineering talents obsessively trying to do these things for centuries.

Every engineer knows now that there is no such thing as a 100-per-cent efficient machine or mechanical process. All work, all conversion of materials, involves a net cost, a net loss of energy. That is why there will be no technological quick fix to the coming energy crisis. In the end—and it is not so very far away now—we will have to fall back on the efficient use of scientific and engineering knowledge to tap into the world's renewable energy sources, the free energy that comes from the sun and from the earth's rotation, and the weather and currents that those natural energy-drivers create.

What kind of a world will it be then, after the petro-economy sputters to an end? Even if it is possible, theoretically, to convert to a renewable energy-based world economy, can we get from here to there without terrible dislocations on the way? Will there be more wars over shrinking resources, *Mad Max* scenarios of a world fighting over diminishing stocks of oil?

The alternative, even scarier, scenario than peak oil is global warming caused by carbon dioxide emissions, leading to accelerated and catastrophic climate changes within two generations from now. The peak oil scenario is more bearable to think about, because if oil became a scarce and costly resource first, forcing changes in the way we price and consume it, it might save us before we cook our planetary home. At the moment, it is an open question which will come first: a Noah's Flood, or oil at $1000 a barrel. But one or the other will come, or both at once, and it will happen in our childrens' or grandchildrens' lifetimes. Global warming, unless we cut back sharply and soon on our CO_2 emissions, will involve massive and unavoidable losses of human habitat and civilisational decline.

I thought about how our present, market-driven global society might respond to the stress of adjusting to ever-more-costly oil. Richer countries might try to control what is left, using military power to fend off desperate and starving populations of poor countries. And even within a country, the price mechanism could not be relied on to allocate diminishing energy resources efficiently and equitably. If history is any guide, powerful elites would try to command the lion's share of energy while the poor went cold and hungry. Marie Antoinette nibbled at her cakes while the poor of Paris starved for lack of bread, and bloody revolution was the inevitable outcome. The black people of New Orleans drowned and starved in Hurricane Katrina because no responsible government authority was prepared to pay a few public dollars to hire buses to take them all to safe, higher ground, and to feed and house them once they were there. Incredibly, an American government sat on its hands while its own citizens drowned and starved in their flooded city. That is one possible future.

On the other hand, the modern welfare-state democracies that we have created over the past 200 years, hand in hand with the industrial revolution, could, if they kept their heads and a sense of civic responsibility towards all their people, manage the necessary retro-engineering transitions towards a stable, renewable-energy economy, equitably sharing the social burdens of change. It would require a very different kind of politics to what we now assume to be normal: the politics of managing scarcity, of sharing a diminishing cake.

But I am still an optimist: we could, if we used our brains and consciences, working together as moral communities, finish up with a more balanced, healthy, and sustainable world than the one we have now. Under an unfolding peak-oil scenario, we could still engineer a soft landing, though it would now take a great deal of human wisdom and God's grace to do so.

***

What, one might ask, has all this to do with pilgrimage? Quite a lot actually, because pilgrimage takes your mind into new territory and encourages bold, lateral thinking. It shakes the kaleidoscope of conventional thinking and can offer a piercing clarity of vision of the world, as well as sharpening appreciation of our common humanity—the perspective that must underpin any real change in the way we address the environmental crisis, the biggest of all our problems.

The market mechanism unaided by a sense of universal civil society is not going to solve this one. It is easier while on pilgrimage, rather than being caught up in the realities of day-to-day life at home, to see this truth.

I thought as I walked along on the N630 about how, before the industrial revolution, so many wonderful things had happened in human life without oil. We think that the way we live now is the only possible way to live, but it is not. Most of the world's great achievements in art, music, literature, and architecture had already come into existence before the onset of the petro-economy.

Rembrandt was painting; Mozart was composing his music; the beautiful cities of Europe were being designed and built; Shakespeare was writing his plays, and Montaigne his essays; Jane Austen was writing her brilliant but gentle novels about decent, middle-class people trying to find happiness ... all before the machine age. People were constructing efficient, sustainable systems of water management, agriculture, and animal husbandry. People mostly ate the food and wore the clothing of their region. They lived in houses made of local materials. Agricultural surpluses fed nearby cities, where complex markets and higher cultures developed. There were roads and canals to move any goods around that had to be moved longer distances: high-value goods that could not be produced locally. Travel was a lifetime adventure. Ordinary people did not travel much. The rich, when they did travel, relied on horsepower and windpower. International trade was based on scarce luxury goods—condiments and spices, fine textiles and chinaware, medicines, precious metals.

Al-Andalus in Spain was a good example of that kind of economy, functioning prosperously and sustainably at a high level of civilisation. So too, later, in different ways, were Renaissance Italy, Elizabethan England, the prosperous, bourgeois Netherlands, the early American colonies, and Enlightenment France. Of course, such societies had their seriously dark side—slavery, exploitation and oppression of the poor, and gross inequality. But there are many models of successful pre-oil societies where many people realised their potential to live decent and happy lives.

I also thought about how, if we retain access to enough renewable energy, and the technical knowledge that goes with it, this would enable us to continue to maintain technically advanced civil societies. Our societies as a whole—not just the rich—could continue to enjoy many of the good things we now regard as necessities—modern medicine, telecommunications and multimedia, computer science, and information technology. For none of these sophisticated technologies use much material energy. If we were to steer our renewable energy potential efficiently towards maintaining these sorts of high-technology and low-energy-content sectors, distributing their benefits according to principles of equity and social justice, we could continue to sustain a high civilisational level even as our petro-economy shrinks. This would take intelligent planning, creatively using the taxing and organisational powers of the state to steer these major transitions with an eye to human welfare. It is a big ask, but I believe it would be do-able.

It seems to me that Spain is a country that could manage such a transition more easily than, for example, overcrowded and over-urbanised England. Because the industrial revolution came late to Spain, its population is still quite evenly distributed across the land, with many people still living in or close to areas where sufficient food and fibre could again be grown locally for local needs. There are still precious pools of local knowledge available for reviving efficient, small-scale, sustainable-agriculture and animal-husbandry systems. I did not think it would be so hard for the people of the villages that I walked though in Spain to manage a transition back to a less petrol-dependent economy. There is still enormous human toughness and resilience in those villages. There is still in Spain a living tradition of human adaptability, of improvising solutions, of making do with less in hard times, of sharing what there is and looking after one's neighbours. All those qualities, those kinds of ethics, would be essential in managing a decent and orderly retro-engineering transition to a less hydrocarbon-dependent world.

I thought, for example, of the Andalusian olive industry, those vast, highly productive estates of millions of olive trees, the investment of centuries of work and money, now almost entirely dependent on oil, with every stage of production involving petrol-driven machines and barely a human hand to be seen. I thought about how this industry could manage, with good planning, a progressive, retro-engineered transition back to less use of machines and more use of horsepower and human power. As the price of oil increased, human-powered pruning handsaws could replace chainsaws; solar and windmill electric pumps could maintain trickle irrigation systems; horse-drawn ploughs could again till the land and spread natural fertilisers, instead of tractors spreading bags of artificial oil-based fertiliser. Human hands could again pick and bring in the olive crop, and process and barrel it. And horse-drawn or oxen-drawn caravans could again transport high-quality Spanish olive oil in large wooden barrels for sale abroad, in the colder regions of Europe where olives cannot grow. As fuel oil prices rise, retro-engineering different stages of the olive-oil production cycle would become more economical. Andalucia could gradually be repopulated, as people came home from lost industrial jobs in Madrid and Barcelona to revived rural jobs.

Philosophically, many of us find such ideas of retro-engineering hard to imagine, even terrifying. We have become so used to equating civilisation with more and more use of labor-saving, fuel-consuming devices. Then, paradoxically, we spend hours in expensive gyms or on jogging tracks or on crash diets, trying to restore our lost physical fitness. Retro-engineering could walk us back down the path towards a more natural and healthy utilisation of our own bodies, using the energies God gave us to build richer, more balanced lives. This need not be drudgery. To get to this kind of a world would require far more planning and intelligence than did the fossil-fuels energy revolution, which happened instinctively, fed by the profit motive and without much thought for society. But I believe it can be done if we start with the moral strength to face the issues as they really are.

In thinking about how such a world might look, I went back for possible clues to my experience of an earlier walk I once did—along the beautiful Jomsom Trail in Nepal, which climbs from its lower-valley reaches in the south of Nepal, up along a long, deep, fertile valley, terraced and dammed and irrigated and tilled over many centuries. The trail climbs over 100 kilometres northwards, through the shadow of the Annapurna massif to the east, and the equally enormous Himalayan mountains to the west, up finally onto the high, cold, pre-Tibetan plateau.

It was January, midwinter, yet in the protected valley I saw ripe mandarin trees bursting with orange fruit against the stunning backdrop of snowy peaks. I saw crops of rich, dark-green winter vegetables, green grass, healthy cows and pigs and goats, all bursting with protein. The people were poor because there were too many to feed on the over-subdivided small farms; but the land itself was rich, a Shangri-la of fertility and bounty. I met Australian and Canadian doctors and dentists and nurses, volunteers who had come in on foot for working holidays, tending the people's health and teeth free of charge. I walked through a string of villages and small towns along this valley—places that, at least for some of their inhabitants, offered a surprisingly high standard of living, with ample local hydro-electricity, solid, well-built stone or brick houses, shops and cafés, pharmacies, markets, small hotels and guesthouses with hot and cold running water, radio, television, bookshops, music, and dance.

The truly amazing thing was that there were no trafficable roads into these places in 1997—no cars, no trucks, no buses. In the Jomsom valley, everything and everyone still moved up and down the narrow trail on foot or by single-file caravans of laden donkeys, all carefully negotiating the steep pathways and stairways from one valley level to the next. The terrain was too steep and unstable to build motor roads: to try to build them risked huge landslides and the loss of precious acreages of agricultural tilled slopes. So, at least when I was there ten years ago, this beautiful valley offered a glimpse of how we might live in a world without oil and using limited renewable energy, if we could only manage equitably the social and economic balances and transitions to it.

With such thoughts, I comforted myself as I turned off the hideous N630, plunging with relief into the oak woods, golden wheatfields, and canola flowers of high Castile.

***

I left Calzada de Valdunciel early in the morning, because I had thirty-five kilometres to walk this day, to Villanueva de Campeón. This is a day that I remember vividly: it was mostly a walk though lovely countryside, and it got better as the day went on. I was on a high (about 800 metres in altitude), well-watered, deep-soil tableland. This was already a rich agricultural area in Roman times, on the *Vía de la Plata* trade route, and famous for its wheat, corn, chickpeas, lentils, beef, and lamb. Now it is broad-acre, mechanised, dryland farming, with huge, mobile irrigation rigs rolling slowly across vast, unfenced fields. But where the topography allows, there are little forests and orchards and, as I went further north, increasingly frequent vineyards. I was heading into a quality Spanish wine region, the Douro Valley—after La Ríoja, perhaps Spain's most famous wine-making area.

I passed not far from an unwelcome reminder of the twenty-first century: the menacing, high watchtowers of the Topas high-security prison at El Cubo, Spain's most important prison which, under the US-leaning former Aznar government, had a secret transit role in the rendition of Islamist terror suspects from Europe to Guantanamo Bay and other places unknown. Such rendition flights through Spain, which took place without the knowledge of the Spanish parliament, were being investigated by a Spanish parliamentary committee while I was in Spain. The renditions have now stopped, but I shivered as I saw a helicopter fly at high speed out of the prison.

I stopped at an inn in the village of El Cubo for lunch, and met there two agreeable *bicyclista* pilgrims, brothers in their early twenties, who had spent a year's working holiday in Sydney. They had pleasant memories of Australia, but had never thought of staying there: they had always intended to return to their home and family in Spain.

After lunch, I gradually climbed up a long, gentle hill towards an escarpment. When I got to the top I was rewarded with a magnificent view down into the broad, rolling plain of the Río Douro valley. The valley was not far below—only fifty metres or so—but that height was enough for me to be able to see for miles, until the horizon faded into a hazy pinkish-blue. It was a patchwork, gently undulating landscape of rich-brown, freshly ploughed fields; grasses of different shades of green-gold; flowering canola croplands, vineyards and orchards; forest copses; little, red ochre-roofed white villages in the distance; twisting laneways; and not a bitumen road or car in sight. Far away, one or two little tractors crawled slowly across fields. Kites and hawks circled lazily in the updrafts of the escarpment. I slowly made my way down into the valley, savouring every last step, with remembered music from Beethoven's *Pastorale* symphony ringing in my ears. No photograph could ever capture the serene stillness and peace of that moment: I tried to imprint it firmly on my memory, and it is still there.

Doing Without

Calzada de Valdunciel was an ancient Roman town with a Roman fountain. Villanueva was a 'new' town, established in the sixteenth century. To my untaught eye, they looked equally old. In Villanueva, I stayed in a pilgrim *albergue*. I was now meeting up each evening with two friendly fellow walkers: Richard, a retired businessman, originally from Bavaria, but who had for many years made his home in the Galician seaport city of La Coruña, where he has a large and loving Spanish family; and Aldo, a young Italian from Siena. My walking had been keeping pace with Richard and Aldo for about a week now, since we had met at Calzada de Béjar a few days earlier. Richard had then been walking with a younger German couple from Cologne, but they had left in Salamanca to go home. He was now walking with Aldo. It was still my preference to walk alone, enjoying the solitude and time for reflection on the camino, and keeping to my own speed and walking rhythm, but I had come to look forward to meeting my two new friends in the village inns and *refugios* in the evenings. We had become quite companionable since Salamanca. We ate and drank together and stayed in the same *refugios*. Their common language was Spanish, which Richard spoke fluently and Aldo adequately. I struggled along to speak with them in Spanish, or with Richard in his good English.

We were now watching World Cup football games together every evening, Richard being a great expert on the rules. Finally, that night in Villanueva, he broke the ice, saying bluntly in his honest Bavarian way: 'Tony, don't walk alone any more—why don't you walk with us into Zamora tomorrow?' I agreed, not wanting to be rude, and also thinking it might be time now to try walking again in the company of other pilgrims. Richard and Aldo both looked like quiet, easy-going companions, so I thought, why not give it a go?

It turned out to be a good day into Zamora, which was an easy twenty-four kilometres ahead. Aldo soon lost us—he loped ahead, having a longer stride than Richard or me. He went out of sight behind a low rise. When we topped it, we found a T-junction ahead, with Aldo nowhere to be seen, and no yellow arrow (a rare failure of waymarking). Should we turn left or right? We chose right—incorrectly, as it turned out. We soon came to a village and there, quite foolishly, became lost. We were given contradictory directions by various people in the local bar—it was remarkable how in this village, just a few kilometres off the camino, no one seemed to have much idea of where it was or even what it was. All they knew was the map of the motor roads. Finally, an old farmer gave us more reliable advice, and we carefully navigated our way through lanes and pathways westerly across fields, back until we regained the camino. It was with relief and affection that we saw a familiar yellow arrow again.

We turned northwards, down a deeply gullied ancient track though shoulder-high fields. The Zamora city skyline became visible on the horizon as we drew closer. The path entered the city through an old medieval pilgrim and trade district, San Frontis, south of the River Douro. We reached the river, flowing gently across a low weir, and walked upstream along it to the fourteenth-century stone bridge, where we found Aldo, waiting patiently for us in the late-afternoon sun—he had been sitting there for two hours. On our left loomed the high, reddish-golden ramparts of Zamora castle, the domed cathedral, and the walls of the old city. We walked across the bridge, my spine tingling at the sight of Zamora's medieval walls looming over me, and up a twisting lane into the modestly sized city plaza.

If Salamanca is a Renaissance city, a symbol of proud, imperial, Christian Spain on its victorious march southwards, Zamora feels much older, a city of the medieval age when the destiny of the small Christian kingdoms, León and Castile, on the periphery of powerful al-Andalus, was still being fought out. Zamora took me back to the heroic age of the Santiago pilgrimage, when the fear of being robbed or captured by Moorish raiding parties was still very real.

Zamora figures prominently in the life of Spain's greatest medieval hero-warrior, El Cid (from the old Arabic *el seid,* meaning 'the chief' or 'the lord'). I have never forgotten seeing at the impressionable age of eighteen the 1961 epic Hollywood movie, superbly cast with Charlton Heston as the warrior-knight and Sophia Loren as the love of his life, the breathtakingly beautiful Lady Ximena, niece of King Alfonso VI. Many people think this was the best epic film ever made by Hollywood; and, having recently seen again a remastered DVD version, I think they're right. Interestingly, Ridley Scott was inspired to make his Crusades film, *Kingdom of Heaven,* when he watched *El Cid* again. There are affinities between the two films.

El Cid was a real historical figure. His birth name was Rodrigo Diaz; he was born in Burgos in 1040 and died in Valencia in 1099. A commoner who rose to greatness by his own valour, his bloodline through his two daughters by Ximena entered into the royal families of Europe. One of the greatest epic poems of medieval Europe, 'The Lay of the Cid', was based on his life. He was a brilliant military general, a soldier–mercenary who fought for both Christian and Moorish kings. Initially he fought for Ferdinand I 'the Great', King of León, a key figure in the Christian reconquest who greatly expanded his original kingdom of León, in his lifetime capturing from the Moors most of Galicia and Castile. Ferdinand died peacefully in 1065, rather naively dividing his kingdom among all his five children and directing them to live at peace with one another. Ferdinand's eldest son, Sancho, was left newly conquered Castile; his favourite, second son, Alfonso, got the home kingdom of León; Garcia got Galicia; and his two daughters, Elvira and Urraca, received the city-state dukedoms of Toro and Zamora respectively. But Sancho believed he should have inherited it all. (Was he already thinking of the national interest, I wonder, or was it just the personal greed of an eldest son wanting to have it all?) He made war on his younger siblings.

It fell to Rodrigo Diaz to command Sancho's army. Alfonso was initially defeated and fled for protection to Castile's newly conquered tributary Muslim city-state, Toledo. Elvira and Garcia conceded to Sancho, but Urraca held firm in her well-fortified city of Zamora. Sancho laid unsuccessful siege to the city for seven months, and was assassinated before the walls by a pretended Zamoran traitor who had offered to show him a secret way into the city. With Sancho out of the way, Alfonso came back from Toledo as king in 1072. He inherited all that Sancho had sought—Ferdinand's inheritance. He became Alfonso VI of León and Castile, the second king of expanding, Christian, imperial Spain. Huge further southwards reconquests of Moorish lands were made during his long reign. Alfonso crowned himself Emperor of all Spain in 1077, and died in 1109.

The legend goes that the suspicious and angry Rodrigo Diaz humiliated Alfonso at his coronation in 1072 by making him swear repeatedly on the Bible that he had had nothing to do with plotting his brother's murder, for it was widely rumoured that Urraca and Alfonso had planned the murder together. A vengeful Alfonso soon banished Rodrigo, who spent the rest of his life as a soldier of fortune in the patchwork of states that was then Spain, fighting alternately for Moorish and Christian kings, and earning the love and admiration of all for his bravery and chivalry as 'El Cid'. He later conquered Valencia from a Moorish ruler and became its ruler. According to the legend, El Cid's last battle was there, where he put an invading Moorish army from Morocco to flight by riding out to battle as a dead man strapped onto his horse. It is one of many unforgettable scenes in the movie.

The Catholic Encyclopedia offers this assessment of El Cid:

> Tradition and legend have cast a deep shadow over the history of this brave knight, to such an extent that his very existence has been questioned; there is however, no reason to doubt his existence. We must, at the same time, regard him as a dual personality, and distinguish between the historical Cid and the legendary Cid. History paints him as a freebooter, an unprincipled adventurer, who battled with equal vigour against Christians and Moors ... who plundered and slew as much for his own gain as from any patriotic motives. It must be born in mind, however, that the facts which discredit him have reached us through hostile Arab historians, and that to do him full justice he should be

judged according to the standard of his country in his day. Vastly different indeed is the Cid of romance, legend, and ballad, wherein he is pictured as the tender, loving husband and father; the gentle, courageous soldier; the noble, generous conqueror, unswervingly loyal to his country and his king; the man whose name has been an ever-present inspiration to Spanish patriotism. But whatever may have been the real adventures of *El Cid Campeador*, his name has come down to us in modern times in connection with a long series of heroic achievements in which he stands out as the central figure of the long struggle of Christian Spain against the Moslem hosts.

The encyclopedia comments on the poem 'The Lay of the Cid':

The exploits of *El Cid* form the subject of what is generally considered the oldest monument of Spanish literature. This is an epic poem of a little over 3700 lines as it has reached us (several hundred lines being missing), the author of which, as is not uncommon with works of those days, is unknown … The poem deserves to be read for its faithful pictures of the manners and customs of the day it represents. It is written with Homeric simplicity and in the language of the day, the language the Cid himself used, which was slowly divorcing itself from the Latin, but was still only half developed.

I marveled at Zamora's fiercely contested history. It was a city that had lived dangerously on the Muslim–Christian front line, at the northern limits of the Muslim advance, for

300 years: it changed hands between Moors and Christians no less than six times. The armies of al-Andalus first occupied the city in the late eighth century, not long after they conquered the south. We don't know the date of the first Christian re-occupation, but we know that the Moors took it again in 813 A.D. King Alfonso III of Castile then captured it eighty years later in 893. In a great battle in 901 — the date is still celebrated in Zamora — a Moorish army failed to retake the city. But in 981 they succeeded, completely destroying the city, then later rebuilding it and repopulating it with Muslims. Ferdinand I finally reconquered Zamora in 1062, quite possibly with El Cid, then twenty-two, already leading his army.

There followed a century of rebuilding the city, with Zamora's magnificently romantic Romanesque cathedral built between 1149 and 1174. Zamora's historical importance pretty well peters out after that date. As Spain's royal court and capital moved south, first to Toledo and finally to Seville, Zamora's military significance faded. It was left behind as a forgotten backwater. This is perhaps why this twelfth-century city — built solidly to withstand all future invaders, although, as it happened, the multiple invasions were finally over — survives so well. Walking through old Zamora is like being back in the Middle Ages in a world of knights and jousting and fair maidens and wars with the Saracens. The cathedral is an amazing building, quite different from the grand, late-Gothic cathedrals I saw in Plasencia and Salamanca. Zamora's cathedral looks more like a mosque, with its huge dome, four small flanking towers, and a central tower; or like some fanciful Byzantine cathedral, a fairytale building out of Camelot. Its architecture suggests how

Spanish culture at that time was still Muslim-dominated, even though the military tide had started to turn in favour of the Christian kingdom.

Near the cathedral in the old town precinct, I was thrilled to find a large, walled, stone house with a plaque saying 'This was the house of El Cid'. The whole old-town area is very beautiful, running along the crest of a long promontory ridge overlooking the river, which bends in a serpentine around its base. There is little car traffic here, with many small parks and open plazas around the dozens of palaces, including the palace of the Lady Urraca (who never married, and was rumoured to have shared an lifelong incestuous love with her brother Alfonso), and many churches and convents. Further east is the modern city, which contains many charming late-nineteenth century to early-twentieth century Art Nouveau buildings from a time when Zamora began to prosper again.

Why did Zamora so capture my imagination, perhaps more than any other Spanish city I saw? Partly because I have always loved the Middle Ages, the age of chivalry and romance. But also perhaps because Zamora represents the crucial hinge in Spanish history, the moment at which Spain might have stayed Muslim—as Turkey, the contested borderland at the other end of Europe, stayed Muslim. Muslim al-Andalus was still the most powerful military and cultural force in Spain in the eleventh century, despite the unraveling of the Córdoba caliphate that started in 1031. Al-Andalus might still have recovered its unity and vigour, had it not been for the historical accident of two strong and resolutely expansionist Castilian kings in succession, Ferdinand and Alfonso (with not a little help from El Cid), in launching the Christian imperial project of reconquest from their weak northern borderlands—a project that continued to gather strength and momentum over the next two centuries—at the very same time as fundamentalist Almohads and Almoravids were invading from Morocco, fatally undermining the civilisation of al-Andalus from within.

Zamora was where the reconquest began, but the turn of the tide towards the Christian side was by no means inevitable. Had Ferdinand's self-indulgent plan (for he loved all his children) to divide his kingdom succeeded, the aggressively expansionist state of Castile and León that became imperial Spain might never have come into being, and Muslim states might have recovered their balance and continued to rule much of Spain. The world's history, America's history, would have been entirely different. It is all around you here in Zamora—in the history of Sancho and Alfonso, and their loyal hero-warrior, El Cid.

chapter eleven

From Zamora to the Galician Border

Richard and I had a pleasant Saturday resting in Zamora. We had found a good family restaurant in the northern residential area of the city for a farewell dinner with Aldo the night before. With mixed feelings of anticipation and regret, he was going home to his family in Italy, having walked for three weeks from Seville to here; he planned to complete the second half of his camino from Zamora to Santiago in 2007. That night, we discovered why our three-bedded room in the Hostal la Reina, overlooking the main city square, the Plaza Mayor, was cheap: from about 11.00 pm onwards, the plaza became the scene of a raucous street party that went on till dawn. The next day, wearily asking the hotel staff what had been the occasion, they told me it was like this every weekend night in the plaza. For our second night in Zamora, Richard and I prudently moved to a quieter, two-bedded room in the back of the hotel, where we slept much better.

We headed out of Zamora on Sunday morning, refreshed from the day's break in walking. I was now on my third and last Michelin Orange Series regional maps, of the Galicia region. I had already, with a great sense of pride, airmailed home to my family the Michelin maps of Andalucia and Extremadura, with my completed line of route proudly blazed across them in luminous red highlighter pen. Santiago now seemed much closer, a mere 414 kilometres. Two-thirds of the camino was behind me already.

In good spirits, we headed north again, into more of the familiar dry *meseta* country — did all of Spain look like this? But we knew the landscape was soon to change, because forty kilometres north of here, at Granja de Moreruela, we would leave the *Vía de la Plata*, our long northwards route since Mérida, and strike off west-northwest on a different route towards the passes of Sanabria, through the high mountains of León into Galicia. This was a thrilling prospect now, for though I had grown to love the Castilian *meseta* in all its subtle moods, I was ready for a new landscape, for the green hills and valleys of Galicia, for the Celtic-tinged culture of this very different region of Spain. Zamora was my last Castilian city. My final pilgrimage cities, Ourense and Santiago itself, would both be definitely Galician.

We had an easy, short walk that day to Montemarta. We could not walk far, because the next village with a listed *refugio*, Granja de Moreruela, was another twenty-three kilometres on, and neither of us felt like a long walk that day. More importantly, Australia's second World Cup game, against the favourites, Brazil, was playing at 3.00 pm, and we did not want to miss that game. In Montemarta, we found a hospitable family-run inn on the N630 highway, the Fonda El Asturiano and, after a quick shower in our rooms (single rooms were cheap here), settled into the bar to watch the game. I didn't expect my Australians to win, going up against Brazilian football gods like Ronaldo and Ronaldinho, but they did very well, going down to an honourable 2–0 defeat after keeping Brazil on the back foot for much of the game. My team's standing immediately soared in Richard's eyes. Australia's earlier win over Japan might not have not signified much to him, as he knew little about either team. But our close-shave defeat by the famous Brazilians was a different matter, putting us up there as a serious contender for the Cup. Australia was still in the running to go through to the next round, and so it was a cheerful celebration at the inn that night.

The next day was easy: we halted early, six kilometres short of Granja in the preceding village, Riego del Camino. On the way there, we passed another big reservoir, on the Río Esla, and then an impressive crumbling ruined castle, Castrotarafe. This medieval castle had been a major command post of the Knights of Santiago, protecting this section of the *Vía de la Plata*. The Knights, an order of warrior-monks set up in León and Castile around 1170, had the twin duties of helping pilgrims to Santiago (the hospitaller function) and of protecting pilgrim routes from attack by Moors or brigands (the military function). Their emblem, a red Cross on a white background with fleur-de-lys upper points and a swordblade pointing downwards as the shaft of the Cross, is a familiar waymarking motif on the caminos, and is imprinted on the pastry crust of the famous *Tarta de Santiago*, the traditional, rich, butter-and-almond celebration tart eaten by pilgrims arriving in Santiago. (I took home two for my family and friends to taste.)

The Knights of Santiago order flourished, perhaps because its celibacy rule was initially quite relaxed. The order comprised canons, allowed to administer the sacraments; canonesses, occupied with the service of pilgrims; religious knights living in celibate communities; and married knights. The right to marry, which other military orders of monks only obtained at the end of the Middle Ages, was granted to the Knights of Santiago from the beginning, under the authority of the king, subject only to an obligation to remain chaste during Advent, Lent, and during certain other religious festivals, which they spent at their monasteries in retreat. It is an interesting precedent to look back on now, as the Catholic Church continues to debate the pros and cons of priestly celibacy.

The Knights of Santiago had a smoother history than the tragic order of the Templars. At their height, the Knights were almost a state within Spain, controlling 83 command posts, two cities, 178 villages, 200 parishes, five hospitals, five convents, and one college at Salamanca. The number of knights was then 400, and they could muster more than 1000 armed men. They had properties in Portugal, France, Italy, Hungary, and Palestine. They played significant military roles in the Christian reconquest, sometimes fighting on their own account and sometimes as part of imperial Spanish armies.

After completion of the reconquest, the need for the Knights' military protection of the pilgrim routes fell away, and the order declined in importance. After 1499, their assets were brought under the authority of the King of Spain. But they were still functioning in the eighteenth century, with obligatory service of six months a year in Spanish Mediterranean galleys. They still exist today in Portugal, as a state-recognised Order of Chivalry. The nuns in Granada who gave me my first *sello* obviously have some historical connection with the Knights, but I was never able to find out if they descended from the original Knights of Santiago order of canonesses.

***

On the path that day I met a charming and robust lady, powering along while carrying over her arm a heavy basket of vegetables that she had bought in the next town's market and was taking home to her village, Riego del Camino. She was walking a good deal faster than me, but kindly slowed for long enough to chat and to invite us to stay in the new pilgrim *refugio* in Riego—much nicer and less crowded, she assured us, than the one in Granja. We took her advice, and indeed it was a very comfortable little place, a converted house, and we were its only guests. She popped in later for a cup of tea and a chat with us. It turned out that she was the local mayor, proud of the new pilgrim *refugio* she had just organised. Riego was a village that seemed to be struggling a bit: we saw many empty and dilapidated houses, and not much economic activity. I hope this energetic and charming lady mayor finds more ways to revive Riego's fortunes.

The next day was a testing marathon: thirty-six kilometres of challenging walking. We were leaving the *Vía de la Plata*, which continues due north until it joins the *Vía Frances* at Astorga. We had chosen instead to take an alternative pilgrimage route, north-west to Ourense in Galicia and then on to Santiago. We would not meet the *Vía Frances* at all before Santiago. We were also, at last, leaving the N630.

We walked in a westerly direction, along winding country lanes that at times seemed to be leading us nowhere, skirting the estate of a beautiful and remote ruined Cistercian convent, the Convento de Moreruela. I wish I had had time to go in and see it. Finally, we reached a more significant motor road running downhill to a bridge over a northerly reach of the very large reservoir we had passed the day before. Then we faced an untypical few kilometres of Australian-style cross-country bush-bashing, scrambling up and down rocky cliff-slope paths along the edge of the reservoir that would have challenged horses, and were certainly too steep and rocky for mountain bikes. Then it was mile upon mile of shadeless back roads, walking under a hot, afternoon sun. Castile saved its fiercest heat for the last. The day seemed endless—and we walked for eleven hours that long day, all in hot, dry *meseta* country. But at least we were now travelling due westwards, and the blue mountains of León and the passes over to Galicia were beginning to loom on the far horizon ahead. Towards seven, we stumbled wearily into a highway hotel in Tabara, a largeish village on the main motor highway from Zamora into Galicia, the N631.

***

This might be a good moment to pull together some thoughts about navigation. This is an important practical question for non-Spanish-speaking pilgrims. If you do not have enough confidence in Spanish to ask directions and understand the answers, how do you avoid getting seriously lost? Asking directions can be a problem even for good Spanish speakers like Richard: quite often, a local will say '*a la izquierda*' (to the left) while waving to the right with his right hand, or '*a la derecha*' (to the right) while his left hand points to the left. It is then hard to decide whether to believe the words or the hands!

For me, as an Australian, navigation was perhaps a more serious matter than for my happy-go-lucky European friends, who had an easy confidence that in Europe one is never really lost. Sooner or later, they are sure, there will be a farmhouse or road or village to get directions from and be put back on the right road. For me, brought up on true stories of children and hikers lost in trackless Australian bush and never seen again, not losing one's way in strange places was something I instinctively took more seriously. I hate not knowing where I am.

A fundamental difficulty is the huge variety in the camino, which can be a highway or minor road or rutted rural tractor lane or footpath, or even just a set of directions to walk across a large field looking for a gate or stile somewhere in the far, opposite corner. Many times I had to suspend disbelief: could this faint, almost overgrown sheeptrack meandering up the hill through olive or *encina* trees leading to rusty farmgates into a manure-filled cattle holding-pen really be part of the grand camino across Spain?

One simply has to trust that it is, if the yellow arrows and the guidebook say so. The local Friends of the Camino waymarking societies that have surveyed and waymarked the route in their local area have decided, in their wisdom, where the yellow arrows should be marked. These societies wanted to design routes that would give pilgrims something that is as close as possible to the authentic medieval experience of walking across country from village to village, keeping as far away as possible from busy motor roads. So where the original *Vía de la Plata* was difficult to access because it had been buried under the equivalent modern road, which is often the case—and I don't think anyone really knows where much of the original *Vía Mozárabe* from Granada to Mérida went; it is more of an historical assumption than an exact memory—the local Friends drew on local knowledge to design and waymark the most direct and attractive possible walking routes, using local minor roads and lanes and footpaths that head in roughly the right direction, to create as close an approximation as possible to what the original camino might have been like. This gives rise to some delightful variety of walking, as you move from road to footpath to forestry trail to agricultural laneway to road again ... rarely do you spend the whole day walking on the one kind of route. The camino is almost always an unfolding progression of different kinds of walking.

But, always, the day's camino starts and ends at a main church in a village central plaza, or in cities at the cathedral. These are always the end-points, because it is after all a pilgrimage, and this is what pilgrims do after a day's walking: they visit the local church. The camino, like a Roman or medieval road, tries to avoid serious detours from the most direct, shortest line of walk. So it goes straight up and over the top of hills that are in in the way, rather than curving around them as do motor roads.

Sometimes, in rough terrain with sheep or goat tracks meandering aimlessly around, it can be hard to stay on the right path. You have to put all your trust in the directions indicated by the painted yellow waymarks. They are a metaphor for spiritual guidance in life, in that they are always correct (they never misdirect) and sometimes easily visible, but at other times quite hard to see. On the camino that I walked, they were painted in the oddest and most obscure places—mostly on wayside rocks or trees, but also on fence posts or lamp posts, at the corners of buildings, on street signs, even in treeless wheatfields on drain culverts at one's feet. Sometimes there are too few of them—in some areas, the local Friends seem to have decided to not make it too easy for pilgrims, to make them work at finding the next arrow, which may be several kilometres ahead. In other areas there are yellow arrows everywhere. But that is all part of the fun of navigation—and there is the delight and relief when you spy the next yellow arrow and realise that you haven't lost the track. Sometimes there are yellow crosses, warning not to take a particular road. Sometimes there are puzzlingly bent arrows pointing upwards and then off to the right or left—what do they mean?

A good guidebook is the main back-up to the waymarks. As I got more experienced and developed more instinct for the many moods of the camino, I needed less and less to check back to the guidebook while on the road—it was enough to have read it the night before to get a general sense of the day ahead. But there were times when it was indispensable. As an example, look at this dense slab of instructions from Alison Raju's indispensable guidebook to the *Vía de la Plata,* on a tricky few kilometres between Cáparra and Aldeanueva del Camino:

> 1.5 km later the tarmac ends and the N630 is above you, 20m ahead. Veer to L then cross river (via stepping stones if needed) and then arrows direct you under a road bridge under the N630 on RH side of river/stream. The mountains of the Sierra de Gredos are over to the R in the distance.
>
> On the other side, on your L, is a set of gates (may be locked). Climb over/go through them and head for first electric pylon in field on other side. From there go through gate in the wall in front (at right angles to N630) and turn

R alongside wall. In corner go through gateway and turn L, continuing diagonally R, veering L in front of a ruined building (on your R) then reach a wall by a gateway (on its other side). Climb over wall and turn L—you are now on the *calzada romana*, [Roman road], a wide walled lane, undulating. This is a very nice quiet section with quite a lot of shade—to rest in at least—and which will take you all the way to the outskirts of Aldeaneuva del Camino ...

Navigating these few kilometres with my Swedish friend Marit that day was an exercise for the mind as well as the body. Raju's admirable guidebook itself is not so precise as to make it mechanical and boring to follow. You often have to guess at distances between the features she mentions, and read between the lines of her encouraging phrases. I found that, 'gently undulating' means 'a lot of hills'; 'gently uphill' means 'steeply uphill'; 'steep' means 'precipitously steep' ... Raju avoids lengthy descriptions of scenery and local history. She focuses her text on the basic, navigational landmark data a walker needs, especially at forks or junctions where you need to take particular care. Her guidebooks are packed with essential information for walking pilgrims, and offer just enough descriptive information to pique the curiosity of the reader. A great advantage of her book is that she does not tell you in detail what is coming next.

I found that the best roadmaps, which are a useful supplementary resource to a route guidebook, are the Michelin 1:400,000 Orange series, covering Spain by regions. I used three—Andalucia, Extremadura, and Galicia. These maps don't show footpaths or very minor roads, but they help you to locate yourself in relation to villages and medium-to-large roads and junctions, and to identify distant landmarks (such as mountain summits or lakes). Apart from being useful insurance, they're essential if you want to plan itineraries and side-trips, and to see how far you've come and how far you still have to go.

Finally, it's always helpful if you have an internal sense of general direction aided by a bit of basic solar navigation—which is easier on sunny days, when you quickly get a feel for the rightful position of the sun in the sky at different hours of the day, whatever the season you're travelling in. It can be a useful and reassuring check that you are travelling in the right direction.

And, in the last resort, don't forget the power of prayer, and the scallop shell of Santiago around your neck!

***

Tabara was the end of the hard, dry *meseta*. The next day was a lovely and varied walk on quiet lanes going north again, away from the N631, over gentle ranges of hills; through Bercianos de Valverde, a truly remote village in a valley; entering wine country with picturesque *bodega*s (household wine cellars excavated into the softstone hill slopes); and finally walking downhill through the irrigated fields of a large agricultural area in the fertile floodplain of the Río Tera, to overnight in the substantial riverside village of Santa Croya de Tera. We found a gem of a private *albergue* waiting for us, Casa Anita, near the bridge over the river. It was a business venture—an interesting cross between a tourist hotel (it was the only accommodation in the village) and a pilgrim refuge—built and managed by a charming couple, Anita and Domingo, and their adult children. Casa Anita was large and cool, three storeys high, with its own courtyard kitchen garden bursting with soup and salad greens. The river Tera nearby was large, free-flowing, and clear — the water comes down from the high mountains of León, and the spring snowmelt was still feeding its flow. There was an attractive river swimming spot at the bridge close by the hotel.

We seemed to be the only guests in Casa Anita. Domingo and I warmed to each other at once: he was a charming and knowledgeable host. The next day, I made a diary voice-entry on my MP3 player, and I've transcribed it here to simply let it tell the story of the next two days in all their tumbled immediacy:

22 June: Today has been an amazing day. Yesterday afternoon we walked into Santa Croya de la Tera, a village on the Río Tera, in the middle of a beautiful irrigation area, and of course I am always happy when we come out of the dry scrub into these irrigation areas. We found an *albergue*, Casa Anita, run by Anita and her husband Domingo. It is the nicest *albergue* that we have stayed in: it even has a computer with Internet ... and a comfortable, cool dormitory. We were the only ones there. Good early dinner, and after dinner we went and had a look at the famous stone statue of Santiago the Pilgrim in the church across the river [in the sister village, Santa Marta de Tera]. After that, a special treat — Domingo invited me up to see his *bodega*, while we left Richard watching World Cup football in the village bar. And it was beautiful — a lovely cellar carved out of the hill, very deep under the ground, a vestibule room well set up for parties with a fireplace with

a huge grill, solar-electricity cells powering batteries for lights, and a big kitchen sink, counters to prepare food ... And then we went down, down, steep stone steps into this deep underground *bodega*, about ten metres underground, where the temperature was always about 5 to 10 degrees Centigrade, very cool, with a huge wooden barrel which must have been there for ever, lots of metal vats for ageing wine, and wine in cardboard casks ready to drink. I forgot to say that one of the good features of Domingo's and Anita's *refugio* is a free bar, with casks of red and white wine and chilled bottles of both in the fridge. You can have as much as you like, and it is all from this cellar, their own wine, which they make themselves from their own terrain. So I drank too much with Domingo, and I paid the price this morning: the old Spanish saying, *'noches alegres, mañanas tristes'* ('joyful nights, sad mornings').

But it was very nice up there in the *bodega*. We sat on the bench in front of the bodega, sipping red wine as the sun set over the hills and the surrounding bodegas grew dark. Domingo was very poetical. It turns out he is 63, the same age as me, though he looks about fifty. He said he comes up to his bodega for *'la paz, la silencia, la libertad'* (peace, quietness, freedom). It is where he goes to contemplate and meditate, and enjoy a bit of his own wine as well, I think. Anyway, I'd love to build a *bodega* like this at home. It has an air vent, a high chimney-shaft, so that there is always some circulation of air down into the cellar, not so much as to make it hot, but enough that it doesn't get stuffy down there. And the air in the bottom of the cellar was wonderfully cool and refreshing. Domingo said the cellar had been made by hand more than 100 years ago, digging down into the soft rock hereabouts. He also said that the people who have these *bodegas* don't have any formal training in wine making; they just all know how to make wine because the knowledge is passed on from fathers to sons.

Today's walk has been amazing; so far we have already walked twenty-two kilometres, all very different. The first ten kilometres or so was through irrigation areas along the river, in green forests fields and villages, finishing up at a beautiful *ermita* [country church] at the end of the irrigation area—locked, but we could see inside the church through a little grille, and leave money in a collection box. Immediately after that the country changed completely: first, dry forest scrubland, and then a real jungle of jumbled trees and vines along the riverbank, a dam wall looming ahead of us. It was almost like the Amazon down near the water's edge. We were having a conversation about anacondas, and I think if my children were here they would have got quite frightened. We climbed out of the river valley, walked over the large concrete dam—an absolute terrorists' dream. Somebody could just drive onto it with a car full of explosives and do enormous damage downstream, but there wasn't a single person in sight, not a guard or sentry, not even a camera.

Then a tormenting four kilometres walking around the edge of the lake; you could see the blue water and empty, sandy beaches. I didn't want to stop and swim because I knew it would be harder to go on afterwards, but I felt like throwing all my clothes off and just falling into the water, it would have been beautiful. Instead I was pounding along this hot, melting, bitumen road. And then we came to this village [Villar de Farfon], and it was my first sight of a deserted village in Spain, and it was very sad, very poignant. There was this lovely old church where we slept in the shady porch for an hour (I definitely needed the rest), Richard on the floor on his sleeping mat, I on a cool stone bench. It was lovely to get my socks off, get my feet up on the rucksack, get my head on my pillow, and I actually slept for an hour like this. There was a pilgrimage plaque there, and I took a photo of it. It says something like: *This village, people don't live here any more. In its solitude, you the pilgrim will find company, and the Holy Spirit will be with you on your journey.* I blinked away tears.

As I walked through the empty village I saw boarded-up houses and broken-down roofs, only three or four houses still being lived in by people who, I guess, were just hanging on through sheer determination—they really don't care if their village is falling down around them. Interestingly, there is still a little government office, a clinic where a doctor comes to see patients; he must have very few around here. It is sad to see a depopulated village like this. There are a couple of active farms on the edge of the village, but I think the people who live there must just think of themselves as farmers, not as people of a village. As a village, it's dead.

Now we are doing the last six kilometres of a very long day, twenty-nine kilometres, to Ríonegro where we hope we will find a *refugio*; there is supposed to be a new one there. Ríonegro sounds like a functioning village; there will be somewhere to stay there. But today I felt really like a pilgrim because it was such a long day with so much variety. Now we are walking through *encina* trees and dry meadows again, lots of wild asparagus, beautiful. And we can see the mountains of Galicia getting closer.

The landscape now was finally changing character as we moved up into the higher-rainfall foothills of the mountains of León. North of Ríonegro, where we were to stay that night, the N631 main road from Zamora merges into a very important east-west road: the A52 motorway from Benavente to Ourense and on to Vigo. To the south of the motorway is a linked chain of huge dams on the Río Tera, holding the winter snowmelt from the mountains of León. South of these dams is the wild Sierra de la Culebra: dry, unpopulated mountains that are still home to the largest population of wild wolves in western Europe, on the border with Portugal. The remote north-eastern Portuguese region of Tras Os Montes ('across the mountains'), with its regional capital at Braganca, was about thirty kilometres to the south of us. Our camino was now winding in and out of the A52 motorway, sometimes along the now little-used older trunk-road N631, and sometimes going off on walking paths to the left or right.

These are the Sanabrian borderlands: fertile, well-watered mountain valleys rich in history where Castile, Galicia, and Portugal meet. Nowadays this area is something of a backwater, but these valleys were frequent battlefields during the early imperial expansion of León and Castile, in the years when Galicia was absorbed into the expanding Castilian empire while Portugal struggled to defend its independence and separate cultural identity. Portugal weakened and temporarily succumbed to Castilian rule in the sixteenth century; but then, in 1640, a great figure in Portuguese history, Duke John of Braganca, grandson of the famous Catherine, Duchess of Braganca, defied the might of Philip IV of Spain by boldly declared himself King John IV of Portugal. There followed a twenty-eight-year war to restore Portugal's independence—a war the Portuguese remarkably won, showing incredible fortitude against the mighty resources of imperial Spain, helped a little by friendly Britain and the Netherlands. There is, in fact, an alternative Portuguese camino route from Zamora to Ourense, running through the Tras Os Montes region and Braganca. I was tempted to take it, but in the end decided to stay on the Spanish route.

It all feels like border country here, because everything is getting greener and more 'European': the landscape becomes more mountainous as the river valley rises and narrows; the vegetation becomes richer. The ubiquitous *encina* trees of the Spanish *meseta* disappear, replaced by a much lusher, more recognisably European, forest ecology in which oaks, chestnuts, and birch trees dominate. Here is a list I found of the diverse natural vegetation of the Sanabria region I was now delightedly walking through:

laburnum, cork oak, heather, Spanish lavender, chestnut tree, cytisus hystrix, white Spanish broom, Scotch broom, striated broom, Portuguese gorse, evergreen oak, erica umbellata, rock rose, broom, thicket, Pyrenean oak, elm tree, Scots pine, Austrian pine, maritime pine, padded brushwood, rosemary, willow, thyme.

To which list I can add that I saw wild iris, buttercups, and silver birch trees. In this granite country, village architecture had changed, too: there were no more whitewashed brick houses. Coursed granite was the preferred building material now, used for solid, unpainted, stone houses with huge window and door lintels of split-stone slabs: houses built to last for many centuries. The villages became more open and spread-out, with more generous gardens and open village commons; again, more northern European in spirit than the densely knit Spanish *pueblo*.

Ríonegro del Puente was charming. We stayed in a tiny *refugio,* with room only for four beds laid side by side, which was an old, converted stone barn, alongside a village *lavanderia* (communal laundry, out in the open). The laundry tubs are made of heavy concrete: ample piped water is freely laid on, and there are built-in, serrated stone washboards for rubbing clothes clean with soap; rinsing tubs below; and drying lines. There I met a woman from the village doing her washing, and we chatted. When I told her I was a pilgrim to Santiago, she spontaneously and sweetly said to me: 'Thank you for all the hard work and prayer you are offering up to God for us in making your pilgrimage.' It was a revelatory moment, because until then it had never occurred to me to think of my pilgrimage as a sacrifice and prayer offered up to God and to help others. But it was a lovely thought, and it left me feeling glowing. I mumbled something to the effect that I was really enjoying my pilgrimage walk, that it really wasn't a sacrifice at all ... but I thanked her for her kind words.

Ríonegro was a pretty town, a stone village in a soft, green valley. It had a fine, large church — how did such small villages always manage to have such impressive churches? — and also a bar–grocery store combined. It was the only shop in the village, run by an attractive young Bulgarian woman named Sofia, partnered with a local Spanish man, and her sister

Olga who was on a long-term visit. Both young women were blonde, pretty, and cheerful, and they were the main attraction that kept the bar and shop humming. Although the only hot food on offer (it was a small place) was pre-packaged toasted sandwiches, the chilled beer and wine was good. I talked to Sofia: she said it was a good life in rural Spain, people were kind to her, and she had learned Spanish and wanted to settle here. It is interesting to see how eastern European immigrants are coming into Spain in quite large numbers to fill useful economic niches in such villages that are struggling to hold onto their populations and services, as young Spanish people drift away to better jobs and more money in the cities. The local council, understanding the importance of keeping a bar and shop going for the population of about 400 people in and around Ríonegro, sensibly offered this building to Sofia at a nominal peppercorn rent.

We walked on the next day to an equally friendly village, Cernadilla, with a spic-and-span, large, newly restored municipal *refugio* for pilgrims in the central square—it was really quite palatial, and Richard and I once again were the only pilgrims there. It had a large dormitory, magnificent hot showers, and a communal kitchen and dining area, all cleverly retrofitted into an old building. We went to evening Mass, ate well, and watched more World Cup football. Then, on the next day, passing through a string of villages close together now in this lushly forested valley, Richard got ahead of me; I wanted to walk slowly and enjoy the beautiful terrain here. I visited the parish church of Otero de Sanabria, with its famous wooden wall-carving portraying seven sinners in the fiery furnace. Actually, it is a sweet little carving: the seven naked men and women have their hands clasped in prayer, and are submerged waist-down in what looks more like watery waves than a fiery furnace: they look calmly contemplative rather than suffering. It might just as well be a picture of a river baptism.

Onwards, to the large and impressive regional hilltop town of Puebla de Sanabria—much more than a village, but not quite a city. I found Richard and several other pilgrims already ensconced in a comfortable pilgrim *refugio* within a convent, the Colegio de Nostra Señora de las Victorias, near the castle and cathedral on top of the hill in the old town.

This town's records go back to 569 A.D. On a steep granite bluff hundreds of feet above the Río Tera stands a twelfth-century Romanesque church and a dramatic sixteenth-century castle out of Verdi, built by the powerful Duke of Benavente. I think this castle was built more as a political assertion of Spanish sovereignty than for serious military defence, because the medieval age of castles and sieges was now over. This castle has several little windows, even a romantic balcony, let into its high walls that grow straight out of the granite cliff below: it is a fanciful, Alexandre Dumas sort of castle, the kind of place in which you can imagine D'Artagnan creeping into a lady's bedroom and then hurriedly escaping down the castle wall using a rope ladder or knotted sheets. The castle is a bit Hollywood, but great fun.

Puebla de Sanabria was a picturesque, neat town, and it all looked busy and prosperous, if perhaps a bit touristy: the sort of place that comes alive at weekends with lots of short-term visitors. The hinterland of Puebla de Sanabria has good roads into an attractive mountain region of high alpine lakes, scenic walks, and even skiing in winter.

The next day was a short walk (though we did at one point

get a bit lost—there are many lanes and villages confusingly spread all around the rich valley here, and the waymarking was sparse) on to the village of Requejo de Sanabria, on the main A52 road at the foot of the first mountain pass. On this our last night in Castile, we happened on a gem of a commercial *hostal*, the Restaurante-Hostal Tu Casa ('Your Place'), run by a charmingly hospitable and dignified *patron*, Francisco Fernandez Pequeño. His wife cooked us up a magnificent dinner on the *menú del dia*. I was now sad to be leaving my Spain of the past seven weeks, to be going into the different culture of Galicia. Francisco was a real Castilian, a man of great natural presence and graciousness. He recognised me—we had both been at the same Mass the evening before (a Saturday) in Puebla de Sanabria.

The next day, we had to cross not one but two mountain passes—a marathon thirty-four kilometres, with nearly 1000 metres' vertical climb, all on the now-disused former highway N631 that had been replaced by the motorway. We crossed two high passes, the *Portillo de Padornelo* at 1329 metres, and the *Portela da Canda* at 1262 metres. The day was pleasantly cool, but it was not particularly attractive country. The mountains were quite barren, their great original oak and chestnut forests having been greedily clear-felled in the industrial revolution, then left to sheep and goats and never properly replanted. I saw a lot of erosion. There were some recently planted young pine-forest plantations, but many of these had been burned out—the hilltops were drying out from declining rainfalls in recent years, and had suffered badly from forest wildfires a few years before. It was a sad, damaged landscape.

* * *

To while away the climb, Richard and I talked about our lives. We already knew that we had much in common: we had both travelled widely; we enjoyed challenging exercise; and we took comfort and pleasure in a rich, old-fashioned family life at home, enjoying the company of a loving wife, children, and grandchildren. We were both old-fashioned family men, maybe even a bit patriarchal, Christian in spirit yet worldly and practical at the same time. Yet our life experiences had been, in important ways, very different.

Richard had lived in the world of international commerce. He was well settled now, retired with his wife in a comfortable apartment in La Coruña, with their children living not far away. His peak career years had been spent with Spain's largest fishing and fish-exporting company, but he'd spent his entire career in international marketing all over Europe, about which he told me many interesting tales. (He speaks four languages fluently.) He is naturally conservative, not too keen on the present Spanish government, but not thrilled by the alternative either. Basically, he mistrusts politics and government. On the other hand, my whole career had been in politics and government. We were both quite naive about one another's worlds.

But what came through to me, as we got to know one another better, was how well Richard has balanced his life. Superbly fit at seventy, he also knows how to relax and to enjoy his well-earned retirement. Comfortably off, he is not greedy to own new things or to have new holiday experiences. His pleasures are simple and homely: enjoying good company, and good food and wine; being with his grandchildren;

staying at his country-retreat farmhouse; and going on regular distance-walks with friends to keep fit. He has walked four different caminos to Santiago already, totalling some 3500 kilometres. Every now and again, when he feels the old urge coming on, he says to his wife, 'I'm off again on the camino', and away he goes for a few more weeks with his old, homemade rucksack frame, in his spartan T-shirts and shorts. He is physically as tough as old boots, stocky but with no surplus fat at all, and a gentle and civilised man. He grew up in Bavaria, so he must have spent his first nine years of life under Nazi rule, and the rest of his childhood under the privations of early post-war Germany—but he never talked about those times.

What was most striking to me, during our time together, was how his mobile phone rang hot with calls from family members and friends, including many men and women from his former company, asking how he was faring and when he was coming home. It was clear that many people loved and cared about Richard. And this got me thinking—here was a man of seventy, strong both physically and morally, still inspiring his friends, attracting great affection and loyalty, making a powerful contribution to the happiness of those around him, part of a rich human community of people who clearly needed his strength and love as much as he needed theirs.

I looked back by comparison on what I had to show for my thirty years in Australian government service. I asked myself, how many real friendships had I kept up from those long years of shared public working life? Had I let old friendships atrophy and wither on the vine, that I should have valued more? What was the quality of my family life—was I giving enough time and love to my family to go on earning their love in return? Richard may not know or want to know as much as I do about politics, but he knows a lot more than me about building and nurturing a good personal life around yourself. I learned much from his example.

He also taught me a lot about stamina and self-discipline, as much moral as physical: pacing yourself at night, eating and drinking in moderation, saying no to the third or fourth glass of wine, having fresh fruit instead of a rich ice-cream dessert. It is not that Richard was an ascetic or a kill-joy—he enjoyed these pleasures as much as anyone—but he understood that pilgrimage was a serious business. One was asking a lot of one's body every day, so one had to treat it with care and respect.

We did not talk all the time—indeed, for a lot of the time we walked either in companionable silence or some distance from each other, one of us (more often Richard) setting the pace and jauntily striding out ahead, listening to his favourite radio talk-programs. We would always, sooner or later, meet up again during the day. I found that you don't need to chatter all the time on the camino to enjoy the comfort of a travelling companion. We did most of our talking of an evening, in the bar and over meals, when we were not watching World Cup football, which was often. Thank you, Richard, for your company and friendship: I won't forget you.

chapter twelve

Into Galicia

I had crossed the León Mountains into Galicia, and Santiago was only 210 kilometres ahead, possibly only a week away. The end of the journey was now distressingly close. It had seemed only yesterday that I was far back on the Spanish *meseta*, on the road from Baños de Montemayor to Salamanca, feeling that so much journeying still lay ahead of me. That had been two weeks ago. But where had those two weeks gone? Had my feet taken wing as my soul drifted through time and space?

I was being reminded again of the sad truth that the second half of any life, even a pilgrim's little life, goes more quickly than the first. The real midpoint of life is not the chronological midpoint, in your forties. It is at about age 25–30, when you foolishly think that the best years are ahead, and old age and death are still far away. Time on my pilgrimage had sped up now, just as the years of normal life speed up as you grow older. I wanted to cry out: Please God, slow down the clock! Make my life pass more slowly again, the way it did when I was young, and every day seemed dreamily repetitive and long. Bring back those sublime, endless days of childhood, and bring back my idyllic month of ambling through Andalucia and Extremadura, those days of walking with little thought of destination, when it still seemed Santiago was half a continent and a lifetime away.

I understood now that the real midpoint of my camino had been back around Mérida, a month and 600 kilometres before. I had still thought then that endless miles of walking lay ahead, but remorseless time had now caught up with me. How space and time had played tricks on me. I had started off in Granada with the fear of not being able to make the distance to Santiago, which then seemed impossibly far, and I had thought then that the only possible strategy was to take each day as it came, one by one, not thinking about the final goal. Now that the journey was nearing its end, my mind was reaching for a similar protective logic. As I felt the panic of my approaching 'little death' in Santiago, I tried to put that knowledge out of my mind, savouring each precious day that was left as it came, determined not to think about the journey's end.

But Richard was already planning ahead, talking enthusiastically about us being able to reach Santiago in six days, if we managed to walk thirty or forty kilometres a day. He had helped me build up to a high level of fitness now, and we both knew my body could do it with him. He was keen to get home: his wife and family were awaiting him in La Coruña, he had a beloved granddaughter's birthday party coming up in La Coruña in ten days' time, and he also wanted to fit in a final walk from Santiago to Finisterre. He was keen to press on as fast as possible.

I knew that, God willing, Richard would enjoy more pilgrimages to Santiago. Richard was too nice a man to ever say anything, but he had been holding back his pace for me since we started walking together a week before. I had to make a hard decision now that I would ask him to go on alone ahead of me. Much as I was enjoying his company, and the challenge of pushing my body to its limits, I knew that I really needed to experience the final days of this pilgrimage at a more leisurely, meditative speed, to try and recapture that magically suspended state of being, the high spiritual awareness, that I had briefly glimpsed in the wondrous week between Baños de Montemayor and Zamora. I wanted to go back to slow, reflective, solitary walking, because I knew this would probably be my last time in Europe and my last pilgrimage. I didn't want these precious final days to be swallowed up in a blur of fast walking and evening exhaustion.

Was I being selfish? Yes. But I knew Richard would manage the last few days well on his own, and I knew he was keen to get home. So, on our second night in Galicia, at Campobecarros, I told Richard. He received the news with great grace and charm. The next day, I got up early for breakfast with him and to farewell him. It was a necessary parting, but a sad moment for me and, I think, also for him. For all their brevity, pilgrimage friendships can grow to be real and strong.

***

We had walked down from the high passes into Galicia, and at our first Galician stopover, Vilavella, we had watched Australia lose 1–0 to Italy in the *Octavos* ('Round of Eight', that is, eighth-finals) of the World Cup football. It was a tensely exciting game, with no scores by either side as the game drew to its end. But then, in the final ten seconds, Australia incurred a questionable penalty right in front of the goal it had successfully defended against every Italian attack for eighty-nine minutes and fifty seconds. It was an infuriating way to lose a close game. As Italy in later days cruised through an easy quarter-final win against an outclassed Ukraine, and then achieved two cliffhanger victories over Germany and finally France to win the 2006 FIFA Football World Cup, I could not help feeling some chagrin at the fickleness of the sporting gods. How far might Australia have gone if it had had no last-moment penalty awarded agaisnt it, and if it had then achieved the miracle of defeating Italy in overtime playoffs? Could we have gone to the quarter finals, the semis, even to the very final? But that is the World Cup, in all its glory and frustration for every team but the winners. Better luck in 2010, Australia! Clearly, six weeks of pilgrimage and contemplation had not purged me of my native competitiveness and will to win.

Richard was immediately and loyally supportive. 'It's a scandal!', he exploded. 'What did that umpire think he was doing? The Italian just fell over. There was no Australian foul at all!' Most others in the bar agreed. Uncomfortably, it was a Spanish referee. Someone (not Richard or me) raised a Machiavellian conspiracy theory: an Italian was due to referee the Spain–France *octavo* game the next day—could it be that the Spanish referee had offered Italy 'a little favour' at the end of the Australian game, in the hope that his Italian counterpart might kindly reciprocate in any tight calls the next day? Of course, I refused to consider that such skullduggery might ever be possible in a World Cup! And, in the event, the next day France rather easily knocked out Spain 3–1, so the theory was never tested.

***

On from Vilavella, and we were soon climbing westerly again, away from the A52, onto the old pilgrimage route that runs across high hills from A Gudina to Xunqueira de Ambía, seventy kilometres of the most beautiful walking country on my route so far, along the high treeless ridge of the *Sierra Seca* ('the dry mountains'). The deep valley town of A Gudina was still shrouded in deep fog as we passed through at around ten in the morning. As we climbed up to the ridge at 1000 metres, it cleared to a perfect sunny but cool day. The breeze was fresh and invigorating. There were magnificent views along our path, northwards to the impressively high mountains of León with their traces still of winter snows, and southwards into the endlessly receding blue ranges of Tras os Montes in Portugal. The old nineteenth-century railway from Galicia to Zamora, now rarely operational, snakes along this ridge, in and out of winding tunnels. A few tiny railway-maintenance villages cling precariously to life along its track, inhabited by a few old people, and their sheep and goats and cows and pigs. This is a bit how I imagine walking the English Pennines might be, on top of the world with all spread out to see, villages and forest copses far below in the folds of the valleys, the odd shepherd up above, herding his sheep.

We were walking the old trail that poor Galician agricultural labourers took to in the nineteenth century, walking across the mountains to find seasonal work for cash in León and Castile, harvesting by hand their huge summer-cereal crops in the days before mechanical harvesters ended that kind of work. After that, poor Galicians were forced to emigrate to survive; large numbers went to Argentina.

Campobecerros was a pretty and relaxed hill village, with half-timbered houses and large gardens. I had a comfortable room in the friendly local *pensión rural*, the Casa Nuñez. The next day, alone again after Richard had left, I went back to bed for a rare sleep-in, and then set off on an easy fourteen-kilometre day's walk to Laza, passing two villages on the way, Portocambo and As Eiras. From now on, villages would become more frequent as I came down from the mountains into more fertile and populated valleys nearing Ourense.

In Portocambo I lingered for a while in front of a lovely old church, Saint Michael the Archangel, reading the local families' gravestones. They were building new houses on the outskirts of Portocambo, solid stone houses, leaving the old houses to crumble away untouched in the village centre. I liked that—the old life fading away as new life grew up alongside it, like a young new sapling growing up and drawing sustenance from a dead or dying tree alongside. It is surely so much better to conserve than to destroy one's family history and memories. I was reminded again of how instinctively Spaniards revere and conserve their past, how they have so far escaped the tyranny of the market-dominated mind. And of how strongly Spanish people value home, family, their village, their local terrain. In front of the church of Saint Michael, I made a solemn vow before God to take better care of my family when I returned home.

Up and over more hills towards Laza, with dramatic upland views again of steeply plunging valleys and pretty villages far below, but also of distressingly large areas of burnt-out young pines—plantations planted at immense effort and cost on steep slopes, but now just blackened stumps on bare, ashen ground. The destruction from huge fires that swept through here a couple of dry summers before must have been immense: I saw workmen still harvesting burnt timber logs as I passed. Global warming again?

But could all these fires have been accidental, I wondered. I had read somewhere that a lot of forest-burning in Galicia had been man-made, deliberate arson. Had some local people resented the steady closure of their free highland sheep pastures with fenced, corporate-owned pine plantations, the closing down of their fragile, agrarian micro-economies in threatened mountain villages? Had some people resented the increased prices of their local land as a result of forestry-led bidding-up of land values? Did they resent the idea of their beloved hill country becoming simply just another supply area for Europe's insatiable appetite for pine newsprint and chipboard? Maybe, I thought, the winds and drought might have been helped along, for every young planted pine tree in these areas to have gone up in smoke so comprehensively. Curiously, there were smaller areas of older natural forest lower down—of mixed oak, chestnut, local native pines—that had not been burnt. Were these areas naturally more fire-resistant, or had local people worked harder to save them, letting the pine plantations go? It was a mystery that I did not have time to resolve. But the thought crossed my mind that if forestry was again attempted here, a better way to go might be to replant mixed natural forests interspersed with open fields, planning it all in real cooperation with the local communities' wishes, to re-create a mixed forest-farming ecology.

I then walked downwards into the sleepy hillside village of As Eiras, an obviously Celtic-derived Galician placename. There is no word like *eira* in the Spanish dictionary. I might mention here some peculiarities of the Galician language, Gallego. It is a Romance, Latin-based language like Spanish and Portuguese, but in some ways is closer to its Latin roots than Spanish is. For example, the word 'lamb', *cordero* in Spanish, is *anio* in Gallego (similar to the Latin *agnus*). 'Dog', *perro* in Spanish, is *can* in Gallego (like the Latin *canis*). Another interesting thing about Gallego is that the feminine article 'the', *la* and *las* in Spanish, become *a* and *as* in Gallego: A Gudina, As Eiras, A Coruña. I went to several village Masses that were held in Gallego; it is an interesting language to hear spoken — not quite Spanish, nor Portuguese, nor Latin.

I lunched in the As Eiras community plaza and picnic area, recently restored with the help of Galician regional government and EU funds. It had stone barbecues and ovens, wooden picnic tables, a children's play area, and a timber viewing deck overlooking the forested valley below, all done in traditional hand-hewn wood and masonry style. In As Eiras, I also encountered a travelling grocery shop — a white van, its back fitted out with ranges of chilled and frozen foods and beverages, fresh fruit and vegetables, standby household items, and little luxury items. There was a good variety of products set out neatly in this little van, which was small enough to navigate narrow, twisting lanes between mountain villages. I had already seen many travelling bakers' vans, selling fresh bread in villages — they have a distinctive horn-signal that sounds like an old steam-train whistle. But this was the first travelling grocery shop I had seen.

I presume that these are all government-subsidised services, part of the policy to look after older people in villages and to help keep village life sustainable. There is no profit to be made here; but, without access to visiting bakers and grocers and health workers, these villages, mostly inhabited now by older and poorer people, and younger artists and craftspeople, would soon shrivel and die. Once again, I was seeing that admirable Spanish community ethic—putting into practice the idea that, as a human society, we are all responsible for one another, including helping our oldest, weakest, or most vulnerable members, to maintain a decent life in their own communities and not to be carted off to nursing homes as their villages shrivel and die around them.

I walked down into Laza, a large, prosperous village in the valley flatlands below, with beautiful old buildings. Laza has a long history as a junction of pilgrimage routes. Alison Raju records that pilgrims coming from Portugal through Chaves and Verin (whether Portuguese or from Andalucia, Extremadura, and parts of the province of Salamanca, who had made detours through Portugal) joined the route I was taking here. In Laza I found a bright new municipal *refugio,* an energy-efficient concrete and steel structure. There I met two young fellow pilgrims, John from Ireland and Marcelino from Bilbao. John and I had an interesting dinner conversation, mostly about modern Irish political history: who had been the truest patriot in the Irish Troubles, Michael Collins or De Valera? John had made an interesting deal with his wife: he was doing two weeks of bicycle pilgrimage before joining his family on the Costa del Sol for two weeks with them on a beach holiday. He said he needed some pilgrimage time, and that this was a good, pragmatic solution.

The next day, I climbed back up into high hills again for a long but glorious day, thirty-five kilometres to Xunqueira de Ambía. Perversely now, having decided two days before that I wanted to walk more slowly, I seemed to be wanting to speed up again: something was driving me forward. Sleeping restlessly, I got up well before dawn, taking care not to wake my sleeping roommates. I set out along a dimly streetlight-lit road, north-west into a deep, narrowing valley, through a village called Tamicelas where I met a farmer leading his mule-drawn hand plough out to work in his fields, then walked steeply left, up and up on rough forestry tracks through pine-forested mountains, to the village of Albergueria in highland pastures at 900 metres.

There I had a mid-morning breakfast of coffee and a homemade Galician tuna-fish pie (which was delicious) in the remarkable Bar Rincón de Peregrinos ('Pilgrims' Corner'), run by a charmingly eccentric local chap whose cosy café is bizarrely decorated with hundreds of pilgrims' individually signed scallop shells hung from the walls and ceiling rafters. We chatted, and after my breakfast he ceremoniously handed me a black marking pen and a new scallop shell—of which he keeps a stock—for me duly to write in my name, city, and country of origin, and date of passage. Up it went on the wall with all the others. You will find it there now if ever you walk through Albergueria.

More high country walking followed, then a short prayer at a huge wooden wayside cross on the crest of the last range, before travelling down again into a huge, flat, fertile plain, with a string of flat, horizontal villages running along the plain's edge into the far distance at the foot of low, fringing hills. The rich valley flatlands were reserved for cropping.

Once again, here was an example of the instinctive good planning of human habitat. How is it that Spain always does this so well?

In the first village, Villar de Barrio, I was directed to a hospitable café, the Bar Carmina, for a late, leisurely lunch. Carmina, a sweet and motherly lady—this seemed to be the favoured eating place for local widowers and bachelors—cooked me up a delicious *caldo*, a Galician speciality, a nourishing soup made from smoked ham, chorizo, white haricot beans, potatoes, spinach, and turnip greens. Served with Carmina's crusty, fresh, village bread and local red wine, it was a richly balanced meal in itself. Replete as I was, she offered me a glass of her potent *aguardiente* spirit with strong, black coffee and fresh fruit to finish with. Gloriously content and at peace with the world, I stepped out into the mid-afternoon sunshine at about 3.00 pm, ready in spirit if not in body for my last fifteen kilometres to Xunqueira.

The yellow arrows pulled me forward, through all those linked horizontal villages that I had seen from the hilltop before lunch. I walked along prosperous hillside streets of substantial, two-storey stone houses with gardens rich in vines, fruit trees, vegetables and flowers, with red and white and pink climbing roses everywhere tumbling over walls and pergolas in exuberant, full bloom. It was siesta time, but children still played, and dogs came out to meet me. I was feeling sublimely, foolishly, happy. It was all so beautiful, such a celebration of human life at its best, and I remember hearing music in my head and singing meaningless ditties to myself as I walked—perhaps too loudly, as I got a few odd looks. Pilgrims sometimes have their moments of madness, especially after as good a lunch on the road as I had that day.

The track veered dramatically left, straight out across the flat green plain for seven more kilometres without a turn. I saw now that this huge, dished plain must have been a lake or marsh not so very long ago, perhaps even within living memory—hence its deep and fertile soil, rich in cereal and legume crops. I glided effortlessly over this plain as if on wings, the seven kilometres going by as if in a moment, then it was up and over a last low range of hills, and down into Xunqueira at about 7.00 pm, still euphoric from the magnificent day. I had been on the track for thirteen hours, yet I felt there were still reserves of strength in my body.

Xunqueira, like Laza, was another biggish village, more like a town, set dramatically on a hillside spur, with a magnificent twelfth-century church that was almost a cathedral, and little plazas ringed by fine, substantial townhouses in the old central area. I would have liked to stay longer and see more of this historic town, but I still had the driving urge to move forward. There was a rather rundown pilgrim *refugio* on the outskirts of the town, and that night I shared it with four companionable Spanish *bicyclistas* who had cycled in a few minutes after me, having ridden that day from A Gudina, sixty-eight kilometres and three days behind me. They invited me to come out and eat and drink with them, but I prudently declined, ate a little bread and fruit from my bag, and went straight off to bed. I slept the sleep of the just, and didn't even hear them coming back in.

I had now come down into the rich south Galician lowlands: fertile, soft, rolling country, with many rivers flowing westwards from the mountains to the sea. From my reading I had associated Galicia with rural poverty, and was unprepared for the great natural richness and beauty of this land. Galicia's nineteenth-century and twentieth-century poverty, which was all too real, was the tragic result of many generations of over-large families and over-subdivision into uneconomic small farms—*microfundia*—that could no longer sustain decent family livings, forcing people out as seasonal wage labourers in Spain and, later, when that labour market collapsed, as forced emigrants to South America. As in Ireland, it was true Malthusian poverty, with population expanding faster than economic sustainability. Like King Ferdinand, Galicians didn't favour primogeniture, the harsh practice of giving the main inheritance to the eldest son and telling the others they must fend for themselves, when one loved all one's children equally and wanted to treat them fairly. Over time, as in Ireland, their descendants paid the price for the Galicians' abundant fecundity and love of their children, as farms became too small to feed whole families.

Now, with agricultural overpopulation no longer a problem in an industrialised economy, Galicia's inherently rich environment is flourishing again. The countryside has a well-cared-for and prosperous look about it. It is being used well, but not abused, for mixed agriculture and forestry. I saw lots of new rural building and renovation going on, good stone houses built to last, and well-tended family vineyards and orchards and vegetable gardens in what seemed an almost Elysian environment. Southern Galicia feels like an Ireland that has been towed 1000 miles south to a warmer, gentler climate, a land well warmed and watered by the Gulf Stream, but—at least in this summer season—without Ireland's chilling mists and rains. I don't know what southern

Galicia feels like in winter—no doubt it has its share of cold and rainy days—but I cannot imagine that these lowlands would ever be as bitterly cold as Ireland can be. In terms of a nurturing environment for human life to realise its full potential, the beautiful south Galician country that I passed through in this last week of my pilgrimage must be about as good as it gets anywhere in the world.

How Irish is Galicia? I found many interesting echoes of Ireland, especially in the Galician folk music: richly complex and melodic music for voice, bagpipes, flutes, violins, guitars, and kettledrums, played and sung by highly talented groups with names like Luar na Lubre and Milladoiro. There are traditional tunes with names like *Crunia Maris* (the Latin name for 'La Coruña') and *Canteixiere*, *Devanceiros* ('To our ancestors')—music that hits you right between the eyes with its hauntingly stirring Celtic harmonies and dissonances, the thrilling contralto voice of the female lead singer weaving in loops and strands around the hypnotic instrumental melodies. There are ribald bar choruses and tender love longs; instrumental jigs so like Irish jigs, yet wilder and more anarchical; strange Galician lyrics that sound like medieval Latin ... this is music of the Middle Ages, brought back to life, and no wonder it is wildly popular among young European folk-music lovers. Galicia has big annual folk festivals that bring people and musicians together from all over Europe. I'm hearing some of Luar na Lubre again now on a CD as I type this, and I'm weeping again for the sheer joy and delight of this brilliant music ... music that I first heard over dinner in a little bar near Lalín in Galicia.

And the Galician people are stunning—those slim and gorgeous white-skinned Celtic girls with their wild tresses of curly red or jet-black hair, their cool, greeny-blue eyes, Celtic genes gloriously mixed with blood-lines from everywhere in Europe—blond-haired and blue-eyed descendants of Goths and Visigoths and Normans, dark-eyed Spaniards from León and Castile, olive-skinned Portuguese. So many people have come to enjoy and husband this beautiful land of Galicia; there is such a glorious blending of humanity here.

Galicia is not Spain, any more than Portugal is Spain. But it is part of Spain, in that strange paradox that lies at the heart of the Spanish constitution, of there being many nations within the one Spanish Nation. There will always be a tension in Galicia, as there is in Andalucia and Catalonia and the Basque country, between the facts of being Spanish and Galician at the same time. In Galicia I saw some angry juvenile graffiti on both sides of the national argument. I hope it will never be expressed in serious vandalism or separatist violence, but rather in an energetic and creative resurgent regionalism. Galicians, especially younger ones, are justly proud of their language and cultural heritage; glad that it is recognised at last, after years of suppression, as one of the great Romance cultures of Europe. Realistically, Galicians understand that their political destiny lies within Spain as part of a liberal, non-authoritarian, non-constrictive Spain that is itself part of a liberal-democratic European Union.

Ironically, Franco was a Galician from Ferrol; and, from the very start of the Civil War, the conservative and church-influenced Galician political elite supported the Nationalist rising. Yet Franco suppressed Galician culture as ruthlessly as he suppressed other regional Spanish cultures. It was all part of his iron Spanish centralism

Galicians will never again accept second place for their

language and culture. From the other end of Spain, the great Andalusian poet Federico Garcia Lorca loved and admired Galicia for its uniqueness. Just before the Civil War broke out, Lorca wrote his 'Six Galician Poems' in 1935, composed in the Gallego language as his tribute to Galicia. One of them is 'Chove en Santiago' ('It's raining in Santiago'), which Luar na Lubre later set to music. It is one of their most-loved songs now:

Chove en Santiago
meu doce amor.
Camelia branca do ar
brila entebrecida ao sol.

Chove en Santiago
na noite escura.
Herbas de prata e de sono
cobren a valeira lúa.

Olla a choiva pola rúa
laio de pedra e cristal.
Olla no vento esvaído
soma e cinza do teu mar.

Soma a cinza do teu mar
Santiago, lonxe do sol.
Ágoa da mañán anterga
trema no meu corazón.

(Lorca, 'Madrigal â cibdá de Santiago')

Lorca never translated these six poems into his native tongue, but I found a Spanish translation by Juanfer Puebla, which is nearly as beautiful as the Galician original, on a Spanish poetry website:

Llueve en Santiago
mi dulce amor.
Camelia blanca de aire
brilla temblorosa al sol.

Llueve en Santiago
en la noche oscura.
Yerbas de plata y de sueño
cubren la luna nueva.

Mira la lluvia por la rúa
lamento de piedra y cristal
Mira el viento evanescente
sombra y ceniza de tu mar.

Sombra y ceniza de tu mar
Santiago, lejanía del sol.
Agua de la mañana antigua
tiembla en mi corazón.

I also found an English translation, by Catherine Brown, which inevitably loses the poetic rhythm of the Romance versions but retains something of the poem's beauty:

Rain falls on Santiago
my sweet love.
White camellia of the air,
the veiled sun shines.

Rain falls on Santiago
in the dark of night.
Grasses of silver and dream
cover the vacant moon.

Look at the rain in the street,
lament of stone and of glass.
See on the languishing wind
shadow and ash of your ocean.

Shadow and ash of your ocean,
Santiago, far from the sun;
water of ancient morning
trembles in my heart.

Lorca was thrilled that under the short-lived republic, Galicians, like Andalusians, were starting proudly to rediscover and revitalise their national cultural roots. He would be glad that Galician culture is now flourishing again. And its great cities—Santiago, Vigo, Ourense, Pontevedra, cosmopolitan La Coruña, Ferrol, and Lugo—are both Galician and Spanish in spirit, important elements in the rich multicultural mix that is Spain.

chapter thirteen

Walking with God

It's time that I tried to say something about the religious ideas I took with me into my pilgrimage, where I stood in relation to my Catholic faith before I started the journey, and what impact the pilgrimage might have had on me—for this book would be incomplete and less than honest if I were to remain silent on such matters. These days, fortunately, we have pretty much left behind the inhibitions of the quite recent past, when it wasn't considered good manners in English-speaking countries to talk about religion, politics, or sex. Nowadays most people talk easily enough about politics and sex, and we are recently becoming less constrained from talking about religion, the last taboo.

Religion starts with family. I was baptised as a newborn baby at St Canice's Catholic Church, Sydney, down the road from St Luke's Hospital, where I was born in 1943. I was brought up a Catholic with loose but real connections back to my father's Australian Irish–Catholic tradition. My mother, Minnie Kevin, and grandmother, Josephine Schick, with whom I grew up in Sydney, were well-educated, culturally sophisticated women, of Viennese–Jewish cultural background but not practising Jews. My father, Charles Kevin, had always wanted me to be a Catholic, and my mother honoured her promise that I would have opportunities to grow up as one. It was a marriage whose formative years were disrupted by long wartime separations. My parents married in London in March 1939, on the eve of World War II.

My father spent the war as an Australian naval officer and in secret intelligence work. I learned years later from the official biography after his death—he had never told me anything of this—that in 1941 he helped set up the Commonwealth Security Service, which worked out of Melbourne. These secret duties kept him away from my mother and me for most of the war years. I always understood that he had spent the war at sea as a lieutenant on a minesweeper in the Indian Ocean, and he was in fact on active naval service at sea for a year in 1942–43.

To my mother's enduring sadness, my parents effectively separated in 1947 after eight years of marriage, when I was four. My father was then Australia's first head of diplomatic mission (his title then was official secretary, effectively charge d'affaires) to the newly independent nation of India. Conditions were still very unsafe in Delhi then, so my father sent my mother and me, first for a few months in Ceylon while waiting to see if security improved, and finally back to live in Australia for the rest of his three-year posting. My mother and I did not see him again for the next three years, and my parents never lived together again after he returned from India to duties in Canberra in 1950.

After a few unsuccessful attempts by my mother to re-establish a family home in Canberra—my father had gotten too used to his independent single life by then, and could not handle the stresses of a domestic life with his volatile and eccentric Viennese wife—we stayed on in Sydney, living with my grandmother, whose flat was always a home and a safe refuge for me.

Many years later, my parents were finally divorced—an acceptance of facts—at my father's volition. He remarried in 1963, to Therese Wilson, a beautiful and charming woman he had met in Ceylon (Sri Lanka), when he was Australian high commissioner there from 1959 to 1961. Therese had two daughters, Tammy and Naomi. Naomi is my cherished little sister, living in Australia now with her husband, Deve Mahesan, and their daughters, Lara and Tatiana. Naomi had some happy years as a child living in our father's home during his last posting as Australian ambassador to South Africa. She has the warmest memories of him. He died of cancer at age fifty-nine in 1968, the year I began my Australian foreign affairs career. Therese died a few years later. I am sad that I never really got to know my father as well as I should have. We loved one another, and he was as good a father to me as he could be in our damaged family circumstances, but our relationship was never easy.

My early school years were in non-Catholic schools. As a boy, I was taught most of what I know about my Catholic religion by an outstanding Jesuit, Father Michael Scott, headmaster of Campion Hall, a Catholic primary school in Sydney not far from my home and school. At my father's request, I would visit Father Scott in his study for an hour's regular teaching, one on one, every Saturday morning. They were stimulating conversations rather than lessons, and I greatly looked forward to them. Scott was a charming and perceptive man who knew exactly how to make the best use of the limited time he had to teach me. With his help, I went through the Catholic sacraments, starting with First Communion at age eight. I have retained a respect and affection for the Jesuit order ever since.

I spent my three final high-school years attending a well-known Jesuit boarding school in Sydney, Saint Ignatius College, Riverview. I drifted away from religious observance at university, and married in an Anglican church in Northern Ireland. I have two sons, Patrick and Charles, from that first marriage to Valerie Russell; and three young grandsons, Patrick's sons, Jonathan, Sam, and Max. I didn't return to the practice of Catholicism until my early fifties, under pressure of a series of emotional hammer-blows, years of deep loneliness and distress and flawed judgement following the death of my beloved second wife, Jennifer Cushman. Instinctively, I reached back into my past, to my childhood Catholic religion, seeking the help of a divine Friend.

My reawakened Catholicism grew stronger during a challenging final ambassadorial posting to Cambodia (in 1994–97), as I wrestled with official detachment and cynicism in the face of great human distress, and as I took my first tentative steps towards taking on responsibility for a new, adoptive family. In Phnom Penh I started going regularly to Mass again, at the weekly English-language Masses conducted by the US-based Maryknoll Fathers' Mission to Cambodia. An impressive Maryknoll priest from Vermont, Father Jim Noonan, baptised my adopted Cambodian baby daughter, Vanny: it was a moment of re-invigorated faith for me. After retiring from the Australian foreign service in 1998 and beginning a new life as a private person back home in Canberra, I became a regular Mass-goer with my young children Vanny, Raingsey, and Julius in my local parish church of St Christopher's, and we draw joy and comfort as a family from that. My wife, Sina, is a loyal member of Canberra's Cambodian Buddhist community. On festival days I go happily with her to our local Buddhist temple, and she comes with us to Mass on special days, too.

I am not a fervent or doctrinaire Catholic, and have never experienced any dramatic 'born again' experience of rekindling of my religion. It has been a more gradual thing, a gentle re-orientation with and re-affirmation of the 'faith of our fathers, living still, we will be true to thee till death', in the words of that stirring Irish hymn we used to sing at Riverview. In recent years I have felt a growing, quiet conviction: 'Yes, I really do believe in God, and I do believe in the essential elements of my faith—a faith which is Catholicism'. Going on pilgrimage to Santiago was a natural step in my life's spiritual path over the past few years

I'm still probably an unusual sort of Catholic, as indeed my father was. He used always to stand at the back of the church so as to be able to slip out of Mass unobtrusively during the sermon, across the road for a quick milk-shake! He had strong views on the separation of church and state, and resented being told by priests how to think about politics or how to vote, as some Australian bishops and priests were still wont to do in the 1950s. He loved the remote mystery, dignity, and universality of the Latin Mass, and he felt the loss of it when the language of the Mass became vernacular English.

My nonconformity takes different forms from my father's. I enjoy the stimulus of good sermons (or, as they are now called, homilies), and I am comfortable hearing Mass in my own language. However, I still remember and love the familiar words of the Latin Mass that I experienced as a child, so going to a choral High Mass is a special joy for me. I have a problem with personal Confession (or, as it is now called, Reconciliation). The notion that one should regularly confess one's sins to God through the intermediation of a listening priest, another human person, strikes me as burdensome on both confessor and auditor. It seems to me that, just as one prays to God privately, one may properly confess to God privately, and the idea that one should tick off one's card with a priest before taking Communion is discomfiting for me. I make my private confessions to God before and during Mass, and I receive Communion with a clear conscience.

I suppose the other odd thing about my Catholicism is that I have absolutely no interest in converting anyone to my faith. I love my church because it works for me, for my family background, culture, and personal values. I love its universalism; its tireless and culturally sensitive good works in helping the poor and sick and homeless (work that I came to know and admire in Cambodia); its total absence of racism or any sense of European superiority over other cultures; its fearless affirmation of the equal dignity and worth of every human person in this world; and its firm precept that we are all brothers and sisters under God. Catholicism's unshakeable affirmation of our common humanity under one God is, for me, the most precious precept of my religion, the mainstay of my faith.

I know this: we will need to hold firm to that universal value in coming years, as global warming accelerates, sea levels rise, and as Hurricane Katrina-type cyclones and coastal inundations become more frequent and permanent. Will we rich countries respond to the human suffering from those predictable disasters selfishly, circling the wagons and driving the starving and homeless away from our defended *laagers*, or will we respond as one human family? I know my church's answer, and the answer that many Australians of religious or non-religious belief would instinctively give, for we are or we used to be a generous and fair-minded people. I don't yet know what answer my government would give.

To me, the idea that one should be going around the world trying to convert people does not sit well with Catholicism. One could argue that God in His divine wisdom wanted to make room for all the world's great religions and belief systems, even for humanist and atheist philosophies; and that God in His wisdom will decide if and when people should choose to transfer their allegiances from one religion to another. I admire the way that Catholic priests and nuns and lay people work selflessly in Cambodia to help people in need, without asking anything in return. And I have to say that I am uncomfortable with the approach of some Christian missionary enterprises working in poor countries, which quite unashamedly hold out material inducements in the form of assistance with sustenance and children's education to those who convert to their offered faiths. I think that offering such deals is missing the essence of Christianity, in which one gives without expectation of reward.

Do I then believe that one religion is as good as another? In a way, I do, but not to the extent of that very funny scene in the Beatles' movie *Help!* when the Anglican bishop is having a cup of tea in his garden with his guest, a high priest of the murderous Indian cult of Kali (gleefully played by Leo McKern), amiably comparing the theological merits of Christian worship and ritual human sacrifice to the goddess

Kali. Obviously, religions have to be compatible with core human ethical values: to love your neighbour, to forgive those who have sinned against you, to help the poor and homeless and suffering, to honour and cherish your family. But all of the world's great religions, and secular humanism as well, inspire such values. The ethical systems, the precepts on we may try to live a good life, that grow out of the three great Abrahamic religions of Judaism, Christianity, and Islam, and out of the great Eastern religions or philosophies (Hinduism, Buddhism, Taoism, and Confucianism) seem to me similar in their essence. These great world religions have stayed the course for thousands of years. Religions that call on people to do violent and unnatural things such as engaging in human sacrifice or ritual suicide or self-castration have short lives, and are not serious ethical alternatiives.

If I respect all the world's great religions as I do, what is it about being a Catholic that is important to me? Why don't I wander around the smorgasbord table, visiting churches and synagogues and mosques and Eastern-religion temples at random? Simply, I think, because I feel most at home in Catholic churches, places of worship that embody the belief system and language that I grew up in, and that helped shape my personal morality. My Catholicism is an important part of my childhood memory. It helped to make me the person I am, and its yeast continues to ferment in me as I grow older. By my choice, it is the moral yardstick of how I live.

My mother's maternal grandfather (the family name was Keller) was a German-speaking reform rabbi in Bratislava, the 'city of brotherly love' that is now the capital of Slovakia. Her father was a wealthy Viennese spirits distiller, Julius Schick, who came from an upper-middle-class, secular

Jewish background She grew up in Vienna in the 1920s as a tolerant humanist, a strong believer in modernity and internationalism and human progress. She rarely, if ever, went to a synagogue. If she had any religious belief, it was in some vaguely understood 'universal spirit' or 'life force'. Talking about a personal God used to embarrass her. I think that, like a lot of Europeans in the early twentieth century, she found organised religious observance archaic and unprogressive.

Her generation's optimism was shattered by her forced flight as a refugee from her home city and nation, and by the ensuing Nazi Holocaust in which most of her aunts, uncles, and cousins who did not get away in time perished. I don't think that my mother ever recovered from that horror, about which she would not speak easily, though she did lovingly show me old photographs and tell me the names of her lost relatives and childhood friends. I think she spent the rest of her life wondering what had gone wrong with her beloved high-German culture. She was a highly educated and artistic woman, brought up to read Goethe and Schiller and Kant (I still have leather-bound sets of the German classics at home—I cannot read them, but cannot bring myself to sell them), to draw well, and to play the piano music of Beethoven and Schubert and Chopin. She died in 1971 in Sydney, a sadly wounded and bewildered woman, a casualty of anti-Semitism and the dislocations of war. I gave her little comfort: in those years, I was mostly selfishly absorbed in myself and my new career as a young, ambitious Australian diplomat.

My father had a firmly instinctive Catholic faith—I think for much the same reasons as I do now, that it was a strong part of his family history and culture—but he never would have claimed that his faith was either provable or disprovable. He would not have thought either proposition was worth wasting time discussing. Religious faith was just that—a leap of faith, and a precious gift from God. It was enough, for him as it is now for me, to try to live a good life without fretting over trying to 'prove' that God exists. I remember vaguely a religion class at school, when a priest took us carefully though one of the most famous attempted proofs of the existence of God—I think it had something to do with Swiss clocks—but in the end he concluded rightly that all these ingenious 'proofs' somewhere along the line always required an act of faith.

So Catholic Christianity works for me, but I am also comfortable with and respect what I know of Protestant Christianity, Judaism, and Islam. I see the three great Abrahamic religions as one family, all growing out of the same hugely creative cultural melting-pot of the ancient world of the Mediterranean and Near East—the world of the great cities of Babylon, Jerusalem, Damascus, Antioch, Athens, Rome, Alexandria, Mecca, Byzantium, Cairo, Baghdad. These three religions, all claiming to possess the sole revealed truth, have coexisted uneasily around the Mediterranean Basin and Levant for over fourteen centuries now; sometimes in great cruelty and bloodshed, but at other times in peace. To me, the many things they have in common are far more important than the differences that separate them. I think those of us who believe this are going to have to go on defending that belief bravely, as the voices of anti-Muslim prejudice grow louder and harsher.

I abhor extremism or fundamentalism in any religion. Although fanatical abuses can happen in all religions—think of recent years' Buddhist mob violence against Tamils in

Sri Lanka, and of similar Hindu abuses against Muslims in India — the Abrahamic revelatory religions seem to have been more prone to religious fanaticism and violence than the generally more contemplative Eastern religions and religious philosophies.

Historically, Jews have often had more to fear from Christians than from Muslims. Islamic rulers have usually provided a more tolerant and nurturing environment for vulnerable Jewish minorities, and it is only since the establishment and expansion of the state of Israel, and the great injuries that this state is causing to displaced Palestinians and to the people of Lebanon, that relations between Jews and Muslims have become so toxic in recent years.

Christian anti-Semitism, on the other hand, has been an ugly cultural reality in many different forms over many centuries. That is why I think the currently popular but misleading phrase 'Judaeo–Christian civilisation' has little historical validity or substance.

Spain between the eighth and the fifteenth centuries was a viable 'Judaeo–Christian–Muslim civilisation', when the three Abrahamic religious communities lived together in peace and mutual respect, and together achieved a high level of civilisation. For most of the history of Islamic-ruled states, until very recently, minority Jewish and Christian communities could usually live securely and with respect for their faiths, as long as they were loyal to the state, observed its laws, and did not proselytise.

It was only for about a century and a half, and after many centuries of intermittent profound mistreatment by their Christian neighbours, that Jews in western and central Europe enjoyed a brief interlude of institutionalised acceptance and full human rights in what could be called a Judaeo–Christian civilisation: this lasted from around the time of the French Enlightenment until the Nazi nightmare. But European anti-Semitism never went away completely in these years, and in Eastern Europe and Russia it remained endemic.

Now, in some 'Judaeo–Christian' Western states, Muslim minorities are becoming the new scapegoats—'the new Jews', increasingly mistrusted and excluded and at risk of victimisation, as Jews used to be in Europe. We are still living through a continuing, tripartite, historical tragedy involving the three Abrahamic religions, in which Muslims are now the main victims. The unconscionable attempt by some Western political leaders, who should know better, to emphasise and politically exploit the 'otherness' of vulnerable Muslims living in Western multicultural societies is cruel and disgraceful.

I welcomed Pope John XXIII's ecumenical movement and the miracle of the Second Vatican council from 1962 to 1965, because they affirmed in the church's doctrine and practice values that I had absorbed as a child from both my parents in their own different ways: tolerance, acceptance of human diversity, celebration of our common humanity, respect for other races and cultures and religious traditions, and a religious culture of openness and generosity. It is wonderful that these values, pressed vigorously by that great reformist pope, have now, under the three succeeding popes, become firmly entrenched in Catholicism, confirming it as a truly universal religion.

I think that part of Catholicism's tremendous staying-power in the world, its ability to surmount long periods of schism and corruption and institutionalised intolerance and cruelty to non-Catholics, is that its central theology offers wonderful gifts to every person at every stage of life.

I am no theologian, but the thought came to me during my pilgrimage walk that the doctrine of the Holy Trinity, the three Persons in one God, has huge inner power and strength, because it satisfies all of our spiritual needs: for a God the Father, who is a safe refuge and a strong patriarch who lays down the rules for a good life and protects us as a father from harm; for God the Son, Jesus, our hero and friend, who came to live among us on this earth and sacrificed His life to redeem our sins; and for God the Holy Spirit, the quiet voice of our conscience, the cool, soothing breath that steals into our hurt souls. We reach out to each of the three Persons in God at different times in our lives, according to our needs at those times. And Mary, the Virgin Mother of God, not a goddess but certainly the most loved and cherished of all the Catholic saints, satisfies our widespread human yearning for a spiritual mother figure, a yearning that has given birth to many 'earth mother' cults and religions over the ages. Catholicism, for me, has it all.

Finally, there is my proud knowledge that Christianity has generated many things of great worth and beauty during its twenty centuries of existence. In music, in art and architecture, in literature—in our whole European civilisation—the church's beneficent influence has been a profound inspiration to high culture. Yes, Christianity has been responsible for terrible things, too: the encouragement of ruthlessly bloody Crusades and other wars of religion; inquisitions; and persecutions of non-conformists and religious dissenters. But when I walk into a cathedral or Spanish village church, when I hear a sung Palestrina or Bach or Mozart Mass, when I gaze on a Michelangelo painting, when I read a John Donne or

Gerald Manley Hopkins poem, I feel I am part of something glorious, an enterprise so grand that it cannot be simply human in origin. I cannot prove this—I just know it in my heart. Faith makes us stronger and better than we could be on our own. It inspires us beyond the material and the selfish, to higher levels of aspiration and creativity. It transforms our lives into something meaningful.

***

When I decided to go on pilgrimage, I didn't know what to expect of it, except that I was sure it would be healing and strengthening to my bruised beliefs in my society's continuing worth. That is why I wanted John Eddy to bless my pilgrimage before I set out. As John prayed that God bestow on me the gifts of my pilgrimage and protect my family while I was gone, I bowed my head humbly, knowing that something important was about to happen in my life.

And it truly did. But, as I have explained, there was no magic, revelatory moment in Spain; rather, it was a series of little steps forward, towards a slowly opening door. My pilgrimage opened my heart wider to God; it washed away my emotional constrictions and defence mechanisms; it enabled me to pray more freely and unforcedly than ever before in my life. It gently but insistently urged me to confront my life, warts and all. Everyone I met on the pilgrimage played a part in this: the Mother Superior in Granada who put the first stamp in my passport, and all the priests on the way to whom I introduced myself in churches after Masses and who blessed my journey; Juan, the innkeeper in Alcaracejos who was the first person in Spain to hail the inner significance of what I was trying to do; the hospitable lay brothers at Alcuéscar; Marit and Karin; Tim and Liz; Richard and Aldo and Nigel; the woman at the *lavanderia* in Ríonegro; John and Marcelino in Laza; the man in Albergueria who hung up my scallop shell on his ceiling; and every fellow pilgrim or villager or innkeeper or *hostalero* I met who wished me '*Buen Viaje!*' on the way.

Going to Mass often, both in village churches and in awe-inspiring city cathedrals, was a wonderful spiritual nourishment. I felt so at peace with myself attending these Spanish Masses. The last time I went to Mass so regularly was as a boy at Riverview, where it was part of the obligatory daily routine. I chafed under the apparent burden then, and it meant little. But it wasn't at all a burden in Spain, and it meant a great deal. When I arrived in a village, I would ask if there was an evening Mass: if there was one I could attend, I gladly did so. I bought a little Spanish prayer-book so that I could read the liturgy in Spanish and take part in the congregation's spoken prayers. It was a wonderful thing to recite in Spanish the Lord's Prayer with congregations whose worship of God I was privileged as a pilgrim to share:

> Padre nuestro, qué estás en el cielo,
> santificado sea tu Nombre;
> venga a nosotros tu reino;
> hágase tu voluntad en la tierra como en el cielo.
> Danos hoy nuestro pan de cada dia;
> perdona nuestras ofensas,
> como también nosotros perdonamos a los qué nos ofenden;
> no nos dejes caer en la tentación,
> y libranos del mal.

Then there were the prayers at wayside crosses, of which I passed a great many. I got into the habit of making the sign of the cross and offering a short prayer at every wayside cross or church that I passed. At first, I felt self-conscious at such public affirmations; but after a while it came to be natural.

In Spain on the camino, I was living my religion rather than thinking about it at an intellectual level. The pilgrimage wasn't a mental exercise in theology on the move. I was not working through ideas about religion and politics, or religion and society. I was giving that part of my brain a rest. What was happening to me was a felt thing.

***

My daughters Vanny and Raingsey were confirmed while I was in Spain. I was sad to miss their preparations and Confirmation Mass with their schoolmates and families, but it was wonderful to be able to share it with them from a distance as a pilgrim, praying at this special time in my life for this special time in their lives. In Córdoba, I found confirmation presents to airmail them: for Raingsey, a little silver bracelet of Santiago scallop shells; and for Vanny, similar silver earrings and a pendant of a scallop shell set inside a Star of David. I also sent them prayer cards from Córdoba showing the Holy Spirit as a dove, sending down as flames His seven gifts: *sabiduría, inteligencia, consejo, fortaleza, ciencia, piedad, temor de Dios* (wisdom, intelligence, good counsel, fortitude, science, compassion, and the fear of God). On the back of the card was the text of a Spanish prayer that I recognised as the Latin prayer often set to music and sung at High Masses: *'Veni, sancta Spiritus'* ('Come, Holy Spirit').

Later, I found that this mighty prayer, one of the greatest masterpieces of sacred Latin poetry ever written, was most probably composed at the height of the twelfth-century Christian renaissance by an English priest, Stephen Langton, Archbishop of Canterbury, who died in 1228. These were, of course, the great years of the pilgrimage to Santiago. The prayer reads as powerfully and beautifully in Spanish as in its original Latin:

Ven, Espíritu divino,
manda tu luz desde el cielo.
Padre amoroso del pobre;
don, en tus dones espléndido;
luz qué penetra en las almas;
fuente del mayor consuelo.

Ven, dulce huésped del alma,
descanso de nuestro esfuerzo,
tregua en el duro trabajo,
brisa en las horas de fuego,
gozo qué enjuga las lágrimas
y reconforta en los duelos.

Entra hasta el fondo del alma,
divina luz, y enriquecenos.
Mira el vacío del hombre,
si tú le faltas por dentro;
mira el poder del pecado,
cuando no envias tu aliento.

Riega la tierra en sequía,
sana el corazón enfermo,

lava las manchas, infunde
calor de vida en el hielo,
doma el espíritu indómito,
guía al qué tuerce el sendero.

Reparte tus siete dones,
según la fe de tus siervos;
por tu bondad y gracia,
dale al esfuerzo su mérito;
salva al qué busca salvarse
y danos tu gozo eterno. Amén.

After I came home, I found an English translation on the Internet, but it was a bit too florid for my taste. I would rather give you, in all humility, the rough-cut and doubtless highly inaccurate translation that I made while in Mérida from the Spanish, with the help of my pocket dictionary, and sent by letter to my daughters, asking that they read it in time for their Confirmation Day:

Prayer for Your Confirmation Day

Come Holy Spirit, and send Your light down from Heaven. Father, Who loves the poor, take us into Your hands. Light, enter my soul; fountain of good counsel.

Come, gently lodge in my soul, relax me from my labours, be a cool breeze in the hottest hours, the joy which dries my tears and strengthens me in my struggles.

Come deep into my soul, Divine Light, and enrich it. See how empty man is, if You are not with us; see the power of sin, when You do not breathe upon us.

Water the dry land, heal the sick heart, wash our stains away, melt our coldness with Your warmth, tame our restless spirit, guide us if we stray from the true path.

Share Your seven gifts with us according to our faith as Your servants, through Your goodness and grace reward our efforts; save those who seek salvation, and grant us eternal life. Amen.

Not wanting to leave my five-year-old son Julius out of it, I sent him a postcard of Juan Pablo II, 1978–2005, and some Spanish football shorts. I had met Pope John Paul II when he visited Poland in 1992, at a reception for ambassadors to Poland hosted by the Papal Nuncio in Warsaw. One of my greatest treasures now is a framed photo of the pope shaking hands with me on that day. It hangs above Julius' bed now.

On the day that Vanny and Raingsey were confirmed, 4 June, I was praying in the great cathedral at Plasencia, asking God to protect them and give them good and happy adult lives. I can truthfully say that my prayers were with them all the way during my weeks in Spain, and I believe the Holy Spirit came into us all on this special day.

Now, as Santiago was finally approaching, I felt that my heart was as cleansed and refreshed and open to God as it was ever likely to be in this life on earth, and I was happy.

chapter fourteen

Pilgrimage's End

Now I walked from Xunqueira into Ourense, an easy twenty-kilometre morning walk, mostly gently downhill, along quiet minor roads undulating through hills and valleys, past small farms, lush gardens, and vineyards, through increasingly built-up country that gradually merged into the garden suburbs of Ourense, a substantial city of 96,000 people. I passed a hairdresser and had my first haircut in Spain, the short-clipped cut from eight weeks before in Australia having grown shaggy. Then I walked on into the city through an attractive old stone village, Seixalbo, on a road which led me directly into a long downhill avenue to the Río Miño.

At the busy city junction at the bottom, I veered right, walking uphill along a long, stately avenue flanked by six-storey apartment buildings and street-level shops, until I found at the very top of the hill my pilgrim *refugio*, a comfortable dormitory in the Convento San Francisco, a substantial, old sandstone building overlooking the old city which is built on slopes down to the river below, facing a range of higher hills across the river: a beautiful setting for a city. I settled in, showered, rested, and went out in the early evening to go to Mass in the Cathedral of St Martin and to see the town.

Ourense was a warm and welcoming city, filled with young, stylish, and vivacious people. It had the feel of a university town. Around the Romanesque thirteenth-century cathedral was an attractive pedestrian precinct with sophisticated clothes and jewellery boutiques, bookstores, and restaurants and bars. It was a youthful, lively, and happy crowd strolling around, and it all somehow reminded me of my student life at Trinity College, Dublin, forty years before.

I went and sat in the main city park. All the sidewalk cafés were filled with people, and there was an exciting buzz of movement and voices and laughter as dusk came on. People were casually and comfortably elegant, cool, even hip. I was struck by the kind of urbanity that I had last seen in Córdoba, at the other end of Spain. At 10.00 pm on a Friday night, here was a wonderful diversity of people enjoying themselves together in the streets of old Ourense: young courting couples; groups of girls or young men getting together in readiness for a night out on the town; family groups of parents and grandparents and uncles and aunts sitting together and enjoying the company of their young children; and older people quietly watching and enjoying it all—the rich human texture of a civilised small city. There was a sense of fun, of warmth and love in the family groups, of a pleasurable tingle of sexual anticipation in the young people at that wonderful time of life when every night out is a potentially life-changing experience ... but I saw no alcohol-fuelled aggressiveness or anti-social behaviour. I saw a human society at peace with itself.

I wondered if we could ever again recapture in our brittle

and suspicious Anglophone urban cultures that vital capacity to relaxedly enjoy one another's company in city streets. Could we regain that precious quality of community life in an integrated civic society, without cordoning ourselves off into mutually exclusive and wary demographic boxes: slick young urban professionals, competitively flaunting their brief moment in life of mindless affluence; moody and alienated young outsiders looking on in resentful poverty and disappointed hopes; worried young couples stuck at home in their mortgaged-to-the-hilt houses, eating cheap, fast-food takeaway meals and watching cheap, rented DVDs, trying to keep costs down; the forgotten old in their lonely flats and retirement homes; and bored, neglected children sitting alone, playing games at Internet consoles—all wondering where real life and community had gone?

I made myself shrug off such negative thoughts, and found a restaurant that advertised its speciality of the house: spicy mussels in white wine. It was quite full, a jolly place and, as we were near the Atlantic, only about 100 kilometres away, I thought it would be safe to try the mussels. They were delicious.

***

Walking out of Ourense very early the next morning, down through the still dark and sleeping city, I met young revellers still coming out of the nightclubs and calling in at all-night cafés for a reviving early-morning coffee. Then I walked across the Roman pedestrian bridge. How these great Roman bridges have survived in Spain! I mentally ticked off those I had walked over: in Córdoba, Mérida, Salamanca, and now

Ourense. I walked on through nondescript northern apartment and industrial areas, nearing the looming escarpment. I crossed under a railway line and walked straight up a killingly steep road, about 500 metres' height gain in two kilometres, onto the high plateau and countryside again. Then I drifted along dreamy country lanes, away from main roads and with hardly any traffic, to a pretty stone humpbacked bridge over the gently flowing little Río Barbantino, into a small village called Ponte Mandrás. I was just ninety-five kilometres from Santiago now—I had passed the 100 mark.

It was lunchtime. Ponte Mandrás had a friendly tavern, but it had no beds. I had to go on, another six kilometres to Cea, where I knew there would be a *refugio* and where the local, crusty, wood-fired sourdough bread is justly famous. I stopped in at the bar at Ponte Mandrás for a cheese *bocadillo*, two hefty slices of fresh *pan de Cea* with deliciously salty *manchego* sheep's cheese in between, and a glass of robust young local red. The good folk in the bar companionably urged me to come back in the evening—it was the local saint's day, so there was to be *música folklorica* with Galician bagpipes and dancing. I saw the bandstand already set up in the little plaza, and said I would try to come back. I walked on to Cea, crossing back over the main Ourense–Santiago road, the N525, on the way.

Somehow, Cea as a place didn't work for me. I was the only pilgrim in the *refugio* that night and, unusually, I felt lonely and low-spirited. The hostalero on duty hospitably shared his frugal dinner with me—tomatoes, cold chicken, bread, fruit. I recognised within me a mood I remembered from my younger days of impending separation, the bitter-sweet feeling towards the end of a holiday with a loved one from whom one knows one must soon be parted. I rang up a local taxi and went back to Ponte Mandrás to seek an evening of fun and folk music. The people I had met in the bar at lunchtime were there again, and seemed delighted to see I had returned to their village. We had good conversations over more local wine. I met a vivacious fifty-ish lady who had come back to live in this her native village, from where she had emigrated to Latin America many years ago. She told me that Venezuela had been fun then, but Spain was a better place to live now. This was a theme I heard often from returning emigrants to Latin America: a lot are coming home, voting with their feet, as Spain becomes more politically and economically attractive. The band did not show up—it turned out they were not expected till midnight, as they were much in demand and had several other engagements first. It was going to be a very late-night party in Ponte Mandrás. I couldn't stay for it—not with thirty-five kilometres' walking ahead of me the next day. Regretfully, I called up my taxi and went back to sleep in Cea as the villagers of Ponte Mandrás prepared to dance the night away.

Sunday was quite a hard day, from Cea to A Laxe. Though never very far from the main road, I was hardly aware of it. There was more climbing—up to a plateau at 800 metres. I was walking across the grain of Galicia, north-westwards through a region where all the mountain ridges and intervening river valleys ran south-westwards, and so it was up and down all the way. It's why the Moors found this region so hard to conquer and hold: geography favoured the defenders.

As I moved up into the high tableland, a deep mist came down, and I could barely see ten metres ahead. I was now walking with the help of my staff along deep-furrowed, rich-green mossy laneways lined with ancient trees and fieldstone walls, dripping wet in the mist, fern-fronded and boggy underfoot. It was intensely romantic, Tolkien country, where one might expect at any moment to encounter Frodo Baggins fearfully sheltering from the Dark Riders cantering along the unseen crests above. It was heartbreakingly beautiful, the stuff of childhood dreams and Celtic fairytales, and my soul was like a quivering violin string. I was trying desperately to lock this beauty into my memory, taking photo after photo as my heart broke and my eyes filled with tears.

Finally I came down off the misty high plains, emotionally wrung out but still physically strong, and into the more familiarly beautiful valley and thus into the small village of A Laxe, where I found another pilgrim *refugio*. The mountain fog had lifted, and so had my mood. A late-afternoon sun was shining warmly. It was a relief after so many empty or near-empty *refugios* to find that I wasn't alone here—there were about fifty exuberantly happy high-school teenagers from the Ourense region, girls and boys together doing a short school-holiday pilgrimage walk to Santiago. A lovely bunch of kids, they had filled the hostel to capacity, and I was lucky to be offered a bed next to one of the accompanying young teachers in a packed dormitory. I knew it was going to be a noisy night.

I headed off to a contemplative dinner in a quiet local bar. The charming young woman there made me up a tasty potato omelette and salad, and with a half-litre of wine I was soon content. She was playing a tape of melodic Galician folk music, and that is how I first came to hear the stunning sound of Luar na Lubre. I wandered back to the *refugio*, steeling myself for a restless night. But fortune smiled—the *casita,* the lady caretaker of the refuge who had dropped in to check that everything was alright for the young pilgrims, took one kindly look at me and decided to offer me the special privilege of a locked-access suite for disabled pilgrims. It was a quiet room with a private bathroom, an executive suite all to myself, and I slept like a log.

The next day was relaxed—no more high hills, just a gently undulating thirty kilometres along quiet paths to the crossing of another big river valley, the Río Ulla, with a bridge and village at Ponte Ulla, my last overnight stop before Santiago. Again, it was beautiful, soft country, mostly off the highway, through villages and farms, across streams, past stables and high-trellis vineyards. The farmers here like to get their vines up high into the sun, and to grow green vegetables during winter in the sheltered spaces underneath the vines. The camino at times itself passed under canopies of trellised vines growing across lanes; they were bursting with bunches of ripening grapes. Harvest was about a month away. The young pilgrims from A Laxe soon passed me—I had left the *refugio* earlier than them, but they were faster on the path—with many cheery waves and '*Buen viajes*'.

As I neared Ponte Ulla, the path plunged down into a deep ravine, slanting down towards the river. I could hear the roar of rapids below. Finally a bridge came into view. I crossed it into the village, where I found a truly delightful little family pensión, the Restaurante-Hostal Ríos, in the lee of the bridge. After the past five nights' sleeping in pilgrim dormitories, I was more than ready for the comfort of a well-appointed hotel bedroom. Luckily, the innkeeper's wife was happy to do my laundry. I was determined to enjoy my last night on the camino. It was a marvellous dinner, another Galician *caldo* hearty soup, with delicious cheeses and country bread, and fresh, sweet cherries still in season.

After dinner I rang home to tell the family I would be arriving in Santiago the next day. Things were not too good at home: Sina told me that all the family had come down with debilitating winter colds, and that this week she had had to take my five-year-old Julius to hospital to check out a severe flu. Now that she knew I was nearly in Santiago, Sina could safely tell me news that she had not wanted to burden me with before: she was feeling increasingly tired and run-down, and she really hoped I could try to come home soon, because all the family missed and needed me. Could I possibly change my flight bookings, still nearly two weeks away? Of course, I promised to try. My pilgrim life was drawing to a rapid end as real-life family responsibilities re-emerged.

The final day, a Tuesday, was just twenty kilometres into Santiago. The camino kept its surprises till the end: it was so hilly that the city did not come into view until I had crested the last of many ridges on that day, a final low saddle about three kilometres from journey's end. There, suddenly, the city was at last before me, ranged along a hillside that faced me across a final valley. I saw the dreaming fairytale spires of Santiago Cathedral at last, and I felt—what? Joy, pride of achievement, sadness, fear, excitement at the sight, loss—a welter of indescribable emotions flashed rapidly through my mind, in the end settling as a kind of resigned acceptance that this was how it had to be.

I walked slowly and thoughtfully down the valley, along the ancient cobblestone road, the Calzada de Sar, into the old Sar district of the city, across a dammed stream and then up the hill opposite, through the great walls of the old city, towards the Plaza de Cervantes. There were tourists around me as I walked, and people sitting in cafés, but I hadn't seen any arriving pilgrims yet because I was coming into the old city from the south, and the main pilgrim route the *Vía Frances* comes into it from the east. In the hot early afternoon it was uncannily quiet in the city.

I walked into the Plaza de Cervantes and then, with shocking suddenness, they were all there: hundreds of fellow pilgrims, as if from another planet, streaming into the city in great numbers from the road to the right, the endpoint of the *Vía Frances*. I knew now, irretrievably, that this wasn't my special personal pilgrimage any more, that I was only a tiny part of a mass movement that belongs to the whole world. I heard the sounds of Spanish and French and Dutch and German and English in every accent, everyone so brisk and cheerful, purposefully striding into the city towards the cathedral. I felt like Rip Van Winkle who had just woken up, surrounded by so much efficient motion. I mechanically joined the current moving towards the cathedral—people of all ages, shapes, sizes, and nationalities, with packs large and small, with all manner of staffs and hats, with beards, with bicycles, with short hair or long hair or no hair—humanity in all its amazing diversity.

And suddenly I was there, in the magnificent cathedral plaza, three hours too late for the 11.00 am daily pilgrim Mass, but in time to find the official pilgrims' office, where I would get my *credencial* book stamped for the last time, receive my *compostela* (the certificate of completion of pilgrimage), and be listed for announcement at the next day's Mass. It was all happening fast; too fast. I mutely passed my *credencial* across to the woman behind the counter. We had a short conversation; others were waiting in line behind me as she carefully inscribed in pen on the ornate *compostela* certificate my name in Latin, *Dominum Antonium Kevin* (every pilgrim gets the courtesy title of *dominum,* meaning in this case 'clergyman'), and handed me the precious document in a protective cardboard tube.

'So you've really walked all the way here from Granada?', she asked me.

'Yes, I have', I said.

'Well done!'

'Thank you, señora.'

I stepped out into the hard street sunlight, blinking away tears. It was done, yet I still felt no sense of triumph—just another sudden onrush of sadness and loss. I wandered through the town, heading west into the modern commercial and residential district. I had an address for a pensión where I had already made a phone booking from Ponte Ulla. It was pretty down-at-heel, and cost a lot for what it was; but accommodation in Santiago is a sellers' market in this peak season of pilgrim arrivals two weeks before the feast day of St James, and I was in no mood to fuss over a few more euros.

I went off to collect my three parcels from the post office, the twelve kilograms of excess weight that I had shed and sent on ahead during the journey, from Madrid Airport, from Córdoba, and from Mérida. Miraculously, all three parcels were waiting patiently for me in the *recogida de correos* section of the post office. Here in Santiago, post office staff were used to holding pilgrims' packages for weeks on end. It was fun unpacking them, like meeting old friends again—all those things I thought I would need on the way, but that it turned out I obviously hadn't needed.

I found an Internet café, and over the next couple of hours worked to reorganise my flight bookings. All London-to-Sydney flights were packed full, July being the peak month for flights from Europe to Asia and Australia. The first booking I could get—and I was very lucky to do so—was five days away, on Sunday. I rang my good friend Jean, who lives near London, and she kindly invited me to stay with them over the weekend; it would be good to wind down with congenial company in quiet Buckinghamshire before the long flight home. I booked a flight from La Coruña to London on Friday, and that left Wednesday and Thursday to fill. I would stay three nights in Santiago, attending the Pilgrims' Mass the next day, Wednesday, and taking a one-day bus trip to Cape Finisterre on the coast on Thursday. With everything settled at last, I relievedly rang my family with the good news. They were thrilled that I would be coming home in only six days, and their joy began to lift my spirits, too. I had found my main purpose in life again—to try to be a good father to my young children—and my mood of despair finally lifted. God's wind filled my sails again.

***

The Pilgrims' Mass the next day was two hours of unalloyed happiness, a thrilling and unforgettable experience that I will never forget. I was glad, as it turned out, that I was attending the Mass on the day after I arrived. Twenty hours and a good overnight sleep in the city was enough time for my volatile end-of-pilgrimage emotions to begin to settle. As I entered the cathedral and found a seat in the main nave near the altar—I went half an hour early at 10.30, and it was just as well that I did, as the cathedral filled quickly—I saw hundreds of pilgrims walking in, still hot and flushed from hurrying to reach Santiago in time, still carrying their rucksacks and hats and staffs. A nun with a guitar was leading rather lugubrious community hymns (I already knew that most modern Spanish church music is drearily forgettable), but the sense of building expectation and excitement in the pews was palpable; it was like waiting for the curtain to rise for a first-night opera performance. Priests in red and white vestments began to gather before the altar, and then suddenly the grand cathedral organ rang out, filling our ears with rich, triumphant blocks of chords, and it was under way at last—our great Pilgrims' Mass.

As the Mass got under way, there was no homily, but rather a series of congratulatory announcements from the pulpit. It was all in Spanish, but I got the gist of it. This Mass was to thank and honour us, we pilgrims who had now fulfilled our solemn promise to make a camino to Santiago for the glory of God. We were being congratulated and thanked for our courage, our fortitude, our endurance, and our sacrifice in completing our arduous journeys, which were testament to our sincere love of God. One isn't used to hearing words of such praise from church pulpits—usually, one is being exhorted to do better. But here was sincere, unqualified praise and admiration for what we had all done. The lady washing clothes back at Rionegro del Puente had got the theology of pilgrimage exactly right

Suddenly, I realised what this was—it was a welcome home. We were like Olympic athletes being welcomed back into their communities, like a victorious school football team home from winning the trophy, like soldiers home from the wars. No wonder it felt so wonderful—we were actually the heroes on this day! The priest went on to read out the honour roll. On the *Camino Frances*, so many pilgrims had arrived today: so many from Madrid, so many from Barcelona, so many from France, so many from the Netherlands, so many from Germany ... I waited impatiently to hear the announcement ... 'and on the camino from Granada, one pilgrim from Australia'. Like an excited schoolboy, I nudged my friendly Dutch neighbours. 'That was me! That was me!' I whispered proudly, and they smiled warmly at me. The Mass passed by quickly, in a mood of exaltation and joy. Soon it was time for Communion, and we all filed forward slowly for our Bread of Life.

It wasn't over yet: still to come was the famous Santiago ceremony of swinging the mighty incense-brazier, the famous *Botafumeiro*, through the cathedral. A massive brass censer, which must weigh close to a tonne, is lowered on pulley chains from above, the incense is lit inside it, and then it is swung by eight priests pulling on ropes, faster and faster, in wider and wider sweeping arcs up and down the main nave, filling the whole cathedral with the sweet, smoky scent of incense. Finally, the priests stop swinging, and the censer begins to slow down. It takes some time to come to a halt, because it has so much weight and momentum at the end of its long chain, like the pendulum of a grandfather clock. At last it is hauled in and stilled, and the pilgrim Mass is ending. The priests file out, and we queue up for our last ritual blessing—to hug the venerated, many-centuries-old statue of a seated Santiago behind the high altar.

I couldn't believe I was indulging in this medievalist

superstition; but here I was, queuing up with every other pilgrim, waiting my turn to climb up the narrow, winding stairs behind the altar, to pass my hands around the broad shoulders of Santiago from behind, to hug him like an old friend, to whisper to him, 'We did this together, my friend!', and finally to float out, out of the great cathedral for the last time, into the bright sunlight of a Santiago afternoon. My years had melted away from me; I felt young and strong and fresh again, ready for a new world. My pilgrimage was finally, exuberantly, over.

chapter fifteen

To Finisterre and Home

There wasn't much more that I wanted to do in Santiago. It isn't just a pilgrimage centre: it is a major modern Spanish city, the capital of the Galician autonomous region, home to 80,000 people and a major football team, and a centre of commerce, government, and education. But none of that interested me any more. I was already mentally preparing myself for the return home, and I was starting to disengage from Spain. So I did what many pilgrims do after Santiago—wind down by going to Cabo de Finisterre, the End of the World, the farthest-west promontory of the European mainland: the place from where it was once believed, if you sailed westwards, you would soon fall off the edge of the world. Finisterre is a Romance name that also evokes the Celtic twilight of Europe, the ancient mysteries and legends, and Tolkien's Land of the West where Frodo and the Elves sailed into the afterlife. I would have liked to walk to Finisterre as Richard was doing, a 100-kilometre walk from Santiago; but there was only one free day, so I did the next best thing and went by bus.

I caught the first bus at 6.00 am. Seeing the country rapidly sliding by me through bus windows felt strange. Somehow it wasn't real anymore; it was more like watching a travel documentary on television. Looking out vacantly, I barely recognised the Galician countryside that had been wringing my heart just two days before. Already I was disengaged, in that bland tourist mood of 'if this is Friday, it must be Belgium'. Sitting in that bus was like being on Prozac—all feeling was deadened.

After a couple of hours, the sea at last came into view. Soon we were in Cee, a sheltered fishing village at the head of a great wide bay, protected from the Atlantic's huge winter storms by the southwards-jutting mountainous promontory of Cape Finisterre. From Cee, the road wound around the shore of the bay for fifteen more kilometres. On my left were quiet bay beaches, with gently lapping little waves. Soon we were in Finisterre, historically a dirt-poor fishing village, but now a bustlingly prosperous little tourist resort.

I shouldered my small daypack, and set off on my last walk in Spain, from the village up to the lighthouse on the high barren cape. The road climbed and climbed; soon I was hundreds of feet above the sea, with a magnificent view opening up of a richly indented coastline running southwards beyond the bay, and receding ranges of mountains eastwards toward Santiago and beyond towards León. I rounded a last point, and saw the lighthouse ahead. And here was a powerful image of Santiago, a modern bronze sculpture of the beloved apostle dressed as a Galician fisherman, wearing a mariner's sou'wester and rain-hat, bent over double against an oncoming storm, straining to keep his footing and make progress. It is a moving statue, and a reminder to me that today's weather was really all wrong for this place.

I should have seen Finisterre on a cold, wet, windy day, with wild Atlantic waves breaking fiercely on the rocks below, and clouds scudding across a leaden sky. Instead it was a calm, cloudless, sunny day, the sea was bright blue, and the waves were lazily curling onto the rocks below as seagulls circled below me in gentle thermals. Only when I rounded the lighthouse and looked out west to the Atlantic side of the cape did I see a few whitecaps, and get a sense of the strength of the sea. Never mind; it was still Finisterre.

I listened for a while to a Galician piper, and then left the tourists to climb up a minor road to the top of the hill behind the lighthouse. I'm glad I did, because from the top I now saw in front of me, far below, an inviting ocean beach, not far from the village. I carefully picked my way down a rough, eroded track—the last thing I wanted to do was to break a leg on my last day in Spain—and found myself finally on a sea-bleached pine boardwalk leading down to the almost empty beach.

There were a very few people sunbathing, and no one in the sea at all—deterred by a stern warning notice that the ocean currents here were strong and dangerous, and that this beach was not safety-patrolled at all. I reached the beach, stripped off my pack and shirt and shoes—I had worn light summer shorts that day, in case I had a chance to swim—and plunged into the waves for my immersion in the Atlantic Ocean, the pilgrim's last ritual. I didn't stay in long, because the water was freezing, and the beach fell away steeply into deep water. I went in no further than waist-deep: the waves were strong, and I felt a dangerous backcurrent tugging at my legs. After a couple of breathless whole-body plunges, I was soon back on the safety of the beach.

I walked along, collecting bleached, white scallop shells. At the south end, in a sheltered area I had not seen from the hill, was an encampment of young backpackers. They had set up tents and a fireplace, some were playing beach volleyball, and some were just lazing. They were a happy international bunch, relaxing after their pilgrimages—French–Canadians, Germans, Dutch ... the pilgrimage makes nationality unimportant. I met a young French–Canadian woman in the rocks, and we talked about how the pilgrimage had affected each of us. Though strangers, there was an immediate intimacy of a shared profound experience. Then I walked slowly back along the boardwalk to the village. I had fish soup for lunch, and then, at the bus-stop, a welcome surprise: Tim and Liz, my good camino companions from Wales whom I had last seen many weeks ago in Montemayor, were waiting for the same bus, the last bus of the day. On the way back to Santiago, we talked about what we had all been doing and how we were feeling now, and then I walked back with them from the bus station into Santiago, over a hill and through a park from where we had a beautiful last view across to the cathedral spires. I left them at the pilgrimage office: we didn't swap addresses, but I hope someday they may read this book.

***

There is really little more to tell: a few hours the next day in the sophisticated metropolis of La Coruña, Galicia's largest city, awaiting my flight to London; a relaxing weekend with Jean and her husband John in Buckinghamshire; the long flight to Sydney; and the last bus trip home from there to a final, blissful reunion with my beaming wife and children at the Canberra bus station. It felt indescribably good to be home safe in the bosom of my family, back on parental duties. I thanked God for His protection of us all in the nine weeks that we had been parted. I never wanted to leave my family for so long again.

***

So what was it really all about? What did I bring back from Spain, from my pilgrimage adventure, that is of lasting value? Can I sum it up? Can I share it? Should I even try, or should I just leave off here, letting my readers draw whatever they want to from what I have set down in this book so far? Being an ex-public servant, in the business of crafting words all my working life, I itch to attempt a conclusion.

Spain taught me that a country and its culture can go through hell on earth and still come out at the end as a decent and caring human society. Human societies have enormous recovery powers, and I believe this is a gift from God. It gives me hope that my country and other Anglophone countries that are going through a time of political and moral decline at present, of fear and moral indifference and selfishness, will recover. From the Inquisition to the Civil War and then a whole generation of fascist rule, Spain had everything thrown at it. And yet it has come through now as a gentle, human, and decent society, a country as far as I could tell that is at peace with itself and with the world. Of course, I did not see the major urban agglomerations of Spain, and I do not doubt that big cities such as Madrid and Barcelona have major problems of organised crime, drug abuse, child abuse, etc.

But, as a whole, Spain seemed to me to be a country whose political morality these days is to be admired.

I believe something that Thomas Jefferson said in 1772: 'A nation, as a society, forms a moral person, and every member of it is personally responsible for his society'. The greatest recent test of the morality of Spanish society was the Madrid train bombing by Islamist terrorists—a shock every bit as great to Spaniards as 11 September 2001 in the USA or the London Underground bombings in 2006. Spain's reaction was quite different: not vengeful, not mindlessly and implacably war-like, but immediately ready to confront the policies that had led to this tragic political crime of mass murder. Spaniards instinctively understood from their history that revenge was not the answer. An eye for an eye and a tooth for a tooth could only prolong the evil. They knew that the Spanish government had invited this crime by former prime minister Aznar having imprudently involved his country, against the weight of public opinion, in the US invasion and occupation of Iraq. The Spanish people well understood what the people of Iraq were suffering daily, and how the Palestinians in the occupied territories and Lebanese were suffering. Spain withdrew from the Iraq occupation in an act not of cowardice or selfishness, but of great nobility and wisdom. Spain has learned from hard experience that good ends do not justify evil means. In Anglophone countries with less tortured recent histories, our leaders have forgotten this lesson.

I saw a civic contentment in Spain, a sense of balance and pride in one's own local place, of viable small communities: a rural confidence that is harder and harder to find elsewhere, as the driving force of unchecked city growth and economic rationalism sucks country towns and villages dry of real economic life and social hope. I saw a mature, non-doctrinaire understanding that if everything in life is left to market forces, people who need and have a right to public protection will not be protected as they should be: that there has to be a 'Third Way', a social morality that draws on the best features of both capitalism and socialism.

I saw a proper pride and self-sufficiency in national languages and cultures, and a sturdy sense of independence. Spain does not see itself as a country on the periphery of an Anglophone-dominated world, but as the centre of its own vibrant—for once, this over-used word is exactly right—Hispanophone world. For an Anglophone like me, to experience this world for a few weeks was both humbling and reassuring. I am glad there are still alternatives to Anglophone culture; our shrinking planet would be so boring if there were not. Spanish culture, even though it has many correspondences and overlaps with international Anglophone culture, is not derivative. It stands proudly on its own achievements.

Spain is a religiously based society, a society whose Catholicism is still rich and strong, but that at the same time offers the full freedom of political and multicultural pluralism. I saw no oppression of gays or lesbians in Spain; no heavy-handed censorship; no religious prejudice; no impediments for Protestants or Jews or Muslims to practise their religion; and the choice of a secular system of education for those who want it. The free-thinking, freewheeling Spain of Pedro Almodavar's films does exist: Spain is now a genuinely liberal-minded country, and a country that is able to laugh at itself.

I don't propose ever to emigrate to Spain; my future belongs to my own country and culture. But my few weeks in Spain as a pilgrim gave me a glimpse of what is possible in society—of better approaches to dauntingly huge problems, if we can only liberate our thinking from familiar assumptions and stereotypes about how things have to be. We don't have to accept stress and unhappily alienated affluent societies, or the daily disappointments of our joyless consumerism. There are other answers, if we dare to ask the right questions.

Soon after I returned home from Spain, a new Catholic bishop was installed in my diocese of Canberra–Goulburn, Mark Coleridge, an impressive man who has spent many years of his religious career working out of the Vatican. He gave a thoughtful and broad-ranging homily at his installation ceremony at my church, St Christopher's Pro-Cathedral. At one point, he said something that resonated remarkably with my own feelings after two months' walking through Spain:

> I ask the question: Where and how does Australia stand at this time? In some ways, we are like Abraham, 'our father in faith' *(Roman Canon)*. He was a rich and successful businessman. Yet something gnawed away at him deep down; something was missing. In the midst of plenty, there was a lingering unhappiness, a sense of failure, of life slipping through his fingers. He had everything except a child and a land of his own; and without these in his culture, he was a man in whose life death had the last word and a man therefore who was wounded deep within, slowly bleeding to death.
>
> So too Australia is in many ways rich and successful, and there is much of which we can be rightly proud, as

Abraham was no doubt. Yet there is also something missing deeper down: we sense it in public life and we feel it in the privacy of our heart. We have a bit of fun but not much joy; we get on well enough with others but struggle to find love; we know little conflict but do not find peace; we have endless options but do not feel free; we move but we do not advance. Like Abraham, there is the wound deep within, and so we just get on with business, proving how rich and successful we can be in a world where fear and greed loom large. There is no hope of the fullness of life we long for deep down—the joy, the love, the peace, the freedom; there is no hope of healing. Or so at least it seems. But precisely at this point of seeming hopelessness, God speaks a healing word—a word of promise to Abraham, 'I will give you a child and a land', and a word of hope to Australia, 'I will fill the muted void'. This word comes from nowhere and opens magnificent and unexpected horizons of hope. It overturns the conventional logic which says that nothing else is possible, so just get on with business. This word is the wisdom of the Cross *(cf. 1 Cor 1:18-25)*, and it's the only wisdom to which the Church can lay claim.

I believe that God spoke a healing word to me in Spain. God restored my hope in possibilities for the fullness of life. I don't yet know if the pilgrimage will make me a better person. It has already made me a happier, more relaxed person. I appreciate more intensely the blessings of every extra day spent with my family, the rich joys of ordinary family life and domesticity, of every precious day in which my young children grow up in my care. I am happier in my Australian society, despite my keen knowledge of its present serious problems.

I think my pilgrimage was, indeed, in Frank Brennan's memorable words, a precious opportunity to 'take my life for a walk', to unflinchingly hold up to the light memories of past relationships and responsibilities, to examine how well or badly I met those challenges—and how I would try to do better in future, try to heal old wounds and prevent new ones from forming. The pilgrimage to Santiago can teach humility, charity, wisdom, patience, and endurance; in fact, if I look at the list of the seven gifts of the Holy Spirit, I see them all now as central to my pilgrimage experience. It was, truly, a humble search for Wisdom, Intelligence, Good Counsel, Fortitude, Science, Compassion, and the Fear of God.

'Science' is an intriguing word in that list—not a word one usually associates with spirituality. I think of the 'science' of the Muslim, Jewish, and Christian communities in al-Andalus, working together harmoniously in the disinterested pursuit of knowledge and the maintenance of a civilised, tolerant society. Or I think of the 'science', the mental and physical challenge of navigating one's way and husbanding one's bodily strength through a 1200-kilometre pilgrimage walk. And, finally, I think of the science that the human race will need if we are to navigate our way as civilised and caring societies built around the principle of the common humanity of every person on this planet, through the terrifying challenges that are coming, of global warming and fossil-fuel depletion.

Hard times lie ahead, times that will require every ounce of wisdom and goodness we have. And we will need God's help. It cannot be by science alone that our species will survive these great perils. The great error of the eighteenth-century Enlightenment was to think that science could do it all alone.

It is science allied to the other six precious gifts of the Holy Spirit that we will need to exercise now.

My pilgrimage was a miraculous gift from God, an opportunity to better understand the importance of the gifts of the Holy Spirit. I had to allow myself time and space, alone in a foreign place, to be open to that miracle. I had to be ready to take the risk of trying to talk to God alone.

The pilgrimage has given back to me, at the age of sixty-three, what we all seek: the gift of a *mens sana in corpore sano*, a healthy mind in a healthy body. God willing, I may hold on to that gift for some years to come, more time in which I can cherish and protect all my family.

We are not so far, after all, from the medieval religious vision of the purposes of pilgrimage: repentance, expiation of sins through sacrifice, self-knowledge, and the hope of salvation through prayer and good works. That is what the pilgrimage to Santiago meant to pilgrims in medieval times. In the end, for all the pleasures of travel that I had on the way, that is what it meant to me.

And to you, dear readers, a final word of thanks for sharing this experience with me. It wasn't in the end so exciting a story—no life-threatening moments on the way, no encounters with robber gypsies, no holiday romances with dark-eyed, shapely Spanish ladies, not even many interesting conversations to recall. But I hope it was still an absorbing armchair journey for you, as it was for me to experience its reality. Pilgrimage is about sharing as well as about 'company in solitude', and I hope by this work of reportage and reflection that I can share my experience with as many people of goodwill as possible. *Buen viaje, peregrinos!*

Notes

The Confraternity of Saint James (London) is a good starting-point for information about the caminos, travel guides, and credencials. Its website address is www.csj.org.uk/

This not being in any way an academic book, I have not used footnotes. I owe much to Wikipedia as a short-cut to factual knowledge, and to other Internet sources as noted, and to the following copyrighted books and maps:

Alison Raju, *Vía de la Plata—The Way of Saint James: Seville/Granada to Santiago*, a Cicerone Guide, 2nd edition, London, 2005

María Rosa Menocal, *The Ornament of the World: how Muslims, Jews, and Christians created a culture of tolerance in medieval Spain*, Back Bay Books, Little, Brown, New York, 2002 (paperback)

Antony Beevor, *The Spanish Civil War*, Cassell Military Paperbacks, London, 1999

Easy Learning Spanish Dictionary and *Easy Learning Spanish Grammar*, Collins, London, latest reprints 2005

Berlitz Spanish Phrase Book and Dictionary, Spain 1998

Michelin roadmaps, 1:400,000 Orange Series, 'Regional—España': 578 Andalucia, 576 Extremadura, 571 Galicia.

The poetry by Federico García Lorca quoted on pp 66–7 is reproduced with the publisher's kind permission from 'Romance de la pena negra' ('Ballad of Black Pain'), pp 564–5, from *The Gypsy Ballads, 1924–1927*, translated by Will Kirkland and Christopher Maurer, in *Collected Poems* (rev. bilingual edn), Farrer Straus Giroux, New York, 1991, rev. edn 2002. The poem (in Galician) on p 251 and the English translation on pp 252–3 are taken from the same book.

My dedication of this book to Amy Banson requires some explanation. Amy is a student in her early twenties at the Catholic University of Canberra. She walked 1463 kilometres over two months, all the way from Brisbane to Canberra, at around the same time as I was walking in Spain. Amy walked to honour the memory of Clea Rose, another Canberra university student, aged twenty-one, who died after an irrecoverable brain injury that was caused when she was knocked down soon after midnight on 30 July 2005 by a speeding stolen car, driven by a fourteen-year-old boy, which was being pursued by a police car through a pedestrians-only area of Canberra City. Neither car stopped after Clea was hit. Amy was one of the first people on the scene. She comforted Clea, a young woman whom she did not know, and tried to help her. Clea never regained consciousness. After three weeks in hospital in a coma, Clea died.

Clea Rose's tragic and pointless death has haunted me ever since. To me, it symbolises the callous cruelty and indifference to human life of our aggressive, machine-driven, and speed-obsessed age. Amy's walk, which she called 'Walk with a Rose', was sponsored by many Canberra businesses. It attracted huge community support along the way from Brisbane to Canberra. It also raised a lot of money for the National Brain Injury Foundation, which seeks to raise awareness of the plight of people with an acquired brain injury.

I learned from newspapers about Amy's walk, and I phoned her in its final days as she was nearing Canberra, not long after my return home from Spain. It was a privilege to be invited by Amy to walk for a day with her. I cannot think of anyone more appropriate than this inspirational young woman to whom to dedicate this book. Amy Banson is the truest of pilgrims, and young people like her offer hope for a better world.